A World Without War

Syracuse Studies on Peace and Conflict Resolution
Harriet Hyman Alonso, Charles Chatfield, *and* Louis Kriesberg,
Series Editors

A World Without

How U.S. Feminists and Pacifists Resisted World War I

WAR

Frances H. Early

Syracuse University Press

First Edition 1997
03 04 05 06 07 08   9 8 7 6 5 4 3

The paper used in this publication meets the minimum requirements
of National Standard for Information Sciences—Permanence of Paper
for Printed Library Materials, ANSI Z39.48-1984.⊗

Library of Congress Cataloging-in-Publication Data
Early, Frances H.
A world without war : how U.S. feminists and pacifists resisted
World War I / Frances H. Early.
p.   cm. — (Syracuse studies on peace and conflict resolution)
Includes bibliographical references and index.
ISBN 0-8156-2745-9 (cloth: alk. paper). —ISBN 0-8156-2764-5 (pbk.: alk. paper)
1. World War, 1914–1918—United States.   2. World War, 1939–1945—
Women—United States—History—20th century.   3. Pacifism.
I. Title.   II. Series.
D570.1.E27   1997
940.3'16—dc21   97-16767

Manufactured in the United States of America

For Abe and Ida Kaufman

and

In Memory of June Figg

Never doubt that a small group of thoughtful committed citizens can change the world. Indeed, it is the only thing that ever has.
—Margaret Mead

FRANCES H. EARLY is professor of history and chair of the History Department at Mount Saint Vincent University in Halifax, Nova Scotia. She is the editor of *Immigrant Odyssey: A French-Canadian Habitant in New England* by Félix Albert and is the 1989–90 recipient of the Charles De-Benedetti Prize in Peace History. Early presently serves as president of the Peace History Society (formerly the Council on Peace Research in History).

Contents

Illustrations

xi

Acknowledgments

This book represents the culmination of a scholarly project begun almost a decade ago. Along the way, I have been assisted by a number of institutions and individuals.

Financial backing came from the Social Science and Humanities Research Council of Canada Research Grant Program. A Teaching Relief Stipend, awarded by the Research Committee of Mount Saint Vincent University, provided me with additional time for writing.

Numerous archivists were most helpful, especially Peter Filardo at the Tamiment Institute Library of New York University and Jean Soderlund and Wendy Chmielewski at the Swarthmore College Peace Collection. I also appreciate the proficient research of archivists and collection curators who assisted me in procuring valuable photographs: Gene DeGruson, Pittsburg State University Axe Library; Tim Ericson, Golda Meir Library, University of Wisconsin at Milwaukee; Margaret Jessup, Sophia Smith Collection, Smith College; Joanne Dougherty, Smith College Archives; Tom Rosko, Seeley G. Mudd Manuscript Library, Princeton University; and Joselyn Clapp at the Bettman Archive. Historians Paul Avrich, Blanche Wiesen Cook, and Robert Cooney also helped me secure photos. Margaret Rockwell Finch, Joyce Fuller, and John Recht graciously permitted me to reprint pictures from their family collections.

Over the years, scholarly support and encouragement came from many individuals. My debts in this respect are too numerous to cite in their entirety; however, I do wish to give special recognition to some individuals. The members of the Halifax Women's

History Reading Group offered constructive advice on portions of my manuscript. Kathleen Kennedy, John Chambers, and David Patterson commented incisively on some chapters.

Harriet Hyman Alonso, Lawrence Wittner, Janet Guildford, Abe Kaufman, Ida Kaufman, and an anonymous reviewer were conscientious readers of the near-final version of my manuscript; this study has benefited greatly from their suggestions. I have had the best of research assistants, and I thank Jennifer Curran and Madeline Conrad for their cheerful and efficient help; Madeline, who labored tirelessly and enthusiastically at my side for several years, brought not only zest but discernment to her work. Ann Pelley and Terry Paris, the reference librarians at Mount Saint Vincent University, were unfailingly helpful. I have appreciated the exacting professionalism of Syracuse University Press and thank particularly Executive Editor Cynthia Maude-Gembler for her support of my project. I am pleased that my study has been included in the Syracuse Studies on Peace and Conflict Resolution series; Harriet Hyman Alonso, one of the series editors, has evinced unswerving faith in the scholarly value of my work.

A special joy of mine has been the opportunity to meet with and learn from individuals who were in some way a part of the history that I have attempted to bring to life in the following pages. I am most grateful to the late Howard Moore and his wife, Louise Moore, Abe and Ida Kaufman, Margaret Rockwell Finch, and John Recht for sharing their time and insights with me. As well, inspiration to write this book owes much to the exemplary activist lives of two esteemed friends, international feminist pacifists Muriel Duckworth (Halifax, Nova Scotia) and Berit Ås (Oslo, Norway); I thank each of them for helping me to see that a world without war is not only desirable but possible.

It is customary and most appropriate to thank family members for their own steadfastness of purpose when a research project of "longue durée" reaches completion. My partner, John Figg, has been a generous supporter of my work, and his wisdom and fine sense of humor have helped provide needed perspective on life at critical stages in this study's history. My dear twelve-year-old daughter, Jasmine Figg, accepts my scholarly preoccupations with wonderful grace; over the course of her childhood, Jasmine has absorbed a great deal of my passion for past times. Her justifiable impatience with the time spent on this study has perhaps hastened its completion. My parents, Ruth and Shep Kinsman, maintain a keen interest in and engagement with my scholarly endeavors. I value their consistent support.

My life has been immeasurably enriched by my close friendships with Abe and Ida Kaufman and with my mother-in-law, the late June Figg. I dedicate this study to Abe and Ida and in loving memory of June.

Frances H. Early

Halifax, Nova Scotia
April 1996

Introduction

I first stumbled upon the history of the New York–based Bureau of Legal Advice while studying the papers of Tracy Mygatt and Frances Witherspoon, feminist pacifists who were activists for suffrage, socialism, peace, and civil liberties during World War I and the period surrounding it. My discovery of the Bureau's existence led me from Mygatt's and Witherspoon's archives at the Swarthmore College Peace Collection to the substantial papers of the legal aid bureau that they established, which are housed at the Tamiment Institute Library on Washington Square at New York University. It was not long before I was immersed in a tumultuous, disturbing era. I caught the spirit that animated the exciting and uplifting but tension-charged lives of World War I peace and civil liberties activists. Emerging from the library on Washington Square daily after long hours of research, I found the mental switch to the present disconcerting. Frances Witherspoon and Tracy Mygatt had shared an apartment just around the corner from the library, on Waverley Place; I could easily imagine what my life might have been like had I been a part of the wartime radical pacifist subculture. After a time, I knew where people such as Witherspoon and Mygatt lived and worked and which restaurants and cafés they chose for meetings and social gatherings. It seemed strange to be returning to my accommodations at the YWCA on Forty-seventh Street. Was it not time to meet my comrades for a late "working" supper?

In addition to identifying with some remarkable people, I soon recognized that I was recovering an important chapter in U.S. social history. The Bureau of Legal Advice was a small, poorly financed, but highly effective civil liberties association, sponsored initially by the radical wing of the peace movement. It was actually the first of its kind to offer free legal service to victims of government repression and to conscientious objectors. However, it had been ignored or misrepresented in the standard histories of the civil liberties movement right up to 1990.[1]

In part, the Bureau's historic invisibility has been due to the largely unconscious propensity of historians to study organizations that endure over time and that demonstrate a record of long-term achievement. Hence, the history of the American Civil Liberties Union (ACLU), founded in the same period as the Bureau of Legal Advice, has attracted the attention of scholars; the Bureau of Legal Advice, in existence for a relatively short time (from 1917 to 1920), has not. In addition, a rich, almost overwhelming documentation exists on the ACLU and its leaders. Historians, bound by the methods of their craft, choose topics with an eye to the evidence available for study; many scholars of the past would agree with G. R. Elton's blunt, tendentious statement: "Historical study is . . . the study of the present traces of the past; if men [*sic*] have said, thought, done or suffered anything of which nothing any longer exists, those things are as if they had never been."[2]

Even so, in the case of the Bureau of Legal Advice, records do exist. There is a small collection on the Bureau at the Swarthmore College Peace Collection, and the main papers are, as already noted, at the Tamiment Library. Is there, then, an additional reason why historians have been remiss in acknowledging the Bureau's history?

The male-centered nature of historical inquiry, not necessarily a lack of evidence, predisposes scholars—even today, after twenty-five years of creative feminist historical scholarship—to assume that some things are "as if they had never been." Historians, not expecting to find women active and innovative in civil liberties work, have not found them to be so. To be sure, the very women who were themselves the actors have unwittingly abetted in their own invisibility: few activist women of the world war era, relative to men, have written their memoirs. A similar trend holds true in relation to private papers on deposit in archives. Those of men predominate; being valued, they have survived—along with their bias. I have been alternately fascinated and frustrated, when studying the writings of men such as Roger Baldwin, Norman Thomas,

and John Haynes Holmes, to discover that they consistently belit-
tled, slighted, or ignored their women comrades in the movement.
The women who left their impressions, on the other hand, gave
full credit to their male counterparts. Time and again, then, historians (including myself) consulting such sources are led ineluctably
back to literature authored by men and to the archives of the
organizations in which they were active. In this way, efforts to
recover women's involvement and leadership roles in this period
are confounded. An added measure of determination and persistence is required to circumvent these conceptual and methodological pitfalls. An ability to read between the lines, to pay attention
to what is not recorded or stated explicitly, is also an asset. In fact,
without it, we are left with an incomplete understanding of the
past.

My interest in women's history and my commitment to feminist scholarship has guided my decision to trace the connection
between women's antiwar activism and the emergence of civil liberties organizations in the United states during World War I. My
strategy has been to focus on the history of the Bureau of Legal
Advice, a mixed-gender organization created as an auxiliary to
groups associated with the feminist-oriented, left-wing antiwar
movement. This approach has allowed me to demonstrate that the
contributions of left-liberals and socialists to the birth and development of the civil liberties movement has been greatly underestimated. It also permits me to explore in some depth the role of
women as civil liberties activists in this period.

At one level, this book is an organizational history of the
Bureau of Legal Advice. However, because of the Bureau's close
working relationship with other civil liberties groups across the
country, notably the National Civil Liberties Bureau (the forerunner of the ACLU), its history becomes intertwined with the larger
movement and becomes thereby more than that of one group. The
Bureau's executive secretary, Frances Witherspoon, was a seasoned
political activist and moved easily in feminist, socialist, and pacifist circles, and so the story of the Bureau enhances our knowledge
of how a variety of radical people and groups responded to the
development of a militarized and repressive state during the war
years.

Most intriguing is the opportunity this study provides to observe and to analyze women's political activism and evolving
thought in difficult circumstances at close range. In the midst of
the traumatic yet energizing crisis of the home front war, women
involved in civil liberties work developed a way of thinking and of
acting in the world as serious-minded, pragmatic activists, which
built upon but went well beyond the legacy of Progressive era
white women's politics. Most shared a background of activism in
the prewar women's movement, particularly in suffrage work; their
feminist commitments were wide-ranging and informed by left-
wing or socialist thought. They shared a liberal-progressive faith
that people of good will could create an equitable, socially just
society, a position shaped (in part) by their privileged upbringing
as members of the white, well-educated middle class.

The socialist proclivities of these activists took their thinking
further and helped them to recognize the dynamics of economic
and political power in society: they understood that the good in-
tentions and actions of a handful of like-minded reformers would
not bring about a cooperative commonwealth. They believed that
the analysis of power relations, the development of new social policies, and the organization of disadvantaged groups were necessary
steps if society was to be reconstituted along more egalitarian
lines. The idea of social revolution brought about through legal
means was not the stuff of dreams but of long-term commitment
and creative activism. For a short moment in history—before dis-
illusionment with the Russian Revolution set in—such women
found it possible to consider themselves both progressive and socialist or, in terms they used interchangeably, both liberal and
radical.

In the hurly-burly of wartime activism, Bureau women did not
find time to think deeply about their civil liberties work in feminist terms. If they had been asked to do so—which they were
not—probably most would not have been able to articulate a feminist position on civil liberties. Bureau spokespersons, notably
Frances Witherspoon, spoke instead of the erosion of "traditional
freedoms." Nonetheless, Witherspoon and other socialist-minded
members of the Bureau's executive committee comprehended that
classes and groups without political and economic power in U.S.
society had never enjoyed the freedoms of the Bill of Rights except
fitfully, at the sufferance of the ruling elite. Inchoately, women

civil libertarians seemed to comprehend that in demanding civil liberties for others—immigrants, labor radicals, political dissidents, critics of the war, and conscientious objectors—they were gaining something necessary for their own liberation as women.

Civil liberties activism represented a new direction for women, but it also existed on a continuum of political praxis. Women civil libertarians put to effective use their experience with grassroots organization-building and feminist networking; they knew how to galvanize public attention through dramatic events (such as "theme" parades, demonstrations, and petition campaigns); and they were adept at surviving personally and organizationally on slender funding. The isolation and estrangement that they experienced as outsiders in a nation awash with wartime patriotic frenzy and intolerance helped to build a sense of community and to mitigate ideological and class differences that surfaced among them when the Bureau began to attract some working-class women to its work.

Sexual politics were a part of movement work. Women operated differently from men in some ways, they were sensitive to the tendency of men to assume leadership rights and to expect women to do routine jobs, and they sometimes set their priorities differently. These realities impinged on day-to-day existence for both women and men and are important to elucidate for what they reveal about the values, perceptions, and aspirations of the people involved.

Personalities are central to historical narrative, and the dynamic interplay between the personal and the political in people's lives emerges as a central theme in this study. The women and men we meet here struggled to sustain a peace culture in the midst of war; this process of building peace required, in part, the fashioning of new gender identities. Movement individuals embraced this daunting personal challenge, and the structure and focus of this book help us observe this development at an individual level. The history presented here should teach us some important lessons about ourselves in relation to our own painfully imperfect, insecure, and war-haunted world.

A World Without War

Prologue

April 2, 1917, was a balmy, welcoming spring day in Washington, D.C. However, the five thousand people who stood together in front of the Capitol that morning had not come to the city to enjoy the cherry blossoms or to revel in the ending of winter. Instead, as delegates of the Emergency Peace Federation, they were there to participate in a "Mass Meeting for Peace" and to lobby against U.S. entry into World War I. Inside the Capitol, Congress debated whether to commit the country to war. A reporter for the New York *Evening Post* attempted to capture this moment in words: observing the "great, silent bannered mass" that appeared to be guarding Washington throughout the warm spring day, it seemed "impossible that it was war that these people were protesting, or that this was anything but the setting for a charming picture."[1]

The women and men who made up this improbable tableau had traveled to the Capitol from a number of eastern cities in a last-ditch effort to witness against war. By and large, they were representatives of a new, youth-flavored, left-leaning, largely middle-class and white peace movement that had sprung into being in response to the outbreak of war in Europe in August 1914. In the evening, after a full day of demonstrating and lobbying individual members of Congress, the social workers, progressive reformers, intellectuals, representatives of the clergy, socialists, feminists, labor leaders, and cultural radicals who made up the peace delegation rubbed shoulders in a meeting and rally at Convention Hall, craning to see and concentrating to hear the speeches of prominent antiwar spokespersons such as Emily Greene Balch, Rabbi Judah

1

Magnes, and David Starr Jordan. The Emergency Peace Federation resolutions committee presented a number of statements, which the demonstrators enthusiastically adopted. The twin themes of peace and freedom resonated in the resolutions. War, as an institution, was condemned: "All history, and more particularly the frightful waste of life and property in the present world war, has proven the utter futility of war as a means of settling international disputes or of vindicating national honor." Individual liberty, the perceived heritage of the American political tradition, was proclaimed and set against the frightening reality of a society readying itself for war, which "would mean the nullification of the First Amendment to the Federal Constitution . . . because under the guise of fighting for the democracy of other peoples, we would fasten upon ourselves a militaristic imperialism." Arguing that "the great majority of the people of the United States are opposed to war," the resolutions contained suggestions for diplomatic action to avert it.[2]

Among the people attending the rally that night were two young peace activists, Frances Witherspoon—Fannie May, to family and friends—and Tracy Mygatt. Journeying from New York City, they came as members of the Emergency Peace Federation executive committee and as special delegates of the Woman's Peace Party. Because Witherspoon's father, Samuel A. Witherspoon, had been a U.S. Representative from Mississippi before his death in 1915, his daughter knew many of his former colleagues in Congress—an asset for the peace cause. She and Mygatt, along with a large number of peace delegates, chose to remain in Washington after the mass meeting to lobby insistently against war in the corridors of Congress.

The hectic days of lobbying passed quickly. Then, in the early morning hours of April 6, Witherspoon, Mygatt, and a few others (including Balch, Louis Lochner, and Jordan) who were observing members of Congress debate the war resolution heard the call to clear the visitors' gallery. Ignoring the summons to vacate the premises, they moved unobtrusively into the gallery and pressed themselves against the wall so as not to be seen. Then they heard the oral vote—for war or against it. Only fifty Representatives and five Senators voted no, among them Montana representative Jeanette Rankin, the first woman to be elected to Congress. "I love my country," she declared, "but I cannot vote for war." The unnoticed little group filed quietly out of the gallery after the vote, but Witherspoon and Mygatt felt haunted by what they had experienced: "The 6th of April that year came on a Good Friday, and therefore to Roman Catholics and Episcopalians like ourselves and to a lesser degree perhaps to some others, the night was a particularly solemn night of betrayal."[3] Feeling "very very depressed," the delegates went back to their hotel and left the city the following day.

Returning to their respective homes, the exhausted peace campaigners found public attitudes hardening against them. As individuals, they faced a difficult decision: Would they support their government or would they continue their antiwar work? Many liberal-progressive supporters of Woodrow Wilson who had been active in the antimilitarist movement since 1914 stood by the president and accepted Congress's war decision. They chose patriotism over dissent—a few enthusiastically, but many with troubled hearts. Only a small left-liberal and socialist contingent of peace activists and a tiny group of clergy stood apart, resisting the lure of Wilson's insistent crusade to "make the world safe for democracy."

Those who opposed U.S. participation in World War I were also particularly sensitive to the problem of maintaining civil liberties in wartime. It was not long before people discovered that public criticism of Wilson, of the war decision, or of conscription could lead to police or citizen arrest and a stiff prison sentence. Peace organizations soon found it difficult or impossible to book lecture halls, and mob violence quickly became an omnipresent threat whenever antiwar activists sought a hearing. After the war declaration, immigrants, labor leaders, and political radicals of all persuasions were automatically suspect.

Two weeks after her return from the Capitol, Fannie May Witherspoon experienced at close range the growing repressiveness and violence of the times. Out for a walk, she unexpectedly met a friend on the corner of Fifth Avenue and Forty-second Street, opposite the New York Public Library. While chatting, they noticed that an army recruiting meeting was taking place across the street. A Dutch man approached Witherspoon and her friend as they paused at the corner and in broken English began to ask them questions about the war. Suddenly a police whistle sounded and several recruiting officers descended on the stranger; they grabbed him, threw him unceremoniously into a van, and disappeared quickly. The astounded women discovered that he was being taken to a nearby police station. They hailed a taxi and arrived at the police precinct in time to be told that the Dutch man was in transit to Bellevue Hospital for "mental observation." Witherspoon later recalled:

> So we said, "Well, it's our duty to see what's happened to the poor creature." We got into another taxi and went over to Bellevue, and to this day I don't know how we managed to get past all the doors and so on, but we got right into the place. Our poor Dutch friend was already in those awful pyjamas and the kinds of things that they put on people when they bring them in. He was absolutely terrified. He was a stranger in this country, an alien, and so we telephoned to a lawyer with whom we were friendly and asked him if anything could be done for this man. He said, "Yes, I'll take it over," and he got him out on a writ of habeas corpus. He disappeared. I don't know what became of him.[4]

Reflecting upon the event, Witherspoon averred that this experience led directly to her determination to establish a legal aid bureau in defense of civil liberties in wartime. Actually, the effect of this incident was not so direct, but the timing was opportune; at this moment, the necessity of protecting civil liberties on the home front was being discussed in the antiwar circles in which Witherspoon traveled. Within a short time, Witherspoon was asked by the Woman's Peace Party and the Emergency Peace Federation to organize a legal aid bureau to defend individuals whose civil liberties were at risk during the war. The "implacably gentle" yet determined young woman agreed, resolving to see the war madness through to the end.[5]

⊰ 1 ⊱

Fannie May Witherspoon and the Founding of the Bureau of Legal Advice

The essential history of any life is not the record of its long continuity, but of its high significant moments.
—Frances M. Witherspoon, 1929

When the New York City branch of the Woman's Peace Party and the Emergency Peace Federation asked Fannie May Witherspoon to organize a legal advice bureau, they chose well. A self-described "daughter and sister of lawyers," Witherspoon was familiar with the general parameters of the legal work that she agreed to oversee. Thirty-two years old in 1917, she was poised for what, with hindsight, can be seen as her "high significant moments."

Frances May Witherspoon was born in 1885 in Meridian, Mississippi. Growing to young adulthood in the twilight years of the Victorian era, there was nothing apparent in her white, upper-middle-class background to explain her predilection for unpopular or radical stands. Thinking about her upbringing, she once remarked:

> I am no product of the "Magnolia South." Unlike more aristocratic towns in the state, my birthplace boasted no mansions with stately porticoes. My parents—father, a struggling young lawyer, newly come from that same "Ole Miss" of today's unhappy fame, where he'd been a Classics tutor, my mother, Kentucky-bred and daughter of a fiery naturalized French father, a

5

Confederate officer—reared their family in a plain little frame
house, sans electricity, or even modern plumbing![1]

Despite material modesty, the Witherspoons were a socially
and politically prominent Meridian family. Fannie May Witherspoon's mother, Susan May Witherspoon, was of "aristocratic"
birth, a member of a well-to-do Kentucky family, a Daughter of
the Confederacy and an active clubwoman. She seems to have been
a conventional Victorian woman at the center of Meridian social
and civic life. Fannie May Witherspoon's father, Samuel A.
Witherspoon, was a self-made man of sorts; his father had been a
country doctor. Witherspoon served in Congress for two years,
from 1913 to 1915 (the year of his death). He was known at the
Capitol as "Uncle Sam" because of his name and the auburn whis-
kers that "were thought to create a resemblance to that national
figure." Samuel Witherspoon was also known as "Father of the
Little Navy," the appellation his daughter preferred; along with
four other members of Congress, he criticized President Wilson's
April 1914 order to the U.S. Navy to seize the port of Veracruz,
Mexico, in response to a minor naval incident. This provocative act
led to the deaths of 126 Mexicans and nineteen Americans and, for
a time, brought the two countries to the brink of war.[2]

Witherspoon was inordinately fond of her father and credited
him with influencing her towards antimilitarist thinking well before her college years. Only one letter sent by Samuel Witherspoon
to his daughter has survived; written in a sentimental yet respectful and loving tone to Witherspoon when she was five years old, it
indicates that a strong attachment existed between father and
daughter. No letters of Sue Witherspoon survive, and Fannie May
Witherspoon remained reticent about her relationship with her
mother all her life. Her mother stood by Fannie May during the
difficult World War I years; when Witherspoon set up the Bureau
of Legal Advice, Sue Witherspoon promised to provide bail monies
should she be arrested. Nonetheless, Mrs. Witherspoon had little
sympathy with or understanding of Fannie May Witherspoon's
radical causes. It is probable, however, that mother and daughter
saw eye-to-eye on women's suffrage. By the war era, suffrage was
respectable, even in Meridian, Mississippi.

Witherspoon's memories of her childhood reveal that she was
in some respects a true "Child of the Confederacy," delighted to

wear the stars and bars on Decoration Day and proud that her father was often the orator for this annual event.[3] However, she also set herself apart in some ways and from an early age questioned the racist assumptions that permeated her society and that white southerners, including her parents, took for granted. Witherspoon's sense of uniqueness must have caused some raised eyebrows within the family circle, which included three children, Fannie May, Letitia, and Samuel, Junior. "I was always a queer one," she later recalled; she "wanted to speak English instead of the dialect of the Southern whites or Negroes [and] early questioned the dogma that the college education my dear father insisted upon for me would develop the criminal (i.e. sexual) instincts of the Negro!"[4]

Aside from these comments, we have only a few further glimpses of Witherspoon's childhood. Her snapshots invariably center around her father. Noting that she attended public schools, she remarked that one of those that she attended was named for him. Remembering being thirteen at the time of the Spanish-American War, she described her awe at hearing Samuel Witherspoon denounce it and ridicule Teddy Roosevelt: "Men in uniform [were] to him ridiculous figures."[5]

In 1903, eighteen-year-old Fannie May Witherspoon set off for Quaker-founded Bryn Mawr College, situated near Philadelphia. However, being ill-prepared for postsecondary education, she failed the stiff entrance exam. After further studies, she passed the exam handily the second time, joining the 1904 freshman class in the fall.

Coming of age as a privileged white woman in the early twentieth century meant that Witherspoon, in common with others of her race and class, was positioned to benefit at many levels from the achievements of first-wave feminism. Women's colleges like Bryn Mawr had rigorous intellectual standards and were committed to disproving the Victorian notion of woman's inherent mental weaknesses. Such institutions brought together young women who wished to prepare themselves for a life that would reach beyond kitchens, nurseries, sewing circles, and genteel community service work. The ideal of the New Woman, autonomous, self-possessed, and involved in the public world of career and political action, inspired a whole generation of college-educated women to reject the narrowly constrained lives of most of their mothers and to embrace, in new ways, the complex challenges that their feminist forebears had bequeathed them.

Bryn Mawr, established in 1884, was a prestigious liberal arts school. Its women students constituted a "female world" that served to maintain even as it helped to transform the Victorian sense of women's community. Fannie May Witherspoon, along with many of her classmates, found the college as academy and as community to be a congenial environment for intellectual and personal growth. She majored in English literature and in Latin, noting in retrospect that it was at Bryn Mawr that she "began to think seriously about *Christianity* in connection with the treatment of Negroes in the South—educational, political, even social."[6] She admired the college president, the uncompromising women's rights advocate M. Carey Thomas; by the time she graduated in 1909, Witherspoon, following Thomas's example, was a suffragist. It was at college, too, that she first encountered pacifism as a coherent philosophy. Witherspoon read pacifist literature with keen interest and was fascinated by Stanford University president David Starr Jordan's denunciation of war in his commencement address to her graduating class. Not long thereafter, in a nearby suburb, she was "sufficiently pacifist to hold a soap-box meeting" that echoed Jordan's sentiments.

Crucial to Witherspoon's development at this time was the close friendship she formed with Tracy Dickinson Mygatt, another idealist who shared with Witherspoon a love of literature, a determination to pursue a writing career, and a commitment to work for a variety of humanitarian causes. After graduation, the two young women chose to live together, a decision that resulted in a lifelong partnership—one which, Mygatt once remarked, was the envy of all their married friends.

Tracy Mygatt's ancestors had arrived in the New World in the 1630s and maintained upper-class status down to the time of her birth in 1886. One great-grandfather, Daniel S. Dickinson, achieved political prominence, having been elected attorney general of New York State in 1861. Tracy Mygatt was raised in New York City by her mother, Minnie Clapp Mygatt, widowed when her daughter was four. Mygatt had no memories of her father, and it is a mystery as to whether she knew of his character; in various reminiscences and autobiographical statements, she evaded discussion of him. However, found among her papers at Swarthmore

College, there is a diary of her mother's that covers the years of Minnie Clapp's courtship, elopement, and marriage to Dick Mygatt (or "Werther," as she chose to call him). The diary, initially locked with no key appended, recounted in painful, explicit detail Minnie Clapp's consuming passion for Mygatt and his irresponsible behavior towards her and his numerous betrayals. Dick Mygatt was twenty when Minnie Clapp married him; she was twenty-eight. Clapp's upper-class family disapproved of the flighty, intemperate young man. Once married, Mygatt convinced Clapp to gain control of her inheritance of $10,000. Four years after their marriage, Dick Mygatt died of a brain hemorrhage, most likely brought on as a result of alcoholism and drug abuse; in this short period, he ran through all Minnie Clapp Mygatt's money. Thereafter, for the rest of her life (she lived to be ninety-three), Tracy Mygatt's mother was supported by modest allowances from members of her family. We can appreciate what anguished feelings must have prompted her to write in her diary that she would curb wilfulness in her children (it surfaced early in her daughter's childhood) and teach them "to accept things as they are."[7]

Tracy Mygatt and her younger brother, Henry, led protected childhoods as members of their mother's close-knit extended family. Still, Mygatt—like Witherspoon—remembered experiencing feelings and holding attitudes that set her apart from family and friends. She had vivid memories of passing by slums and seeing wretched women and children as she made her way to an elite, private school in Manhattan, Miss Graham's. The impressionable child liked to think up stories, often keeping herself awake late into the night telling tales out loud to herself in her bed. As an adult, Tracy Mygatt felt torn between her desire to write full time and her sense that she must serve others: "I, who had had so much, ought to help [those who did not]. Incessantly there was conflict,—the feeling of 'noblesse oblige,' and yet the lure of my ivory tower."[8]

It is not easy to get beneath the veneer of gentility and good-works idealism that blocks us from understanding the deeper motivations in both Fannie May Witherspoon's and Tracy Mygatt's characters. Witherspoon's steadiness and determination under pressure contrast sharply with Mygatt's tendency towards self-absorption and temperamentality, especially in the face of frustrated aims. Perhaps Witherspoon's more conventional family life in the

1. *Fannie May Witherspoon in the early 1900s. Courtesy of the Swarthmore College Peace Collection.*

context of her admiration for and even emulation of her successful father helps explain her steadfastness and inner resolve. At some level, Mygatt doubtless absorbed something of her mother's disastrous experience with marriage; this unhappy legacy could have led her to seek out a woman like Witherspoon as a long-term companion, thereby signifying her rejection of conventional heterosexual marital arrangements. Mygatt was probably also influenced by her mother's idealized stories of her intimate youthful friendship with her first cousin, Julia Newberry, who died tragically young at age sixteen.[9] In contrast to Mygatt, Witherspoon identified strongly with her own father and may have felt most at ease in the role of "head," a term once used by a child to describe

2. Tracy Mygatt in the early 1900s. Courtesy of the Swarthmore College Peace Collection.

Witherspoon in relation to Mygatt.[10] Witherspoon also possessed a gift for homemaking that appealed to Mygatt, who lacked the domestic touch.

When speculating about the nature of Witherspoon and Mygatt's relationship, Carroll Smith-Rosenberg's description of the close or romantic female friendships prevalent in the lives of white, middle-class Victorian women springs immediately to mind.[11] To be sure, Fannie May Witherspoon and Tracy Mygatt became devoted companions at a time when the middle-class homosocial construction of gender was on the wane. However, the separatist woman's culture of the nineteenth century had spawned the women's movement, institutions like the women's college, and woman-centered ways of living (such as urban settlement houses and female boarding establishments), all of which carried a "female world of love and ritual" well into the twentieth century.[12] Given their personal histories, therefore, it is not surprising that Witherspoon and Mygatt chose to live together as independent women.

One scholar, Nancy Manahan, has interpreted this relationship as a lesbian one.[13] Lillian Faderman's definition of a lesbian (which provides the framework for Manahan's assessment) as a woman whose chief, sustained love relationship is with another woman does invite us to think of Witherspoon and Mygatt as lesbians.[14] However, "lesbianism" as a concept is relatively recent and is employed by some scholars (often those with a heterosexual bias) to refer to love relationships between women that are explicitly sexual. Documentary evidence and oral interviews with people who knew Witherspoon and Mygatt well do not lead us to conclude that they were lovers.[15] Whether or not we choose to interpret this relationship as a lesbian one, it is incontrovertible that Mygatt and Witherspoon were profoundly loving with one another and committed to their partnership. It is highly unlikely that Tracy Mygatt found men sexually attractive or was ever predisposed to choose a man as a life partner. For Fannie May Witherspoon, a more complex picture emerges.

As a very young woman, Witherspoon fell in love with a married man, her aunt's husband. In 1930, when Witherspoon was 45 years old (Mygatt was 44), the aunt died, precipitating an emotional upheaval in Witherspoon's life. In a bizarre turn of events, her uncle died less than two months later. One of Witherspoon's close friends observed that this unexpected death devastated Witherspoon; the friend had hoped that they would marry.[16] While Witherspoon consulted a "nerve specialist," Tracy Mygatt, in turmoil herself, was comforted and reassured by mutual friends. The crisis passed, and Witherspoon and Mygatt remained a devoted couple for the rest of their lives.

In 1917, when war engulfed the nation, Witherspoon and Mygatt had been together almost a decade. They savored the experience of living and working together during a time when "Boston marriages" were common among women of similar class and educational background.[17] Like many other such women who became political activists in this era, Witherspoon's and Mygatt's close friendships with other women, in the context of a vibrant woman-centered lifestyle, helped to sustain them and give them strength to persevere in radical movements for social change.[18]

The first step that this remarkable couple took after graduating from Bryn Mawr in 1909 was to move to New York City, where Tracy Mygatt took the initiative in establishing (through the donations of philanthropic society women) the Chelsea Day Nursery for working mothers. Soon, however, they returned to Bryn Mawr to experience an "ivory tower" existence. They rented a garret apartment and earned their sustenance by tutoring the children of Bryn Mawr faculty. Becoming restless, they launched into lobbying efforts to amend the Pennsylvania child labor laws. Distressed by the failure of people like themselves to change the laws, Witherspoon and Mygatt embraced women's suffrage as the logical solution. In 1911, they became the first field organizers of the Woman Suffrage Party in eastern Pennsylvania. Traveling through the Amish countryside, sleeping with farm families (sometimes in beds with several children), Witherspoon and Mygatt delivered impassioned orations at grange meetings, county fairs, and old-home celebrations on woman's unique life-conserving role in society and on educated women's responsibility to help uplift their less fortunate sisters. Pragmatic educators, their talks stressed concrete reasons for supporting women's suffrage. In an interview in 1912, Witherspoon commented: "If it is a farming community, we talk of the need of better roads, improved school facilities and of a broadening of the civic spirit of the community, and we tell the people that the ballot in the hands of women of the community will help to bring about these things."[19] Both women also wished to "stir up an interest in the broad humanitarian aspects of government" and sought speaking engagements in schools and colleges.[20]

In 1913, Witherspoon and Mygatt resettled in Manhattan, taking up residence in an East Side flat. They enrolled in a six-month course at the Rand School of Social Science, which was funded by the Socialist Party of America and by various trade union groups so that working people could continue their education. In this heady environment, Witherspoon and Mygatt were converted to socialism and joined the Socialist Party, plunging headlong into propaganda work, particularly among women. Witherspoon wrote back to the Bryn Mawr alumnae bulletin for 1914 that she and Mygatt were "intellectually in perfect accord with our tried and trusted friends the Socialists . . . [who] have the right of it, we think, with their untiring, legal methods of education and organization."[21]

Witherspoon and Mygatt defined themselves as Christian socialists in accord with their strongly-held religious convictions. They, in common with a number of other comrades in the party, sought to square New Testament teachings with the socialist credo. Maintaining membership within the Episcopal Church, they aimed to "bore from within," helping to establish the Church Socialist League in 1914. Earlier, Witherspoon and Mygatt had participated in the "church raids" of 1913: they, along with others, had visited churches during the day, requesting clergy to provide food and shelter for the many unemployed men in the city; at night, when "hordes" of men began arriving at a designated church, Witherspoon and Mygatt were there "smoothing the way."[22] These dramatic raids focused attention on the vast unemployment crisis of 1913, which hit New York City particularly hard. Witherspoon and Mygatt's involvement in this campaign symbolizes their growing commitment to radical social activism.

New York City in the 1910s was a mecca for well-educated, idealistic young people like Witherspoon and Mygatt. In Lower East Side flats, in Greenwich Village lofts and coffeehouses, or in the cramped offices of left-wing groups located in the Ginn Building on Fifth Avenue a few blocks from Washington Square, socialist intellectuals, trade union activists, and cultural and political radicals worked and socialized together at fever pitch. The Socialist Party was at its height of influence and prestige; left-influenced trade unionism was a strong presence; the suffrage movement was accelerating as its expanded base came to include significant working-class, African American, and socialist political support; and a novel concept, feminism—linked to the suffrage cause but going well beyond it—was just developing.

Feminism was a new word in the United States in 1913. It was first used in New York City by women and men who appreciated that a concept and an emerging movement were needed to represent the "uncharted assertions and yearnings not expressed in palpable goals such as the suffrage."[23] As historian Nancy Cott makes clear, feminism was initially left-leaning: "Feminism was born ideologically on the left of the political spectrum, first espoused by women who were familiar with advocacy of socialism and who, advantaged by bourgeois backgrounds, nonetheless identified more with labor than with capital."[24] Left-wing feminists, then, linked suffrage and socialist goals as a matter of course.

In late 1913, the New York state legislature passed a bill that provided for a referendum on women's suffrage in 1915. Within a year, labor leader Theresa Malkiel, under the auspices of the Woman's National Committee of the Socialist Party, organized the Socialist Suffrage Campaign Committee for New York City, with three hundred socialist women pledged to work unstintingly for suffrage.[25] Witherspoon and Mygatt were among this group and within a few months were leaders in the campaign, distributing leaflets, organizing open-air meetings, and helping immigrant women to obtain naturalization papers. By the end of 1914, the socialist newspaper, the *New York Call,* featured a "Votes for Women" column, which in December carried Witherspoon's article "Woman Suffrage: No Longer a Side Issue, but the Main Issue." By February 1915, Witherspoon and Mygatt had organized the Socialist Suffrage Brigade and were recruiting volunteers to take literature, banners, and soapboxes to different districts of the city every Saturday afternoon through November 2, 1915, the date of the referendum.[26] By summer, the campaign was in full swing, with twenty-five to thirty open-air meetings taking place each week.[27] Witherspoon and Mygatt were special editors of a suffrage issue of the *Call* in June.

In a letter to a sister suffragist in her conservative hometown, Witherspoon supplied one memorable view of a brigade action that took place several weeks before the referendum vote:

> The jolliest and most heartening [march] was our walk the other night through the dense East Side where everyone cheered and cheered and the small boys and girls trailed along our lines, and even the old foreign heads of women, done up in their shawls, and the old Jewish fathers with their long gray beards peering out of the windows seemed to do so less in amazement than in positive sympathy with the strange doings of these strange American women. American women, yes, but with hundreds of their own Americanized daughters in our ranks. You can picture for yourself the picturesqueness of the scene as our floats and marchers passed along with flaring torches, gay music, and pumpkin-colored lights.[28]

It is interesting to note here that Witherspoon's letter avoided
mentioning that the activities she described came under the socialist banner.

Witherspoon and Mygatt were immersed in Socialist Party and
suffrage work right up until the vote for women was defeated in
the referendum on November 2, 1915. However, after the outbreak of hostilities in Europe in early August 1914, they also became increasingly involved in the peace movement. For instance,
on August 29, 1914, [Mygatt and Witherspoon participated in the
women's march against war organized by the redoubtable nonresistant pacifist, Fanny Garrison Villard](daughter of the famous abolitionist leader William Lloyd Garrison). A few months later,
Witherspoon published an article in the *Call* that linked women's
suffrage with issues of war and peacemaking. It was her impression
that the European war had "given a distinct impetus to enfranchis-
ing women" on two counts. First, women's suffrage was being seriously considered in some European circles as a means to prevent
future war; the vote would provide "the women who bear the men
who go to war (and who are known to value what they create) a
chance to hold them back from the grave." Second, because of the
absence of men on the home front, European women were proving
their economic importance and political capacity for self-governance:

> If the fruits of this terrible war are evil in every other respect, in
> this one, at least they are good—the disappearance of the fiction
> that women are not in the labor market, but petted and pro-
> tected in homes supported by males. . . . Nor will the question
> of women's capacity as political units ever again seriously enter
> the suffrage question. If they have been able to run the govern-
> ments of these countries alone, is it probable that when but half
> of the responsibility is put upon them in the future they will fall
> down under it?[29]

When Mygatt and Witherspoon arrived in New York City in
1913, the peace movement was in disarray. Male-dominated peace
associations—composed for the most part of lawyers, politicians,
and businessmen who sought to establish a legally sanctioned, warless liberal-capitalist global system—had lost their bearings.[30] The
founding in January 1915 of the feminist-oriented national Woman's
Peace Party marked a new beginning for the peace movement. Its
leaders encouraged cooperation with other newly formed liberal

peace organizations such as the high-profile Henry Street Settlement House Anti-Preparedness Committee, thus helping to forge a peace coalition that was dedicated to protecting domestic reform, discouraging militarism and conscription, and preventing U.S. involvement in the war.

Mygatt and Witherspoon welcomed the development of a broad-based peace coalition in 1915. They joined the New York City branch of the Woman's Peace Party, becoming quite active in this group of like-minded women, many of whom were left-wing pacifists and seasoned suffragist-feminists.[31] They became members of the American Neutral Conference Committee and participated in events sponsored by the American Union Against Militarism. They also maintained their involvement in the Socialist Party's antiwar activities, despite the fact that by the spring of 1915, they had come to see themselves as absolute pacifists; that is, they opposed the use of military force to settle disputes among nations or within a country. This set them apart from official Socialist Party doctrine, which was not pacifist in orientation but judged wars just or unjust according to the class objectives of the parties involved. The party opposed World War I because it was deemed a capitalist-imperialist struggle.

In this same period, another socialist woman, Jessie Wallace Hughan (a school teacher with a Ph.D. in political economy from Columbia University who was also an absolute pacifist), had begun an enrollment group against war participation, the Anti-Enlistment League. When Mygatt and Witherspoon heard Hughan speak on the League, they volunteered to help. Mygatt, along with the eloquent pacifist Unitarian minister John Haynes Holmes, joined Jessie Hughan on the executive committee; Witherspoon became the liaison officer for colleges. The League was not intended to serve as a peace group but represented instead "the banding together in a personal policy of those whose opposition to war has become unconditional."[32] Women as well as men were encouraged to join.

When the League was founded, no other radical (or absolute) pacifist group existed. In time, the League enrolled three thousand people from across the country; because its purpose had been to organize against voluntary enlistment in war, Hughan disbanded it when war was declared and conscription came into effect. In November 1915, however, well before the League had to disband, the

Fellowship of Reconciliation was born, with the aim of drawing into one group all Christians committed to personal renunciation of war. Fannie May Witherspoon, Tracy Mygatt, and Jessie Hughan became charter members.

The impetus for antiwar work in New York City in the months just preceding the war declaration came primarily from the Woman's Peace Party, under feminist-socialist Crystal Eastman's able leadership, and from the newly constituted, mainly female-led, staunchly antimilitarist Emergency Peace Federation. Women peace activists such as Witherspoon and Mygatt were often members of both groups. In the frantic time leading up to April 6, 1917, antiwar women in these associations and others, notably the Socialist Party, formed a close-knit group and mounted a vigorous campaign against U.S. entry into the war.

Mygatt and Witherspoon served on the executive committees of the New York City branches of both the Woman's Peace Party and the Emergency Peace Federation. Witherspoon served as assistant secretary of the Woman's Peace Party for a time, and both she and Mygatt helped to edit *Four Lights,* the uncompromising, original publication of the New York City branch. In a letter of January 13, 1917, to Dr. Maria Montessori, Witherspoon identified the purpose of *Four Lights* as "striking what seems to us a much neglected note of broad internationalism in these days of universal warfare and national strife. Though we hope to have some well known men contribute to our pages, the contributors will be chiefly women, and the issues of feminism and peace will naturally go hand in hand."[33]

Four months after Witherspoon wrote this letter, the United States was at war. Determined to find a new way, the now very diminished peace movement regrouped. In New York City, at the behest of the Emergency Peace Federation and with the cooperation of key people in the Socialist Party and in the Woman's Peace Party, secular and Christian socialists, labor leaders, feminists, and pacifists met at the end of May to establish the People's Council of America for Democracy and Terms of Peace. The new organization, greatly influenced by the dramatic events taking place in revolutionary Russia, strongly disapproved of American entry into the war and resolved to protect democratic rights at home and to plan for a reconstructed nonimperialist, cooperative, international postwar order.[34]

In the meantime, however, between April 6 and the founding of the People's Council on May 31, antiwar groups began discussing the problem of how to maintain civil liberties protections during war. Soon after the war declaration, the federal government launched a well-orchestrated propaganda campaign to win the unquestioning loyalty of Americans.[35] Ugly incidents such as the one Witherspoon witnessed in front of the New York Public Library were reported across the country. The nation quickly became saturated with notions of 100 percent Americanism and unthinking patriotism. Two days before the United States became a belligerent, Woodrow Wilson had predicted that the war experience would change the way people behaved towards each other: "Once lead this people into war, and they'll forget there ever was such a thing as tolerance. To fight you must be brutal and ruthless, and the spirit of ruthless brutality will enter into the very fibre of our national life, infecting Congress, the courts, the policeman on the beat, the man in the street."[36]

In order to protect people against this rising "spirit of ruthless brutality," representatives of a variety of antiwar groups and left-wing organizations supporting peace met at the office of the Church Peace Union in the Ginn Building at 70 Fifth Avenue on April 4 and 5, on the eve of U. S. entry into the war. At this gathering, participants discussed what to do once the country was at war, now almost a foregone conclusion. A joint statement of principles emerged from these deliberations, with a program that had as its main goal "[t]o work for the defense of American ideals and for an early and lasting peace." Those attending the meeting also recognized that individuals who refused war service or who held unpopular minority views would face difficulties in wartime. They pledged to organize "a legal defense and legal advice bureau for the benefit of conscientious objectors and persons who had been deprived of their right of exercising free speech, free assemblage and free press."[37]

The individuals who attended this meeting were committed, seasoned antiwar activists. All were white, most were middle class, and almost half were women. Politically, as a group, they epitomized the left-liberal or socialist antiwar alliance of the U.S. peace movement during 1914–17. Walking into the Ginn Building, they might have smiled grimly at the scrawl emblazoned along one wall by a fanatical patriot of the day: "Treason's Twilight

3. Ginn Building at Fifth Avenue and Thirteenth Street, New York, ca. 1905–1915. This building was dubbed "Treason's Twilight Zone" during World War I. Courtesy of The Wurts Collection, Museum of the City of New York.

Zone." Those entering the infamous building included the "peace twins" Rebecca Shelley and Lella Faye Secor, the spirited and effective young leaders of the Emergency Peace Federation (and before that the American Neutral Conference Committee), and their colleagues representing the socialist-inclined Intercollegiate Anti-Militarism League, Columbia University student Francis Phillips and English professor Henry Wadsworth Longfellow Dana. Also attending were Benjamin Marsh and Joseph Cannon, executive officers of the Socialist Party; Meta Lilienthal of the Socialist Suffrage Campaign Committee; Margaret Lane of the Woman's Peace Party; and Roger Baldwin, an iconoclastic and dynamic social worker recently arrived from St. Louis to direct the American Union Against Militarism, a pivotal liberal antiwar group of the era. Joy Young, a feminist pacifist active in the National Woman's Party and a member of the American Union, accompanied Baldwin.[38] Rabbi Judah Magnes, having returned early from the peace meeting in Washington, D.C., chaired the assembly.[39] Witherspoon, Mygatt, and a number of others were still in the capital lobbying members of Congress and consequently missed this meeting.

During April, several further meetings of these groups and numerous consultations took place in order to firm up plans to establish a legal aid bureau. By May 3, two organizations—the Woman's Peace Party and the Emergency Peace Federation (in one of its last deliberations before evolving into the People's Council)—decided jointly to hire Fannie May Witherspoon to take charge of free speech and free press complaints coming before their respective groups.[40] She accepted the post. On the same day, she wrote to suffragist-feminist and socialist Theresa Mayer that there now existed "a little bureau of legal first aid," which would "perform the initial investigation" of civil liberties cases and then "link up the person in difficulty with some reputable lawyer who will give his services to seeing the case through." It was understood that this service would be made available to "the various peace organizations."[41]

Several weeks later, on May 22, eight women active in the suffrage and peace movements met (again in the Ginn Building) to organize the New York Bureau of Legal First Aid, later renamed the Bureau of Legal Advice.[42] The New York City Woman's Peace Party provided $100 in start-up funds; the Emergency Peace Federation, $50. Suffragist and lawyer Marion B. Cothren was elected chair; socialist labor lawyer and feminist birth-control advocate Jessie Ashley, treasurer; and Fannie May Witherspoon, secretary. The suffragist-feminists, pacifists, socialists, intellectuals, and lawyers who comprised the rest of the Bureau committee were representative of the broad spectrum of New York City's liberal-radical social reform movement of the era.

During these same months, members of the American Union

Against Militarism were also distressed by the growth of a martial spirit in the country and the concomitant erosion of civil liberties. The American Union's directing board included Jane Addams, Lillian Wald, Paul Kellogg, Oswald Garrison Villard, John Haynes Holmes, and Norman Thomas, all leading figures in liberal reform causes. Its executive secretary, Crystal Eastman (the charismatic head of the New York City branch of the Woman's Peace Party), in concert with an energetic new director, Roger Baldwin, skillfully steered their organization towards civil liberties work after America's war declaration on April 6. A subcommittee was formed and Presbyterian minister and pacifist-socialist Norman Thomas quickly began preparing a pamphlet, *Conscription and the "Conscientious Objector" to War.*[43] By May, a Bureau of Conscientious Objectors existed within the Union, with Baldwin at the head.[44] At this juncture, however, a number of board members, notably Lillian Wald and Paul Kellogg, began expressing concern that civil liberties advocacy was hurting the efforts of their group to support Wilson in his desire for a democratic peace and for the establishment of a world government structure after the war. They felt strongly that the American Union should leave the civil liberties field to others. In response, Eastman argued eloquently that the politically liberal American Union could not support idealistic democratic international goals without at the same time attempting to protect democracy at home.[45] Baldwin added his voice, declaring: "Having created conscientious objectors to war, we ought to stand by them."[46] Thomas followed Baldwin's reasoning, adding his perception that if the Union eschewed civil liberties activism, more "radical organizations" would take leadership in this area.[47]

In large part because of Eastman's timely and persuasive intervention with key members Jane Addams, Emily Greene Balch, and Wald, the Union executive board agreed to her suggestion that work on behalf of conscientious objectors and victims of wartime repression remain within the organization. The Bureau of Conscientious Objectors became the Civil Liberties Bureau of the American Union Against Militarism at the end of June, with Baldwin its director. This agreement unraveled over the summer, however: prowar members such as Wald and Kellogg, who kept faith with Wilson, saw the Bureau's work as impeding the war effort, a view that finally prevailed with the Union executive board. In the fall,

4. *Roger Baldwin, ca. 1917. Courtesy of the Roger N. Baldwin Papers, Department of Rare Books and Special Collections, Princeton University Libraries.*

the Civil Liberties Bureau separated from the American Union, becoming the National Civil Liberties Bureau.[48]

While the American Union was sorting out its commitments, Witherspoon convened a conference on July 18 with representatives from the People's Council, the Workmen's Council (an antiwar labor alliance with a large immigrant membership), the Civil Liberties Bureau, and the Socialist Party to discuss the future of civil liberties work and to suggest cooperative arrangements. At this meeting, the People's Council proposed that the Bureau of Legal Advice reorganize on larger lines and promised financial backing if the Bureau admitted representatives of the groups in attendance to its executive committee. It was the understanding of those present that the Workmen's Council, the Civil Liberties Bureau, and the Socialist Party would also contribute financially to the running of the Bureau. The Bureau committee agreed to this arrangement, hired full-time counsel on August 1, and assumed full responsibility for all civil liberties cases in the New York City area.[49] The Bureau's initial aims were threefold: "1) To receive complaints of violations of constitutional rights during the war and to offer free legal aid by referring applicants to counsel for information and legal redress; 2) To serve as legal clearing house for all pacifist organizations and their counsel; and 3) To secure publicity on legal proceedings and legislative measures affecting civil liberties during the war."[50]

The founders of the Bureau of Legal Advice, in common with the executive officers of the Civil Liberties Bureau, recognized from the start the precariousness of their civil liberties mandate in the context of war. Shortly after Congress declared war, it approved measures restricting first amendment freedoms. Then, over the objections and protests of the now quite reduced antiwar forces, Congress passed the Selective Service Act on May 18 and the Espionage Act on June 15. President Wilson let it be known that in his opinion "there could be no such thing" as free speech during war. In his Flag Day speech, given one day before the Espionage Act became law, Wilson declared that he considered the peace movement "the new intrigue, the intrigue for peace," and asserted that the antimilitarists were "tools" of "the masters of Germany."[51]

Fannie May Witherspoon and Roger Baldwin understood that civil liberties activism would inevitably be associated in the public mind with "the intrigue for peace." Accordingly, they were careful to steer their organizations clear of antiwar activities, despite their own resolute pacifist convictions. Especially in the first months after war was declared, Witherspoon and Baldwin also labored hard to establish amicable relations with government officials, particularly with Secretary of War Newton Baker. Initially, War Department officials appeared relaxed about the two groups and indicated that the bureaus might serve a useful function by providing free counseling service to men subject to the draft. Thus, the bureaus headed by Witherspoon and Baldwin enjoyed a certain legitimacy in the eyes of the government, at least in the early months of the war, because they did not publicly criticize the role of the United States as a belligerent. However, other groups associated with civil liberties activism were openly critical of America's involvement in the war and were almost immediately targeted for prosecution. The No-Conscription League provides a case in point.

Organized in New York City in spring 1917 by feminist anarchist Emma Goldman in concert with Alexander Berkman and M. Eleanor Fitzgerald, the No-Conscription League was designed primarily to provide free legal advice to draft-age men. However, League members also spoke out uncompromisingly against the war, viewing it as an unjust capitalist-imperialist conflict. The League manifesto reveals an anarcho-syndicalist critique of capitalism and of the militarized state that was completely at variance with the jingoistic patriotic frenzy sweeping across the country in the spring of 1917. The text of the manifesto represented a challenge to thinking Americans that the war administration was not prepared to tolerate. It read in part:

> We oppose conscription because we are internationalists, anti-militarists, and opposed to all wars waged by capitalistic governments.
>
> We will fight for what we choose to fight for; we will never fight simply because we are ordered to fight.
>
> We believe that the militarization of America is an evil that far outweighs, in its anti-social and anti-libertarian effects, any good that may come from America's participation in the war.
>
> We will resist conscription by every means in our power, and we will sustain those who, for similar reasons, refuse to be conscripted.[52]

Resisting conscription "by every means in our power" was a statement bordering on treason, but despite the danger of arrest, the League organized a mass meeting at the Harlem River Casino on May 18, the day President Wilson signed the conscription bill. About ten thousand people attended, including several hundred policemen and detectives. In her autobiography, Goldman insisted that the speakers at this meeting and subsequent ones, while personally opposed to conscription, did not advise men to resist registration. Like herself, however, they pledged to stand by those who refused to register.

Goldman traveled extensively in the following weeks, setting up No-Conscription League affiliates in cities such as Philadelphia. Two more well-attended meetings of the League were held in New York City, at Hunt's Point Palace and Forward Hall. On June 19, one day after the Forward Hall meeting, Goldman and Berkman were arrested and charged with "conspiracy against the draft." Justice was not served in the trial, and on July 9, Goldman and Berkman were sentenced to two years in prison and fined ten thousand dollars each. The judge recommended deportation at the expiration of their sentences. Two months after its establishment, with two of its three leaders behind bars, the League folded.

Other civil liberties groups, choosing not to take a stand on the war as such, had more success than the No-Conscription League in establishing themselves over the summer months of 1917. The Civil Liberties Bureau, which by this time was defining itself as the national coordinating body for the emerging civil liberties movement, helped similar groups become established in a number of major cities. Particularly active were the American Liberty Defense League in Chicago and the League for Democratic Control in Boston. Meanwhile, the Bureau of Legal Advice, now in charge of all civil liberties cases for New York City, was swamped with work. Defending free speech in the courts and counseling draft-age men became the Bureau's first priorities. The struggle had begun.

ᵃᴴ 2 ᴴᵃ

Free Speech and Personal Behavior
in Wartime

*Let us beware. State or military necessity is the stake
at which every free institution dies, and it makes
little difference if the funeral march be "God Save the
King" or "The Star Spangled Banner."*
—Charles Recht,
"Mobilizing the Judicia," 1918

When the associates of the Bureau of Legal Advice opened their
small office on the eighth floor of the Ginn Building on the corner
of Fifth Avenue and Thirteenth Street, they committed themselves
to protect all individuals whose freedom of speech was in jeopardy;
to render legal service to draft-age men; and to intervene legally
on behalf of individuals, especially aliens, threatened with deportation because of their membership in or activities on behalf of radical and antiwar groups. It was soon manifest that another group,
the families of draft-eligible or drafted men, needed assistance in
filing for draft exemptions or for securing pay allowances and other
legal benefits. In addition, conscientious objectors (COs) to war
who found themselves drafted against their will required assistance
and protection from mistreatment at the hands of the military.

It is important to consider not only the Bureau's official legal
work but also its significance within the larger civil liberties and
prodemocracy movement of the war years, especially in New York
City. Such a perspective permits us to identify the beginnings of

what we might term a peace culture. We are then led to ask: What processes, circumstances, and commitments encouraged the feminists, pacifists, socialists, and left-leaning liberals of this incipient peace culture to maintain their steadfastness of purpose and to actually flourish in the midst of a dominant and aggressively menacing war culture?

On June 3, 1917, the *New York Times* reported rather smugly on the arrest of two young women who had been apprehended the day before for allegedly distributing no-conscription literature at the corner of Broadway and Twenty-third Street. Identified at the police station as Martha Gruening, a writer, and Rose Maria R. Spanier, a student, a charge of "disorderly conduct" had been made against them.[1] Gruening, a founding member of the Bureau of Legal Advice, quickly contacted Charles Recht, a fellow member of the Bureau's executive committee and a lawyer. Recht argued the case before Magistrate Ten Eych, who agreed to have the charges dismissed when the complainant in the case, Louis Horowitz, confessed that a circular had been handed to him at his own request and that he had not seen the defendants pass out the circular.[2] Years later, when writing his memoirs, Recht recalled that this was his "first skirmish with the war machine."

The case was not particularly memorable, but Martha Gruening was. She was a Smith College graduate (class of 1909) and came from a well-known family; her father was an eminent physician and her brother would eventually become a prominent public official. Gruening herself was writing for and helping to edit a short-lived pacifist magazine, *The Dawn,* in Greenwich Village, at the time of her arrest. She held a law degree from New York University (awarded 1914). From 1911 to 1914 and again in 1917 and 1918, Gruening served as an assistant secretary to the National Board of the National Association for the Advancement of Colored People (NAACP); she and the prominent African American cofounder of the NAACP, W. E. B. Du Bois, were appointed by the NAACP to investigate a race riot that broke out in East St. Louis, Illinois, on July 2, 1917. In August 1917, she traveled to Houston, Texas, to report on the race riot there that involved members of the all-black Twenty-fourth Infantry.[3]

In June, during their court appearance, Recht was impressed

5. *Martha Gruening, Smith College Class of 1909.*
Courtesy of Smith College Archives.

with Martha Gruening's character. As he later recounted in his
memoirs, when he tried to exploit her illustrious ancestry in the
trial, she intervened immediately: "My father isn't fighting my
battles," declared Gruening. "Stop it." Recht remembered also that
some time later, when one of the first "Negro dramas" by Ridgely
Torrence was performed in New York, Gruening adopted a child
member of the cast, an African American boy named David Butt:
"She devoted herself to the unique task of being a white mother to
a very dark little boy in a city where prejudice was strong. After
the war, to get him properly educated, she emigrated to France
and until her untimely death continued to be a steadfast advocate
of Negro rights."[4]

Charles Recht was himself an extraordinary individual. A native of Bohemia, this urbane and artistic young man had emigrated to the United States in 1900 at the age of thirteen with his widowed mother, Adele Kraus Recht, and siblings. He was a graduate of a Prague gymnasium and had been rejected for military service in his homeland because of a "narrow chest." Recht was a romantic and ambitious youth. Once settled in Manhattan, he worked diligently at various jobs to help support his family. He became a librarian before he was twenty and put himself through New York University's law school on a part-time basis. The law profession supplied Recht with a living, but his passion was literature. He was a linguist and in 1912 published the first English translation of an August Strindberg play, *Countess Julia*.[5] Recht was also a published poet.

In the immediate prewar era, Recht began to practice law, but he spent much of his free time among literary people. One of his clients was H. L. Mencken, who became a personal friend and "inspiration." Dining with Mencken at the Algonquin Hotel restaurant in Manhattan, Recht conversed with literary figures such as Hendrick Willem Van Loon and Edgar Lee Masters. Masters, a lawyer as well as the author of the celebrated *Spoon River Anthology*, furnished, Recht averred, "an apology for my artistic diversions." As a standby actor for the Provincetown Players (the experimental theater group founded by cultural radical and journalist Mary Heaton Vorse), Recht became acquainted with playwrights Eugene O'Neill, Susan Glaspell, Sherwood Anderson, and Jasper Deeter. He frequented "village spots" and counted poet Edna St. Vincent Millay as a friend, along with other cultural and political radicals of the Greenwich Village set such as John Reed, Max Eastman, Crystal Eastman, Ida Rauh, and Floyd Dell. Recht found New York City fairly tolerant of immigrants like himself in the prewar era, although hatred of foreigners was a palpable undercurrent. Literary America, notably the Greenwich Village youth generation, "welcomed enrichment through the medium of the hyphenates." Thus, for Recht, the period just before the war was one of "roseate effervescence." While law was Recht's "bread," literature was "the jam."[6]

In 1915, Recht married Aristine Munn, a physician and member of a wealthy family, long-established in Rochester, New York. They settled in Yonkers. Munn was appointed director of the New York Beekman Street Hospital, a position she retained even after

6. *Charles Recht in the World War I era. Courtesy of John Recht.*

the birth of their son John in 1916. In later years, she became the first dean of women at New York University.

When war came to America, Recht registered at his local draft board as a nonreligious conscientious objector. In later years, he saw the war as a fateful moment in his life: "The America I wanted to belong to, the literary world, was to be ignored. Creative forces were being mobilized for [war] propaganda."[7] Recht feared for the safety of "the insignificant minority," the pacifists who would oppose the war. He resolved to use his skills as an attorney to aid in their defense. Mulling over why he chose this difficult path, Recht noted that his father Marcus Recht, a lover of German idealist literature who rebelled against political oppression, served as a model. At the same time, Recht's own recollections of being called before the recruiting board of the Austrian army and his hatred of tyranny were contributing factors. In one significant instance, while Recht was a young gymnasium student in Pisek (before he moved to Prague), a trial took place that resulted in the judicial (and almost the actual) lynching of a young, mentally deficient Jewish man, Leopold Hilsner, for the supposed ritual murder of a young peasant girl. Hilsner was found guilty, although his death sentence was commuted by Emperor Franz Josef. This event marked Recht and reinforced other lessons he had learned from his father and from his experience as a Jew in an extremely anti-Semitic culture: "For me, it was the first glimpse of the fact that in political trials, the accused and his lawyers have a more formidable adversary than the prosecutor, and that is public hysteria. That early lesson was to be reinforced in cases I later tried as a lawyer for people called anarchists, communists, and others, vaguely characterized, in general, as subversives."[8]

Soon after coming to Martha Gruening's aid, Recht was inundated with free speech and what he labeled "personal behavior" cases. He was one of a handful of advocates in Manhattan who consistently agreed to represent victims of wartime oppression in the courts. Others included socialist pacifist Winter Russell, also a member of the Bureau of Legal Advice executive committee and its first paid counsel, and Harry Weinberger, a prowar liberal and a staunch civil libertarian who represented (among other radical cause célèbres) Emma Goldman and Alexander Berkman in an unsuccessful attempt to prevent their deportation to the Soviet Union after being convicted on conspiracy charges.

Alongside these men, three women—Elinor Byrns, Adelma Burd, and Jessie Ashley—volunteered their services as lawyers to the Bureau of Legal Advice at its inception. They declined court work but did provide legal expertise from time to time. Byrns, who lived on Staten Island and had an active practice chiefly among women, found court work distasteful; Ashley dropped her professional work not long after the United States declared war so that she could devote herself to pacifist and socialist work; Burd was often in Washington, D.C., in her capacity as an attorney for the War Risk Insurance Bureau and actually moved there during the latter months of the war.[9] Several other women lawyers worked on specific Bureau cases during the war, but it was men—Winter

Russell and especially Charles Recht—who carried on the brunt of the legal work.

From the beginning, the Bureau of Legal Advice possessed a purposeful and energetic style that attracted clients. Initially, the Bureau shared office space with two of the groups that had helped give it birth, the New York City branch of the Woman's Peace Party and the Emergency Peace Federation (which by June had become the People's Council). The newly constituted Civil Liberties Bureau had an office downstairs in the same building, and the executive committees of both civil liberties groups overlapped noticeably. While records do not reveal on which day the Bureau of Legal Advice opened its doors to clients, minutes do indicate that a formal meeting of the executive committee took place as early as May 11, 1917. A report in the fall notes that 431 individuals sought assistance during May, June, and July. Most visited the office two or three times and many came requesting draft counseling.[10] Fannie May Witherspoon, executive secretary, was aided by part-time paid secretarial help, which was at first supplied gratis by the Civil Liberties Bureau; in the fall, the Bureau hired and paid for its own secretary and stenographer. Also on hand were a number of volunteers, including Tracy Mygatt and Bruno Grunzig, a young conscientious objector who worked unstintingly for the Bureau until he was drafted into the army the following spring. Winter Russell became the paid lawyer for the Bureau in August; in the fall, Charles Recht replaced him as chief counsel. During the summer months, Russell and Recht handled a number of Bureau cases.

An early Bureau of Legal Advice pamphlet painted a grim picture of a city and a nation gripped by "an autocratic spirit [that] undermines our national life, influences our minor officials, and permeates our courts." The promulgation of emergency legislation (notably the Espionage and Selective Service Acts) in conjunction with the actions of ill-informed enforcement officers and magistrates created much work for Bureau lawyers:

> Since the declaration of war the courts of New York have been sitting upon cases of persons brought into them on all kinds of irrelevant minor charges where the real question at issue was Freedom of Speech. The offender has spoken in hall or on street corner; sometimes sold a radical magazine; sometimes dared ad-

vocate the repeal of the Conscription Act or voiced a longing for peace. Sometimes the offense has been a conscience which forbids its owner to kill his fellow men.[11]

It was this situation that led Recht to describe his Manhattan office at 110 West Fortieth Street as the "clinic" of the Bureau of Legal Advice. By September 1917, Recht's name was appearing almost daily in the newspapers as the defender of "undesirables." His position with the Bureau had become a full-time job.

In the early months of the war, it became common practice for individuals to be arrested either by private citizens or by police officers under the charge of "disorderly conduct." Martha Gruening and Rose Spanier's case came under this category. Witherspoon recognized that "disorderly conduct" was really a code phrase used by those who wished to curtail free speech. During the summer and fall of 1917, she issued press releases and pamphlets that pointed to the threat to free speech posed by the city magistrates' use of charges of disorderly conduct and "seditious" speech as means for convicting so-called soapbox orators in New York City. Witherspoon insisted that these convictions had no basis in the law and noted that they contributed to a rising level of violence against unpopular public speakers. Charles Recht, under the aegis of the Bureau of Legal Advice, took on a number of such cases in order to test the legality of soapbox oratory convictions.

By September, the combined work of Witherspoon and Recht seemed to have borne some fruit. A New York State grand jury informed the public that street speaking was legal in New York City, even if the content of speeches appeared to be seditious. Sedition was an offense that was punishable only by the federal authorities; the grand jury suggested that soapbox oratory cases either be referred to the federal district attorney for consideration or be dealt with by magistrates under existing laws. It also enjoined municipal government officials to pass an ordinance forbidding street speaking for the war's duration. Thus, the success that the Bureau enjoyed in challenging the illegality of soapbox oratory was checkmated by the grand jury recommendations.[12] Nonetheless, some city magistrates were repelled by the excesses of overzealous and unreasoning patriots and chose to side with the Bureau's broad interpretation of free speech rights in wartime.

The case of Harry Letaner is illustrative. On November 15,

1917, Letaner, a twenty-two year old street speaker, was rescued from an angry mob by a policeman at Madison Square as he discussed the large costs of the war and expressed his doubt that the Allies would be able to repay the loans of the United States. He was brought before Magistrate Murphy, who set bail at $500, pending trial. Recht represented Letaner and bail was furnished, but Magistrate Murphy stated that he expected that Letaner would be found guilty and sent to the workhouse. Letaner reappeared on the soapbox at Madison Square; his theme was free speech, and he criticized Magistrate Murphy, who had gained a reputation for severity in dealing with such cases. Letaner was again threatened by an unruly mob and once more arrested. However, Magistrate Joseph Corrigan, upon hearing the evidence for both cases, dismissed the charges. When "Mr. Fitzgerald," who had made a citizen arrest, protested the outcome, Corrigan responded: "You seem indignant. I do not see anything so bad in what this man has done. It is the right of any citizen to criticize the courts or public officials." Fitzgerald countered with a statement that he had three sons in the army and then remarked that he wished to know how he could prevent the "dirty foreigners from unpatriotic utterances." Corrigan reproved Fitzgerald: "I am not here to tell you what free speech is. What you had better do is to go to the nearest public library and look up the constitution of the United States."[13]

Similar in some respects to the free speech cases handled by the Bureau were those of defendants who were arraigned "not because of any attempt to bring before the public political or other conceptions, but because of individual conduct or individual belief at variance with the popular mind in time of war."[14] Charles Recht called these "cases of personal behaviour in wartime."[15] Recht often won his cases only after much expenditure of time and energy; he claimed a relatively easy victory, however, when a vaudeville actor, Ranislaw Javanovitch, was accused by a stage hand in December 1917 of not removing the cap of his costume to show respect for the national anthem. Javanovitch claimed that he did not recognize the anthem as he walked offstage during a shift in scenes. Magistrate Nolan dismissed the charges. Javanovitch, meanwhile, spent five days in jail, in default of bail.

Much more difficult to defend, because of the prejudice of the presiding magistrate, was the case of Moische Samet, a Galician Jew who had emigrated to the United States after his mandatory service in the Austrian army. At the time of his arrest, Samet was supporting his wife and five children on $14 a week in a basement accommodation occupied rentfree in exchange for janitorial service. On a warm spring evening in June 1918, Samet boarded a Third Avenue street car at Twenty-eighth Street. Exhausted by a hard day's work as an apprentice in the fur trade, he fell asleep against the shoulder of a nativist barkeeper, Michael McGovern, who suspected Samet was not an American citizen. Taking offense at Samet's foreign accent and bedraggled state, he forced Samet to accompany him to the Tenth District Night Court. Once there, McGovern accused a bewildered Samet of having awoken from a sound sleep to shout, "To hell with America." Samet denied the charge, and the complainant offered no corroborating testimony. Nevertheless, Magistrate Francis Mancusco believed the story and was prepared to sentence Samet to the workhouse for six months. However, Recht had been called in at Mrs. Samet's request. He convinced Magistrate Mancusco to permit a probation officer to investigate the home life and habits of Samet before sentence was passed. The officer reported on Samet's exemplary record of behavior and also pointed out the misery that his family would endure without the earnings of its main breadwinner. Magistrate Mancusco finally agreed to dismiss the charges against Samet, mainly on account of the prisoner's children. In his memoirs, Recht quoted in full a letter of thanks that he received from one of Samet's daughters:

June 16, 1918

Dear Sir:
I am thanking you very much for the trouble that you have had in fighting out the case of my father, Mr. M. Samet, and I wish that in every case you shall have good luck and success.
And oblige.

Yours sincerely,
. Rose Samet[16]

Recht's good luck was not to last, however. Four months later he found himself back in Magistrate Mancusco's court, representing another defendant in a personal behavior case. In this instance, Samuel Nikition, a Russian factory worker who had resided in the United States since 1916, refused to buy a Liberty Bond when urged to do so by a group of canvassers in a Greenwich Village theater on October 2. Nikition was severely beaten by an incensed patriot and, after being thrown out of the theater, was rescued by an American soldier and turned over to a police officer. The officer took Nikition to the Tenth District Night Court. Without counsel or understanding of the proceedings (an interpreter gave the accused's testimony), Nikition was convicted and sentenced to six months in prison solely on the statement of his accuser. Recht read about Nikition's case in a newspaper and, after securing the minutes of the trial, filed an appeal. A grateful Nikition informed Recht (who understood Russian) that he had not said, "To hell with America! To hell with Liberty Bonds!" but rather had declared that as a Russian subject it was not his duty to buy Liberty Bonds; the interpreter, however, had garbled his testimony. Judge Crain of the Court of General Sessions reversed the lower court's decision and set a new trial on the ground that Nikition, who was tried immediately upon arrest, had had no opportunity to secure witnesses and to prepare a defense. When Nikition's case was finally heard on July 20, 1919, nine months after the first trial, all charges were dismissed. Some time before this date, Nikition had been released on bail; the interim he spent in jail.

Soon after the Bureau of Legal Advice took responsibility for the Nikition case, Fannie May Witherspoon issued a public statement condemning the spiteful and incendiary words that Magistrate Mancusco had hurled at Samuel Nikition at the time of his first trial. Charles Recht actually wrote to President Wilson about the case. In the Bureau's 1918 yearbook, he declared that the magistrate's behavior was "a sinister commentary on the lawlessness which has invaded our very courts."[17] Mancusco's final words to Nikition were indeed shocking: "I am surprised that the people in the theater permitted you to come out at all. They should have taken you and lynched you right then and there. If anyone was brought before me with a charge of that kind I would send them away with the commendation of the court. Workhouse, six months."[18]

Recht and Witherspoon sought redress for Magistrate Mancusco's flagrant abuse of the law. The president's office had replied that federal jurisdiction did not extend to magistrate court, and so Recht made formal complaint to the Association of the Bar of New York. After sitting on Recht's letter for some time, E. Chrystie, attorney for the grievance committee, wrote Recht in March 1919 that "the facts were not sufficient to warrant any proceedings against the magistrate."[19] Undaunted, within two weeks of making Chrystie's letter public, Witherspoon wrote to Elinor Byrns asking her to look up the law on disbarment proceedings and to advise the Bureau on what form the petition for disbarment should take. In a rather surprising turn of phrase for a proponent of non-violence, Witherspoon informed Byrns (also an absolute pacifist): "The particular scalp we are after is the Hon. Francis X. Mancusco, though we have others in mind."[20] (By this time, widespread violation of civil liberties—anticipated months before by Witherspoon and other movement activists—was in full swing.) There are no further references to this particular magistrate in the records after this date; it is probable that he sat out his allotted term as judge of the Tenth District Court.

The Nikition case and others point to the victimization that many other poor, working-class individuals experienced at the hands of the law during the war, especially those who were of foreign birth. As noted earlier, very few lawyers were willing to defend what the Bureau of Legal Advice termed "officialdom's victims." There was no public defender's office in New York City at this time.

Of course, one did not have to be working class to run afoul of wartime community standards for appropriate patriotic behavior. As in other areas of the country, public school teachers in New York City were expected to be actively prowar. Many teachers were drawn into the vortex of intolerance and hate, but some resisted; such individuals paid a high price for their independence of mind. In New York City and environs, school teachers who were suspended or fired from their positions for opposing the war received support from a liberal press, a determined Teachers' Union, and sympathetic groups such as the Bureau of Legal Advice. Historian Howard K. Beale has pointed out that in New York City, hearings and trials occurred (sometimes with the aid of legal counsel), in contrast to many communities throughout the country where there was no recourse for dismissals. However, the semblance of due process in America's largest metropolis did not affect the outcome: "disloyal" teachers lost their jobs, either temporarily or permanently, because "the decision was determined in advance by the war hysteria of the men conducting the proceedings."[21] Charles

Recht identified teacher dismissals of this sort as additional examples of personal behavior cases.

As one example, the Bureau of Legal Advice took up the case of Gertrude Pignol after she was charged by the New York board of education on April 24, 1918, with "conduct unbecoming of a teacher." Despite Recht's able counsel, she was fired after a board of education trial held on May 7. Pignol had emigrated to the United States from Germany as a young woman and became an American citizen in 1910. She was a firm democrat and a strong critic of German autocracy. At the time she was fired, Pignol had been teaching German and French at the Manual Training High School in Brooklyn for twelve years. Her teaching had received a rating of "superior merit," and she was a respected staff member at the school. In October 1917, however, her troubles began when an anonymous letter by a select group of patriotic teachers denounced her as pro-German in a written complaint to the board of education. Pignol was questioned by her principal, and hostility against her grew among her coworkers. With the apparent sympathy of her principal, Pignol took a three-month leave of absence beginning January 1, 1918.

When Pignol returned on March 15, she was immediately interviewed by her principal, who was openly antagonistic. He asked Pignol leading questions that were meant to entrap her into disloyal utterances. Three days later, she was brought before a meeting of superintendents of schools. At this meeting, Pignol explained that she believed that the United States should not have entered the war and that she did not support U.S. war policies; however, she had never spoken of her personal beliefs in class. In response to pointed questions, Pignol insisted that she had urged her pupils to purchase Liberty Bonds and war stamps but had not bought any herself before she went on leave. In response to a question as to whether she felt justified in combatting the country's decision to go to war, Pignol replied: "No, I do not, and I do not combat it. I only want to have the liberty to keep my own opinion, and if I have conscientious scruples against something, I wish to have the liberty to act according to my conscience." Her answers supplied enough evidence in the minds of the superintendents to move for a trial before the board of education, which occurred May 7, with Charles Recht serving as Pignol's counsel.

At the trial, Pignol admitted that she had reluctantly come to the decision that the United States had been justified in entering the war; her modified stand owed much to her reaction to newspaper accounts of Germany's advance on the unresisting Russian people. Pignol even admitted to buying a Liberty Bond, although she supplied this information hesitantly, not wishing to be seen as yielding to pressure. Nonetheless, as Recht later remarked, Pignol's decision to buy a war bond "did not affect the decision of the Board, nor was it expected that it would. It was clear by this time, that Miss P. was slated for dismissal and any excuse would serve to accomplish that purpose."[22] An excerpt from the trial underscores Recht's assertion:

MR. MCINTYRE [Corporation Counsel]: Are you willing to take part in the crushing of Germany?

MISS PIGNOL: I have stated that I am willing to do all in my power to further the United States in this war.

MR. MCINTYRE: Even to the point of crushing Germany?

MISS PIGNOL: I cannot prevent the crushing of Germany if that is the result of the war.

MR. MCINTYRE: Do you wish to see Germany crushed if the purposes of the United States cannot be accomplished in any other way?

MISS PIGNOL: I do not wish to see Germany crushed, no sir.[23]

Recht considered this part of the record crucial, for "*it was on this that the Board rendered its decision.*"[24]

Gertrude Pignol was not the only teacher so treated. Indeed, she merely had reservations against the war; coworkers who were absolutely opposed to war because of their religious or political convictions met similar fates. Mary McDowell, a Latin teacher in Pignol's school who was a Quaker and a member of the Woman's Peace Party, was suspended, though she was reinstated a few years later.[25] Several respected socialist teachers, all male, were also fired, although not without a great deal of fanfare in the local press.[26] Other teachers who were active in radical causes and were personally against the war lived under constant threat of dismissal. Jessie Wallace Hughan, for instance, almost lost her job; she and a small number of other pacifist teachers earned the ire of school authorities for their refusal to sign the mayor's loyalty oath required of school teachers. Hughan finally signed it, but she added: "This obedience being qualified always by dictates of conscience."[27]

Charles Recht understood why Pignol and other freethinking teachers were fired. In the Bureau's yearbook for 1918, he quoted the words of Dr. John Finley, the Commissioner of Education for New York State, on the wartime obligations prescribed for teachers: "A school-teacher must be absolutely loyal and do with her mind what the soldier does with his body, namely, give it without reserve to the Government."[28] The needs of the militarized state took priority over personal conviction and individual conscience. Historian Kathleen Kennedy has noted that state officials found particularly irksome the declension of some female teachers (like Pignol and Hughan) from a war culture that they were expected to uphold as patriotic "moral mothers." The venom with which Pignol, McDowell, Hughan and other women teachers were attacked adds credence to Kennedy's well-argued thesis.[29] Indeed, the first teacher fired by the New York City board of education was Fannie Ross, an elementary school teacher in charge of seven-year-old children at Public School 88 in Queens. In November 1917, Ross was dismissed from her post for having given advice contrary to the spirit of the draft in her capacity as a registrar for the state census. Her case actually marked the beginning of a systematic investigation into the loyalty of teachers in the New York City schools.[30]

Free speech and personal behavior cases represented a large proportion of the Bureau of Legal Advice's court work. While Gertrude Pignol was the only teacher the Bureau was called upon to defend before the board of education, Recht considered her to be one of the Bureau's most important cases. In other instances, individuals whom Recht defended as free speech or personal behavior cases were arraigned because of their clear connections with domestic politics or with international events. Recht referred to these as political cases.

The Bureau originated at the insistence of socialists, feminists, labor radicals, and pacifists who recognized, as Witherspoon put it, that they would be on "the firing line" at home during the war. With an executive committee of individuals closely associated with the Socialist Party and with foreign-language labor organizations, it was inevitable that the Bureau would take on political cases as part of its mandate. An examination of one such case facilitates understanding of the Bureau's work as part of a larger left-wing prodemocracy movement that developed within the context of wartime exigencies.

On March 7, 1918, a group of Russian workers employed by the Standard Oil Works met in a rented saloon hall in Bayonne, New Jersey, to discuss revolutionary Russia and to organize a night school to help Standard Oil employees learn to read and write Russian and English. The main speaker was Theodore Fedotoff, a young Russian who had emigrated to the United States in 1913 and who was a staff member of *Novy Mir,* a Russian socialist newspaper published in New York City. A fellow Russian, Anton Taichin, who had come to the United States in 1910 and was also a socialist, had made the arrangements to book the hall. While the meeting was in progress, it was invaded by a group of unruly men, who created quite a disturbance; a few minutes later, the police rushed in, the lights went out, and Fedotoff and Taichin were arrested. They were brought to Jersey City and incarcerated in the Hudson County Jail.

On March 9, the defendants were arraigned and indicted under the Sedition Law of New Jersey, an act passed hurriedly several months before the United States entered the war. Fedotoff was charged with "having used such language that from its plain import and effect was intended to foment or encourage opposition or hostility to the Government of the United States and the State of New Jersey." Taichin was charged with "having counselled, aided and abetted [Fedotoff] in his design."[31] Recht served as counsel at the arraignment proceedings. His initial efforts to have the bail of $5000 each reduced were unavailing; however, the Bureau was able to document the substandard conditions at the Hudson County Jail (which housed people labeled "insane" along with other prisoners); bail was finally reduced to $3,500 for Fedotoff and $1,500 for Taichin, and the men were released. By this time, late March, two New Jersey lawyers, Jennie Richer and M. J. Ready, had agreed to defend Fedotoff and Taichin under the Bureau's auspices. The trial was set suddenly for the end of April, and both defendants were convicted of conspiracy to violate the Sedition Law. Two weeks later, they were sentenced to ten years each in the state penitentiary in Trenton.[32]

The Bureau of Legal Advice considered the trial a travesty of justice. In concert with the *Novy Mir* staff and with regional Russian-language socialist federations, Witherspoon worked inde-

7. *Front cover,* The Case of Fedotoff and Taichin, *1918. Left to right: Theodore Fedotoff and Anton Taichin. Courtesy of the Tamiment Institute Library, New York University.*

fatigably to raise funds to appeal the Fedotoff-Taichin case to a higher court. In a pamphlet on the case that was circulated widely in liberal and radical circles, Witherspoon argued convincingly that the young Russian workers had been framed. The prosecution had based its case on the testimony of the three men who had broken up the meeting, who admitted to belonging to a conservative religious organization that was loyal to the czar. Fedotoff and witnesses for the defense admitted that he had stated that the present war was caused by capitalist greed, but they denied that he had criticized the U.S. government and the president, a contention of the prosecution. Witherspoon pointed out that "these comrades are the first to be indicted under the New Jersey Sedition Law"; she expected that they would not be the last to be so charged. Angrily, she declared: "Shall a state law be allowed to stand which forbids residents of New Jersey not only to show a rebellious attitude, but even to offer 'opposition' to State and Federal governments? Is this, or is it not a government of the people?"[33] Witherspoon also contrasted the idealism of the "brave and intelligent young men" with the violence and amorality of the prosecution's witnesses, whom she suggested had probably perjured themselves and, if not "dead-drunk were at least fighting drunk" when they broke up the workers' meeting. She insisted that liberal and radical women and men shared a stake in the fate of Fedotoff and Taichin. Witherspoon concluded on an ironic and insistent note: "Justice, far from being 'without money and without price,' is the most expensive luxury one can afford. The rich man has the wherewithal to obtain it; the poor man only secures it if his friendship [*sic*] dig deep into their pockets and rally to his support."[34]

Witherspoon believed in the power of language to elicit constructive action. She was also a seasoned activist and understood the importance of networking and organization-building. In an undated *New York Call* article, "What It Means to Be a Socialist," Witherspoon reminded her comrades that plans "to convert the world" had to go hand-in-hand with unheralded concrete tasks: "Educate, organize. The words don't thrill, but the result does."[35] In such a spirit, Witherspoon, in concert with Roger Baldwin of the Civil Liberties Bureau, Elizabeth Gurley Flynn of the Industrial Workers of the World, and other labor radicals such as Ella Reeve Bloor (also a member of the Bureau of Legal Advice executive committee), established the Liberty Defense Union in March 1918.[36] The purpose of this national umbrella association was "to organize popular support on behalf of persons prosecuted for their exercise of their constitutional rights of free speech and free press."[37] Baldwin became executive secretary and Witherspoon sat on the executive committee, while three members of the Union's general committee were also members of the Bureau of Legal Advice's executive committee: John L. Elliot (chair of the Bureau), Ella Reeve Bloor, and Bertha Mailly of the Rand School of Social Science. Within a few months, the Union raised almost $6,000 in defense funds.[38]

8. *Elizabeth Gurley Flynn speaking at 1912 Patterson textile strike. Courtesy of Sophia Smith Collection, Smith College.*

Records of the Liberty Defense Union show that the Bureau of Legal Advice received funds on a regular basis. The founding of the Union came in the same month that Fedotoff and Taichin were arrested; by June, the Union had contributed $300 to the Bureau of Legal Advice for costs associated with the appeal of the Russian workers' case. Working closely with the Bureau was the Committee on Defense of Fedotoff-Taichin, sponsored by *Novy Mir.* Correspondence in the Bureau's files indicates that Witherspoon and other Bureau members became quite exasperated with the *Novy Mir* committee. Joy Young, a young feminist-pacifist who had been an active suffragist and antimilitarist before the war and who

9. *Left to right: Annie Clemence, the Dog Picket, and Ella Reeve Bloor, 1913. Courtesy of Sophia Smith Collection, Smith College.*

became acting secretary of the Bureau during July and August 1918 (while Witherspoon took a much needed holiday), wrote disparagingly of the "childish" and "irresponsible" behavior of the *Novy Mir* committee. Its members seemed unable or unwilling to undertake the legwork necessary to mount a successful fund drive.[39] Nevertheless, Witherspoon and the Bureau pushed on with the case and stayed in close touch with Jennie Richer and Jacob Magolis, the New Jersey lawyers retained to argue the appeal. Richer, with Charles Recht's help, prepared the appeal brief. By the end of 1918, when the Bureau's yearbook was printed, the Fedotoff-Taichin case was before the Supreme Court of New Jersey.

10. *Joy Young clad in a white surplice in front of Statuary Hall in Washington, D.C., on the occasion of the memorial service for National Woman's Party suffrage campaigner Inez Milholland Boissevain, December 25, 1916.*

By the close of 1918, the Bureau of Legal Advice had sponsored some forty-five court cases, many of which can be loosely defined as free speech cases (including personal behavior and political cases). Others concerned specific points of law (especially in relation to the rights of aliens during wartime) or court-martial proceedings against conscientious objectors. Charles Recht, retained on a monthly stipend, handled most of these court cases.

When individuals who required the services of a lawyer came to the Bureau office, Witherspoon or other staff people sent them along to Recht's office on West Fortieth Street.

Many people contributed to the survival and achievements of the Bureau of Legal Advice, but the two key players were indubitably Charles Recht and Fannie May Witherspoon. Recht's devotion to the protection of civil liberties in wartime was matched by his skill in the courtroom. He cared passionately about securing justice for individuals and had a knack for securing people's confidence. His integrity of purpose was also appreciated by those public officials who stood apart from the mindless superpatriotism and violence of the times. Fannie May Witherspoon had extraordinary talents as well. As the executive secretary and administrative head, she was responsible to the executive committee for setting Bureau policy; raising funds on a monthly basis to keep the organization afloat; writing press releases and articles for journals; corresponding with other civil liberties and prodemocracy groups across the country; and keeping communication channels open with government and military officials. Witherspoon was an able administrator. She also enjoyed thinking and writing about the law and felt that she possessed a certain competency in this respect; to serve Bureau clients, Witherspoon became a notary public in July 1918.

For the Bureau to run smoothly, Witherspoon and Recht had to create a working partnership. Although their capabilities complimented each other in many respects, there were also points of tension, even discord. Ultimately, however, the partnership flourished. To understand why, it is necessary to look more closely at their respective characters and personalities, as manifested within their evolving relationship.

Witherspoon and Recht were almost the same age and shared common enthusiasms. Both considered literature the "jam" of life and longed, at times, for literary careers. Recht, especially, participated eagerly in the bohemian lifestyle of Greenwich Village and identified with the freewheeling spirit of the cultural radicals who lived and worked there. Although she, too, appreciated Village culture, Witherspoon was more of a political radical and less of a bohemian than Recht. She had spent the prewar years eking out a living with part-time work so that she could devote most of her time to socialist-feminist and pacifist activism, while Recht had begun his professional life as a lawyer and spent many hours in coffeeshops and restaurants discussing literature, philosophy, and history in social groups in which men predominated. Witherspoon spoke of herself as a radical; Recht evaded a label but admitted that others saw him as "a sort of revolutionary-at-large." He joined the Intercollegiate Socialist Society during his law school days but thereafter refused to join any political organization. Witherspoon, by contrast, was an inveterate "joiner." Recht had an ebullient charm, and all manner of people found themselves drawn to this slim and physically graceful young man; Witherspoon was a self-contained and rather formal person. At the same time, she possessed a keen ironic wit and was a shrewd judge of character; of medium build and fine-featured, people found her attractive.

Some movement men of her generation, including Recht, viewed Witherspoon as somehow older than they. Recht, who was thirty years old when the United States went to war (Witherspoon was thirty-two), deferred to Witherspoon's authority in a number of ways and asked for her advice and approval in the way middle-class men of the Victorian era seemed to do with a respected sister or, perhaps, an aunt. There was something of the Victorian woman in Witherspoon's demeanor, but it seems likely that this aspect of her personality came to the fore more in the presence of men than women. Witherspoon, who lived in an enduring and loving relationship with Tracy Mygatt, spent most of her social time with iconoclastic "new women," and in some of her writing addressed primarily to women or on behalf of women, one detects a breezy, fun-loving, and relaxed tone. For instance, she, Mygatt, and others of the New York City branch of the Woman's Peace Party wrote most irreverent send-ups of personalities and events in the journal *Four Lights.*

As their partnership developed, Recht appears to have taken on the role of the flamboyant, endearing younger brother whose lack of attention to detail and occasional thoughtlessness exasperated Witherspoon, who, as elder sister, employed a variety of strategies to secure prompt action or agreement to a plan of her own devising. She could be either most direct or quite roundabout in her dealings with her coworker. Only a few letters exist, all of them from Witherspoon to Recht; most of their communication was by telephone, but when Recht was traveling or when Witherspoon wished to make a point quite plainly, she wrote him a letter. Excerpts from the letters reveal a degree of formality ("My dear Mr.

11. *Left to right: Tracy Mygatt, Fannie May Witherspoon, and Mercedes M. Randall at the organizing conference of the Young Democracy, New York, May 1918. Courtesy of the Swarthmore College Peace Collection.*

Recht") but also a fluid and personal connection between these two very strong-minded people.

It was the habit of the Bureau's executive committee to meet biweekly and to expect a report from Recht, as chief counsel, either in person or in writing. Witherspoon fought against the current in her efforts to secure written reports from Recht when he was out of town and fussed a great deal when the Bureau's chief counsel neglected to return borrowed materials or spoke to the press without consulting her first. For example, in December 1917, Witherspoon wrote to Recht to remind him that she needed to "have carbon copies of every letter, affidavit and other papers prepared by you in connection with the work of the Bureau. . . . I must insist with some firmness that you do this." Then, in a reproachful and somewhat defensive tone, she concluded: "I know that you some time think that I stop at very small points, but indeed, the keeping of an office in shape is not an insignificant matter."[40] Six weeks later, however, Witherspoon wrote to Recht to compliment him on his essay "Mobilizing the Judicia." Calling it "a fine thing," she nevertheless responded to Recht's request for feedback on his writing with the observation that "you have invited criticism and I have a good deal of criticism to offer." After providing some general comments, Witherspoon asked Recht to send her a carbon copy of this first draft: "The fact is, I am rather longing to have a hand in re-writing certain sections of it."[41]

Additional letters and other documents indicate that Recht came to rely on Witherspoon's criticisms and revisions of his essays and that Witherspoon herself relished this collaborative effort between them. She enjoyed writing and possessed a clear, forceful style. She liked to stay in control of all matters relating to Bureau policy, and "having a hand" in critiquing Recht's essays before they were published facilitated this. Witherspoon scolded Recht repeatedly for speaking directly to the press, for she considered this her responsibility; however, when speaking to others, she noted that Recht was merely enthusiastic and tended to get caught up in the moment. Witherspoon never implied that Recht was purposefully overstepping his domain as legal counsel to the Bureau. On one occasion, though, when Recht asked Witherspoon's advice on what to charge a "semi-private" client, she decimated his own reasoning for additional billing (which included the argument that other lawyers in the case were charging more than he), declaring somewhat self-righteously: "Our whole work here is a protest not only against the injustices of the present time, but against the advantage which unscrupulous lawyers and others are taking of ignorance and poverty, and while this is not a Bureau case, and you can put me in my place if you like, your constant appeals to me for advices do seem to give me a certain claim upon it."[42] Witherspoon concluded disarmingly: "If this letter makes you very, very angry, say so. It really is meant in a perfectly friendly way, and with due appreciation of what you have done in this and other matters."[43]

As this last sentence implies, Witherspoon made a point of praising Recht for his achievements. In a letter written when the Bureau was beginning to wind down its activities in 1919, Witherspoon declared: "I want to tell you, as you never permit me to do in person, how delighted I am with our success in these deportation cases and how keen is my appreciation of the big piece of work you have done."[44] By July 1919, Witherspoon, in a change of roles, would ask Recht for his advice on how the Bureau might transform itself into an effective peacetime organization. Nonetheless, in this letter she urged Recht not to let one case "drag along" and to push "promptly and aggressively" on another.[45]

Witherspoon and Recht built themselves into an effective team during their time together with the Bureau of Legal Advice. Their shared commitment to defending the civil liberties of political or social outsiders during the war was reinforced by their mutual connections in the larger movement culture. This antimilitarist, prodemocracy culture was a complex one, with both separatist women's associations (notably the Woman's Peace Party) and mixed-gender groups such as the Bureau of Legal Advice, the Civil Liberties Bureau, and the socialist-leaning People's Council. In New York City, except for the woman-directed Bureau of Legal Advice, men assumed dominant leadership in mixed-gender associations. The male-headed groups received most of the print media's attention. Much to the chagrin of Fannie May Witherspoon and Charles Recht, this uneven reporting pattern was also true for the socialist newspaper, the *New York Call;* in its pages, the Bureau of Legal Advice was frequently confused with the Civil Liberties Bureau, led by Roger Baldwin. Sometimes the Civil Liberties Bureau got credit for work accomplished by the Bureau of Legal Advice.

As early as December 1917, Witherspoon wrote sharply to the *Call:* "Every organization is dependent upon a certain amount of publicity, and I cannot understand why the 'Call' very frequently either does not print our name or else puts [it] in small letters so as to render it inconspicuous. Surely, an organization . . . doing radical work and directly connected with the Socialist Party, should receive the best treatment from the organ of the Socialist movement."[46] As late as July 1919, Recht informed Charles Ervin, the editor of the *Call,* that there were errors in the reportage of a Bureau of Legal Advice court case. In closing, he noted sardonically: "It has become a joke among us to say: 'If the Bureau of Legal Advice does anything, the Civil Liberties Bureau gets a *Call* headline next day.' "[47]

It was ironic that a socialist newspaper consistently underrated the contribution of the Bureau of Legal Advice to civil liberties, especially given that the Bureau was established initially by the left wing of the antiwar movement with the strong backing of the Socialist Party. The Civil Liberties Bureau, in contrast, began as a committee of the liberal American Union Against Militarism, and even when it became independent of the Union, a significant proportion of its executive board were supporters of President Wilson's "war to end all wars." The Civil Liberties Bureau achieved high visibility during the war years as it lent its support to the formation of other civil liberties groups throughout the country, and it developed effective propaganda and lobbying strategies to forward its cause. This accounts in part for the *Call* reporters' confusion. It is also true, however, that socialist men (including those who were editors and journalists) normally saw women like Witherspoon as helpmeet comrades and underestimated their role in the public arena as a matter of course.[48]

Reinforcing the tendency of male socialists to slight leadership qualities in individual women like Witherspoon was the fact that the Civil Liberties Bureau was led by the charismatic and able Roger Baldwin, himself a philosophical anarchist and an absolute pacifist, who was determined to lead the burgeoning movement in defense of first amendment freedoms during wartime. It was up to Fannie May Witherspoon, as the executive head of the Bureau of Legal Advice, to negotiate the slippery shoals of cooperation with Baldwin, her counterpart in the Civil Liberties Bureau. Given Baldwin's character and personal stake in the civil liberties movement, it was not an enviable task. Nevertheless, Witherspoon, true to her own character and commitments, held her course and persisted. Ultimately, she won the grudging respect of Baldwin and a less complicated esteem from Albert De Silver, who directed the Civil Liberties Bureau while Baldwin served ten months in jail (from October 1918 to July 1919) for refusing to submit to a physical examination after registering for the draft. Witherspoon's relationship with Baldwin requires some elaboration, because it presents one telling example of how gendered relations of power played themselves out in wartime movement culture.

Under most circumstances, friends and colleagues of Roger Baldwin responded positively to his intelligence and vivaciousness. Tracy Mygatt, for instance, in a 1966 oral history interview, remarked that the youthful Baldwin was "extremely attractive."[49] However, his imperious, controlling style in certain situations did not go unnoticed. Moreover, he found it difficult to establish egalitarian work relations with strong women. Early correspondence between Baldwin and Witherspoon indicates that he had no wish to see the Bureau of Legal Advice survive. In summer 1917, as an official representative of the Civil Liberties Bureau, he became a member of the executive committee of the Bureau that Witherspoon headed. It was agreed by this time that the Civil Liberties Bureau would coordinate propaganda and lobbying campaigns and the establishment of additional bureaus in defense of civil liberties throughout the nation. The Bureau of Legal Advice, in its turn, would handle all local civil liberties work, including court cases.

As we have seen, when the Bureau of Legal Advice was founded, the New York City branch of the Woman's Peace Party and the Emergency Peace Federation supplied startup funds. Witherspoon required a minimum monthly income of about $600 to run the Bureau; in charge of fundraising, she sought to secure monthly pledges from individuals and from socialist and labor organizations whose members required Bureau assistance. In the early months, she also counted on the financial backing of the newly-constituted People's Council (formerly the Emergency Peace Federation) and the Civil Liberties Bureau, each of which had assured her of a $250 monthly check.

Almost from the beginning, Witherspoon experienced difficulties with Baldwin, who used money as a lever against the Bureau of Legal Advice. Witherspoon found it necessary to write to Baldwin on December 1, 1917, on a number of matters; his brief comments appear penned in along the right-hand margin of the original letter. Witherspoon's third and most important point in the letter was a reminder that the Bureau of Legal Advice had not received "the pledge of $250.00 promised us by your Bureau for November." She expected to use this money to pay Recht's salary. Even though Baldwin's office was just several floors down in the same building, Witherspoon asked that Baldwin "indicate answer to these matters and send back by the bearer." Baldwin's written response to the pledge request was: "Please wait till Monday when my committee meets."[50] Having heard nothing from Baldwin six days later, Witherspoon wrote again. Both her letter and Baldwin's

answer (handwritten at the bottom and on the back of Witherspoon's typed letter) are worth quoting in full.

December 6, 1917

My dear Mr. Baldwin:
    I feel much embarrassed to ask you for that check, but I am
going to do so, as we really need it, and as I understood that you
expected to let us have it on Tuesday.
    If you prefer to send us the whole amount of the pledge for
two months, $500, since it is already the 6th of December, that
would be ever so much better, but do at least let us have the
$250.00 today.
    I am sorry to give you all this trouble. Shall I phone Mr.
Wood direct?

Cordially yours,
Fannie M. Witherspoon
Secretary

Baldwin responded tersely: "We are sending you the check for
$250 today. It is not by any means a *'pledge'*—and the remaining
amount for December is entirely dependent on our raising the rest
of our defence fund. Further, this is only to tide over until the B.
of L.F.A. gets on its own feet."[51]
    Baldwin obviously resented Witherspoon's persistence, and in
their next exchange one month later, he was barely civil. On this
occasion, Witherspoon reminded him that he was two months in
arrears with his personal monthly "pledge." "We are anxious not to
let a single supporter forget the needs of the Bureau," she wrote,
"especially in these trying days of the Second Draft. May we expect
a check for $20.00 from you within a few days?" In hurried script,
Baldwin returned the letter with a testy message: "Did I not agree
to come in among *80* to finance the Bureau at $10 a month? I did
so to help along *that plan*. If it has worked out OK to finance the
work, count me in. If it hasn't, I don't feel as if that amount would
go far to solve the problem and I can't afford to contribute on any
less effective basis."[52]
    Baldwin had hit a sore point. The Civil Liberties Bureau en-
joyed the financial backing of wealthy men like Albert De Silver;
the association Witherspoon headed did not. Witherspoon spent
more time than she wished writing letters to individuals such as

Baldwin requesting small regular contributions. Records do not indicate whether Baldwin decided to honor his monthly pledge to the Bureau of Legal Advice after all, but documentation does reveal that the Civil Liberties Union sent no more checks to Witherspoon's Bureau.

Regardless, the Bureau of Legal Advice pushed ahead. Baldwin remained on the executive committee of the Bureau, and minutes of meetings show that he was reliable and efficient in this capacity. In 1918, when the conscientious objector problem became a major one for the civil liberties movement, the work of the bureaus overlapped more dramatically. Notes back and forth between their offices demonstrate that the Bureau of Legal Advice handled all the legal work for drafted COs from New York City and nearby communities, while the Civil Liberties Bureau concentrated on propaganda.

As noted earlier, Baldwin entered a civil prison in October 1918. By this time, he had grown to respect the work of the Bureau, but he did not like to share responsibility and control. As civil liberties scholar Samuel Walker has remarked, "He never felt he could trust anyone else to direct the civil liberties cause."[53] Nonetheless, he recognized Witherspoon's worth for the movement, after a fashion. In an oral history interview conducted in 1975, Baldwin referred to Fannie May Witherspoon as a "sweet but determined middle-aged woman."[54] He had less gracious things to say about other strong-minded movement women such as the peace twins Rebecca Shelley and Lella Faye Secor, whom he considered "passionate and intemperate."[55] It is interesting that Baldwin, like Charles Recht, viewed Witherspoon as middle-aged in the war era; he was actually one year older than she. In counterpoint to this recollection, Tracy Mygatt recalled in 1966 that "in those days," she and Witherspoon had been young and full of boisterous spirits.[56]

Witherspoon's assessment of Baldwin is also revealing. At least in later years, she praised his brilliant work, but she also found him quite difficult. In a letter written to Shelley in 1932, she remarked candidly: "The peace crowd, the Big Guns, have always been hopelessly anti-feminist. I think even Norman Thomas, much as I admire his perfectly stunning work, is so unconsciously. And of course R.B. always has been."[57]

Movement comrades such as the editors of the socialist *New*

York Call and Roger Baldwin were not the only men to mis-
construe or make light of the Bureau of Legal Advice. In summer
1918, it became obvious that the Military Intelligence Division in
Washington, D.C., held inaccurate views of the woman-directed
Bureau. On August 1, 1918, Baldwin received a letter from F. P.
Keppel, Third Assistant Secretary of War, in which he related that
he had personally received telegrams from the Bureau of Legal
Advice. Keppel explained that he had been informed by the Military Intelligence Division that said Bureau was "part and parcel of
the National Civil Liberties Bureau under your directorship." He
went on to comment cryptically that "the Military Intelligence
Branch feels that the same attitude should be adopted with regard
to it [Bureau of Legal Advice] that has been adopted by the Department toward the Civil Liberties Bureau." Keppel closed with a
promise to "make inquiry with regard to the cases now before us,
but will be glad if you will bring this matter to the attention of
the officers of the Bureau for their guidance in the future."[58] Baldwin answered Keppel's letter the next day. He stated that the Bureau of Legal Advice existed "for a considerable period before the
Civil Liberties Bureau was even organized" and noted that the bureaus worked cooperatively but had different mandates: "They take
care of cases of conscientious objectors in New York City. We handle the cases outside. We once contributed a small amount of
money to them from some special funds." Baldwin declared un-
equivocally that although he was a member of the executive committee, he had nothing to do with the executive work of the
Bureau of Legal Advice. He concluded: "I give you these facts for
what they are worth in determining the Department's attitude toward the Bureau of Legal Advice."[59]

One week later, Joy Young, in her role as acting executive
secretary of the Bureau, also wrote to Keppel. She reiterated Baldwin's points and noted that the Bureau of Legal Advice had written to Keppel in the past to report cases of injustice and had
appreciated his "courtesy." She requested that he inform the Bureau if future correspondence should be directed elsewhere. Young
also enclosed a copy of a letter that she had written to the Military
Intelligence Bureau, which repeated Baldwin's points about the
structure and purpose of their respective organizations. There is an
aggrieved and somewhat defensive tone to this letter; a sense of
noblesse oblige emerges also, as Young attempts to disabuse the

military authorities of the notion that the Bureau's work is disloyal. The words are Young's, but the sentiment was one shared by Witherspoon and by the other members of the Bureau's executive committee:

> This is the only Bureau in New York which does any work for drafted men or attempts to help poor and ignorant ones without charge. A great many lawyers in New York are charging any where from $10.00 to $25.00 to make out affidavits for these poverty-stricken foreigners. We have often found lawyers who will make out affidavits for a registrant, charging him a large sum of money with the promise that he can get for him deferred classification, when the lawyer knows perfectly well the man has no claim and that no amount of affidavits will release him from Class 1 of the draft.[60]

Young added that the Bureau also assisted in working through appropriate channels to straighten out War Risk Insurance allotments that soldiers had made to their families. She concluded with the request that her letter be attached to the Military Intelligence Division's report on the Bureau.

The Military Intelligence Division continued its surveillance of the Bureau of Legal Advice but ultimately concluded that its "parlor socialists" posed no immediate danger to national security during the war and immediately following the armistice.[61] However, relations between the War Department and the new civil liberties bureaus, which had been fairly congenial in the early months of the war, deteriorated in response to the insistent demands by the bureaus for just treatment of conscientious objectors and other political prisoners who were under military authority.

The month of August was a trying one for the Bureau of Legal Advice. With Witherspoon away, Young had to manage an ever increasing clientele, especially with respect to conscientious objectors. In an undated letter to Witherspoon in Ogunquit, Maine, a harried Young conveyed her ambivalent attitude toward Roger Baldwin: "The CO problem worries me frightfully. I am really tied and bound by Mr. Baldwin. I have to consult with him on every detail, and he either assures me 'that it has been attended to' or that he can and will handle it. I try to check him up but never feel quite as satisfied as if I had done it myself. But we work together quite amicably. I certainly respect him for pegging away, even if I

don't agree with his method."[62] At the end of the month, with
Witherspoon still away, Department of Justice officials (who had
become increasingly unhappy with the influence of the civil liberties movement on public opinion) raided the offices of the Bureau
of Legal Advice and of the Civil Liberties Bureau. Young and
Baldwin were drawn together in this drama, and it was Baldwin
who was able to negotiate with the Justice Department for the
eventual return of most of the documents that were seized. Nonetheless, Baldwin's ability to achieve this end might have rankled
Young and Witherspoon; his charm and seemingly spontaneous
sociability contributed to his success with government officials
such as those responsible for the raid, but he was also a privileged
upper-class white man with connections in "high places." Despite
Young's and Witherspoon's equally privileged backgrounds in
terms of family ancestry, their gender disempowered them in significant ways. In a story filled with irony, their very lack of public,
political power sensitized them to the plight of others who were
themselves disempowered by virtue of ethnicity and class. Time
and again, the Bureau women would find themselves turning
weakness into strength.

☙ 3 ❧

Conscription's Home Front Victims and Enemy Aliens

Who will take care of my wife and little children if they take me away?

My wife is going to have a child, but they say that does not matter because I married since May 18th. I can prove I have known her four years. Must I go and leave her alone?

I like America. I'd like to be a citizen here, but I have two brothers fighting for Austria. Please get me an exemption. You see I cannot kill my own brothers.

—Client statements,
Bureau of Legal Advice flyer, 1918

On April 6, 1917, the overwhelming vote by Congress in support of President Wilson's call to arms moved the United States along the path towards universal military service. Until February, both Wilson and Secretary of State Newton Baker refused to endorse plans for universal military training. Nonetheless, in the same month, Wilson directed the drafting of a conscription bill, the final version of which Congress passed as the Selective Service Act on May 18, against the public protestations of antiwar activists and of many socialists. From the start, Wilson and his chief advisors worried that compulsory service went against the "American spirit" of independence and voluntarism. However, in his view, wartime exigency required resolve. Ultimately, Wilson and Baker came to see the draft in terms of overall "manpower" needs, both on the war front and on the home front. According to historian David Kennedy, "Conscription was to serve primarily as a way to keep the right men in the right jobs at home."[1]

The Progressive ideal of a cooperatively-minded, nationally consolidated, and bureaucratically efficient democracy helped the administration secure articulate middle-class allies who were eager to work with George Creel's Committee on Public Information (CPI) to convince citizens of the need for a wartime draft.[2] Wilson asked Americans to rethink the meaning of the draft, insisting that conscription represented a "selection from a nation which has volunteered in mass." Significantly—and ominously—Wilson requested that "every man, whether he is himself to be registered or not [should] see to it that the name of every male person of the designated ages is written on these lists of honor."[3]

June 5, 1917: Registration Day. After weeks of intense propaganda work on the part of the CPI and many volunteer organizations, government officials were surprised but delighted with the orderly turnout of ten million men, aged 21 through 30, who presented themselves to the five thousand local civilian boards established across the country. Each man was asked a set of questions and required to sign a form. Boards then categorized registrants as either eligible or exempt. On the face of things, young American men—indeed, the population at large—seemed to be acceding to the draft. The CPI's national campaign to create a unified populace of unreservedly patriotic citizens was proving effective. Many observers of Registration Day commented on the festive air that prevailed in many communities. The bloody battlegrounds of war were three thousand miles away, and national service proved, at this point, appealing. However, CPI employees, in order to "sell" the war, had to sharpen public fear of a distant enemy; in part, this objective was accomplished by whipping up hatred of Germany and of all things German. Indirectly or subliminally at first, and later more explicitly, loyal citizens were urged to identify the potentially disloyal (and here German-Americans were most immediately suspect) and to rally them to the flag. President Wilson's "lists of honor" implicitly assumed other lists, lists of the dishonorable and of the disloyal.

The threat of the "enemy within" existed in the minds of many Americans well before Registration Day. Fannie May Witherspoon's encounter with the vigilantism experienced by the innocent Dutch man in front of New York City's public library was an early example of the illegal actions that patriotic citizens were prone to take in a society becoming inordinately fearful of internal subversion. Officialdom's victims soon numbered in the thousands in New York City and across the nation, as overzealous citizens and public officials trampled on the constitutional rights of critics of U.S. war policy and their free speech defenders. In particular, foreigners were widely perceived as dangerous outsiders and faced special risks.

When the Bureau of Legal Advice was established, Fannie May Witherspoon envisioned the organization as a crucial link between those on the "firing line in antiwar agitation and larger groups of sympathizers and backers." She anticipated that "not only would justice to the individual perhaps be accelerated, but the Peace Movement as a whole would derive the advantage of having a concrete side to its propaganda."[4] Within a few weeks, Witherspoon recognized that services would be provided to those on the "firing line" that she had identified, notably for free speech victims and conscientious objectors to war. Equally significant recipients would be the hundreds—later thousands—of immigrant, working-class, often non-English-speaking people who began to find their way to the Bureau office for draft counseling shortly after Registration Day. Most came seeking advice because they were noncitizens or "enemy aliens," often with families to support. The Bureau soon appreciated that these people represented conscription's home front victims.

We do not know how many individuals helped in the early counseling work of the Bureau, but Tracy Mygatt was probably a frequent presence in the office. Secretarial help was on hand, in some instances on a volunteer basis. The Bureau was fortunate to secure the part-time secretarial services of Hilda Kovner, a young Russian-born Jewish woman who was active in New York City's anarchist circles and was associated with *Mother Earth,* the journal founded by Emma Goldman; she brought dedication and resourcefulness to her job and aided the Bureau in its networking work with other radical groups and individuals concerned with civil liberties violations.[5] In addition, young men such as Bruno Grunzig

12. Left to right: Harry Weinberger, Hilda Kovner Adel, Sam Adel's niece, and Sam Adel at the anarchist colony in Stelton, New Jersey, World War I era. Courtesy of Paul Avrich.

helped out by counseling conscientious objectors to wartime military service. However, the figure who loomed particularly prominently during this springtime and summer of uncertainty and discontent was Fannie May Witherspoon. She was, simply, unreservedly there.

Records exist for a significant proportion of the Bureau's clients, although many came and went with scarcely a written trace and some records impounded by the Department of Justice were never returned. Excluding the court cases handled by the Bureau's lawyers, who were among the first to seek out the Bureau? What do their stories reveal about the human costs on the home front of this "war to end all wars"? How do their difficulties help us to arrive at new understandings of what it was like to be a civil liberties activist during the war? How can we begin to recognize the spirit of service that Witherspoon and others in her circle personified at a time when critical thinking was not only difficult but dangerous?

The Bureau possessed an executive committee whose members were settlement house workers such as John L. Elliot (also a founder of the Ethical Culture Society); lawyers such as Arthur Leeds, Marion Cothren, and Elinor Byrns; Christian socialist-feminists such as Tracy Mygatt; and Industrial Workers of the World supporters such as Jessie Ashley (also a lawyer). Thus, word of the Bureau's free legal services spread quickly among social reformers, socialists, radical trade unionists, and pacifists. The inhabitants of immigrant neighborhoods in all five city boroughs soon knew of the Bureau's existence. By June, the eleven-story Ginn Building was inundated with confused and needy people who braved "Treason's Twilight Zone" in search of the Bureau's office on the eighth floor. Crowds congregated in hallways waiting for counseling, leading the owner of the building, George Plimpton, to lodge a formal complaint with Witherspoon towards the end of summer 1917, at the insistence of other tenants.[6]

[In its first weeks of existence, quite a number of Bureau clients were men seeking exemption from the draft as conscientious objectors.] In an early press release, dated June 11, Fannie May Witherspoon reported on 42 cases of illegal conduct on the part of clerks at 21 different local draft boards who refused to allow registrants the right to designate themselves as COs (31 cases) or to claim exemption on other grounds (10 cases).[7] The other two major groups to request Bureau help as the summer and fall unfolded were 1) men seeking exemption by virtue of their role as chief financial supporters of their families, often for their wives and children but frequently also for parents and siblings, and 2) men without their first citizenship papers (termed nondeclarants), often enemy aliens, who wished to avoid military service. Supplementing these two groups considerably were the relatives of such men; by winter 1918, mothers, wives, and sisters of registered or conscripted men constituted in some weeks the majority of Bureau clients.

When the exemption-dependency cases of the Bureau are analyzed, the idiosyncrasy of local draft board rulings becomes apparent. Men with dependents were exempted by the Selective Service Act, and some board officials excused all married men in their district from military service,[8] but it was not unusual for local board officials in New York City to draft men with bona fide dependency claims. At some boards, officials cross-examined men quite narrowly as to their spouses' family support networks and ability to find employment.

Unease turned to panic in many family circles after the first order-of-call list was drawn by lottery in the Senate Office Building in Washington, D.C., on July 20. Individuals "called to the colors" in this manner quickly received notice to appear for a physical examination; those who passed the physical had but seven days to appeal their status as conscripts. Once this time of grace had elapsed, appeals could be made only from within the military. Drafted men were placed in class I, those with deferrals in four separate classes. The first draftees began reporting for duty in early August, and by September, 430,000 conscripts were in training camps set up across the country.[9] Ultimately, almost three million men were drafted during World War I.[10]

The actual mobilization of drafted men lacked the carnival ambience that characterized the June 5 Registration Day in many locations. For the most part, though, the process was efficient, conscripts compliant, and families of enlisted men supportive. Nevertheless, in mid-June, five thousand women from the East Side and Harlem petitioned the mayor against the draft and participated in what came to be known as the "City Hall Registry Riot." Beneath the surface, resentments churned, especially in certain immigrant neighborhoods. The *New York Call* reported that delinquency was common in the September mobilization in various boroughs. Moreover, disorderly behavior occurred at a number of train stations as women fought crowds to reach "their men." At one station at Long Island City, several women fainted and ambulances appeared quickly to shift them to nearby hospitals. In Brooklyn, a riot threatened when an angry crowd started to take matters into its own hands: "Mothers, sisters, brothers, other relatives, and friends, as though moved by a common impulse, rushed forward, and stopped the car [transporting conscripts to the train station], calling loudly for their dear ones. And then their rage turned against the men in charge and the crowd called them 'murderers.' Others attempted to drag the drafted men from the car."[11] A threatened riot was avoided, however, as distraught crowd participants eventually broke ranks and bowed to the inevitable.

The family members of enlisted men appear frequently in Bureau files marked "dependency cases." Once their men had been transported to army camps, dependent family members were left to cope with the hardships associated with the loss of the major, often the sole, breadwinner. The salary of an enlisted man was $30

13. *City Hall Registry Riot of East Side and Harlem women, June 16, 1917. Courtesy of UPI/Corbis-Bettmann.*

per month. Even if a soldier sent home most of his pay, an unemployed wife could not survive on this income; a child or children or elderly parents in need of support heightened the dilemma.

When the United States entered the war, the administration immediately began planning for compulsory pay allotments in conjunction with a family allowance system. Legislation was passed by Congress on October 6, 1917, that established mandatory pay allotments for soldiers with dependents as well as a family allowance scheme that provided a modicum of support for dependents, effective November 1.[12] For families whose breadwinners were mobilized in the first months of the war, however, there was no safety net in place. Despite private charity or parsimonious doles from the Red Cross, such families lived precariously. Later, when pay allotments and family allowances were established, bureaucratic foulups led to further frustrations and difficulties for the families of soldiers. Checks failed to arrive in many homes, or families discovered that the amount to which they were entitled was insufficient for adequate sustenance.

Somehow, many of these families made their way to the Bureau of Legal Advice's office, which was open six days a week. Thus, Witherspoon and her coworkers found themselves standing shoulder-to-shoulder on a "firing line" more diverse than that first envisioned by them in the early moments of the war. For every young conscientious objector who came seeking Bureau assistance to avoid the war front, there appeared half a dozen men and women (usually women), often immigrants with poor command of English, who required assistance to survive their embattled existences on the home front.

By fall 1917, the district appeal board of New York City was faced with over five thousand cases, mostly dependency claims. A large proportion concerned the plight of wives, many with children to support, whose husbands had been drafted despite the Selective Service Act's provision exempting them; a significant number of cases involved the dilemma of the so-called "slacker marriage," that is, marriages contracted after May 18, the date the conscription act became law. Further, the district board would not hear oral statements by claimants, requiring instead written affidavits and other documented proof of dependent status. In September, roughly one quarter of the dependency cases heard were reversed, but a large number were also denied because of lack of proper documentation[13]; hence, the Bureau was busily engaged in helping its clients prepare the necessary written forms. Bureau records indicate that despite the clarification of the draft law in fall 1917 by the district appeal board, dependency cases proliferated in 1918.

In July 1918, Mrs. Frank Marcus (we never learn her first name) presented herself to the Bureau with a request that her husband's draft status be changed from class I (conscripted) to class V (exempt—dependency). She was able to produce documents and affidavits proving that she was to be married in a Jewish ceremony in January 1917; however, the wedding had been postponed owing to illness until July 1917, and so the Marcus union was, in the view of the New York City District Appeal Board, a slacker marriage. Mrs. Marcus was pregnant, and this had been sworn to in writing by her physician, but when Mrs. Marcus presented herself to local board #51 to claim dependency exemption for her husband, she was told by the clerk in charge that he did not believe she was pregnant and that the board doctor (who never examined Mrs. Marcus) concurred with the clerk's assessment. She next spoke with the chair of the board, but he refused to take action. At this point, Fannie May Witherspoon appealed to Martin Conboy, direc-

tor of the draft for the city of New York, to take a personal interest
in the case, noting in a letter that Mrs. Marcus had been treated
with "scant courtesy" by local board officials. Conboy replied
curtly that "the question as to whether or not there was any intent
to evade the draft no longer enters into the consideration of marriages contracted after May 18, 1917." The director of the draft
ignored the affidavit of Mrs. Marcus's physician, concluding glibly
that since the "registrant [Frank Marcus] has not satisfactorily
proved to the Local Board that his wife was pregnant the classification was correct."[14] If, in fact, Mrs. Marcus gave birth to her child
while her husband was soldiering (perhaps in France), she should
have received the mandatory $15 per month pay allotment from
her husband's wages as well as a $25 monthly family allowance
(wife and one child). However, $40 was not a sufficient monthly
income to support Mrs. Marcus and her infant, and we can only
wonder how she managed "for the duration."

The vulnerability of married women, especially those who became pregnant after their husbands had been drafted, is a recurrent
theme in the Bureau files. However, Fannie May Witherspoon understood the legal system, kept abreast of official directives, and
was, in many respects, a canny negotiator; her administrative assistant in 1918, Joy Young, shared these attributes. Witherspoon's
handling of the spring 1918 case of Mrs. Harry Mogul, married
after May 18, 1917, to a man drafted but not yet mobilized, is
illustrative. On May 6, 1918, Witherspoon wrote to Leavitt J.
Hunt, appeal agent of local board #132. Conceding that "this is a
case of persons married since May 18th," she also pointed out that
"Secretary Baker's liberal order of January 18th [1918]" directed
that such marriages "be as carefully considered as any other marriages involving dependency claims." Once having established the
reasonableness of her client's request for a change in classification,
Witherspoon struck a note of maternal solicitude. This young
woman, she wrote, "who expects to be confined in July, is very
nervous, and I feel will not be fit for the ordeal before her in her
present state of uncertainty about her husband." "Is it not possible," Witherspoon beseeched, "that you can recommend a further
re-consideration of this case by Board #132 and a decision on the
matter?" Probably in an attempt to manipulate expectations concerning "gentlemanly" sentiment in her client's favor, and possibly
also to suggest a feminist-pacifist perspective on expectant father-

hood, Witherspoon concluded: "Will it not be possible to provide for a delay in the mobilization of the husband? Can he not be left home until the child shall have been born and the wife strong enough to look after herself, as she will be totally unable of doing in the first months of its infancy? There seems to be no family to help this woman either on her side or that of her husband. She has but one sister, a married woman, not in a position to help her in any way."[15]

Responding on May 17, Hunt agreed to recommend to the local board that Harry Mogul's case be reopened and receive a ruling by the district board on an appeal. However, paying scant attention to Secretary Baker's directive that marriages contracted after May 18 be viewed nonprejudicially, Hunt declared that "the man does not deserve much consideration" because "he married her after it was known that he was subject to the draft." His file indicated that Mrs. Mogul had lived for a time with her sister; he suggested "that she could go back there and live . . . the $35.00 that [her husband] would be able to send a month would be enough to board her there." For Leavitt Hunt, it was the soldier who counted: "Every time you pass over one man it means you must take the next man in order and it may well be a question of life and death that you are passing on, which most people do not appreciate, and therefore it is the duty of these Local Boards, in my judgment, to take the men in the order they are drawn unless they come well within the exception."[16] As in many other Bureau files, the final disposition on Mrs. Mogul's request is not known. In a frustratingly large number of cases, clients neglected to return postcards expressly created by Witherspoon to inform the Bureau of a case's outcome.

A more complicated dependency appeal case came to the attention of the Bureau in April 1918. A young inductee, Simon N. Nardone, wrote from Camp Upton, Long Island, that he had been conscripted despite his request at the time of registration for deferred classification on grounds of dependency: "My mother, three brothers and a sister (all under age, still going to school)" had depended on Nardone's income "for support for [the] last 2 1/2 years."[17] He wrote again a few days later to explain the particular difficulty he had encountered in proving the worth of his case: "There was with us at that time a father. And the further fact that he owned a printing shop." Nardone's father had been absent from the home from March 1915 until February 1917, "when by his talented ability to fake he convinced us of his penitence." During this period, the father had been sued in domestic relations court, and after evading alimony payments, he had finally consented "to send home every week the gross sum of six dollars a week!"; further, he had persuaded officials, that his business was not doing well, while (according to Simon Nardone) "all the while he was squandering money on other women." In December 1917, the family had demanded that he provide money to the household: "That request got him going and ever since [that time] he has resolutely decided to give home very little money if any at all." Thus, aware of his father's unreliability as a breadwinner, the young Nardone when he was drafted had left "such an amount of money as would suffice them [his family] until I were to return home again." Within the past week, he had learned that his father had again left home and not returned, flatly refusing to give Nardone's mother any money and even asking "my mother for some money out of what I had left her." The family had written to Simon that the father "has been a beast to the extent of using his *iron* fist." However, because of the very existence of his father, Simon Nardone was not considered the family's breadwinner, thus depriving his family of a family allowance. As he related in his letter to the Bureau, he desired to help his siblings through school, because he had had the good fortune of receiving an education; parenthetically, he remarked that he was below the standard height required of enlisted men.

Witherspoon responded to Nardone, informing him that his mother had already been to the Bureau office. She also related that the local board chair had told her that as long as the father was living it could never award the son, Simon, an exemption, regardless of the fact that the father did not live with or support his family. Instead, Witherspoon explained, the father was to be summoned to court and "compelled to support your mother." She advised Nardone to make application for discharge anyway and to fill out the form for pay allotment based on the need of his mother and the children under sixteen years of age. The Bureau also arranged to help with affidavits, to be signed by witnesses who were not relatives and sworn to by a notary public and to contain the facts as Nardone had related them, noting the names and ages (between eight and sixteen) of his siblings, in addition to relevant household economy information. Nardone had been employed as an operator of moving pictures, earning $28 per week. Household expenses totaled $86 per month (rent, $15; coal and wood, $8; gas, $3; and food, $60); Mrs. Nardone attested that she could not live on a $15 pay allotment (from Simon) and the $40 ordered by the court from her husband (which was never paid anyway).[18] As with so many Bureau cases, the final outcome is not recorded. This case demonstrates, however, that the Bureau under Witherspoon's resolute leadership did not take "no" for an answer. Against the odds, it persisted or advised its clients to persist.

A dependency case with an interesting twist concerned a young Russian-born man, Samuel Lumin, who had taken out first papers for U.S. citizenship, thus qualifying him (as a "declarant") for military service according to the Selective Service Act. Lumin did not dispute the ruling of local board #3 of Bridgeport, Connecticut, that he was eligible for the draft; rather, the complication arose because Yenta Lumin, Samuel's wife, and their children were residing outside the country and were thus considered nondeclarants, precluding them from qualifying for pay allotment and family allowance. Yenta Lumin wrote to the Bureau from Urechie, Russia, in October 1918, that she and her poorly clad, barefoot, and hungry children were living with her mother, who was herself a "helpless" woman without financial support.[19] Witherspoon sought to influence the local board chair to review Lumin's situation, pointing out that if her client had not taken out first papers he could have claimed exemption as an alien. Must his family suffer, she implored, because of his meritorious conduct (that is, becoming a declarant and being ready to serve in the military)? Instead, could not Samuel Lumin's "wife and children . . . be considered declarants on his papers as is the case of wife and children residing in this country?"

In this instance, Witherspoon chose a line of argument—the honorableness of military service—to which she did not subscribe but which she hoped would influence the official in charge. In addition, her request that the wife's citizenship status be linked to that of her husband conflicted with her personal conviction that a married woman's legal or social position be independent of her husband's. In this situation, as in others, Witherspoon put her clients' well-being first and marshalled her arguments accordingly. Again, the disposition of this case does not appear in the records.

Minors sometimes enlisted illegally, and Bureau records contain instances of mothers who sought, often on dependency grounds, to have their sons discharged. For instance, Emma Walsh Kreuger of Brooklyn argued that her fourteen-year-old son was her sole support. On January 7, 1918, the Bureau contacted Captain Frank Maldiner, the commanding officer of the 108th Infantry, regarding William Henry Walsh Kreuger's minority status. The captain replied threateningly that Krueger might be charged for fraudulent enlistment under the 54th Article of War; a few days later, he wrote that an affidavit was required from the stepfather, Fred Kreuger, to the effect that William was a minor. At this point, Emma Kreuger—who had been twice widowed—had to provide her first marriage certificate; an affidavit from her mother that the birth father, William Walsh Sr., was dead; and the receipted bill from the undertakers that Fred Kreuger, the second husband and stepfather of William Jr., had been interred. Only then did Emma Kreuger have the legal right to pursue her request that her son be discharged. By the time this paper work had been sorted out, it was May, and the whereabouts of the 108th Infantry were temporarily unknown to the camp adjutant. The Bureau then wrote to advise military officials in Washington, D.C., that William Kreuger's papers had not been forwarded from France to the War Department. In June, the adjutant general replied that his office did not know where the papers were, suggesting lamely that the Bureau try the 27th Division Headquarters of the Expeditionary Forces. No further documentation exists on this case except for a final letter from Emma Kreuger in which she notes dispiritedly that her young son had ended up, after all, "at the firing line."[20] The war continued for six more months. Did William survive?

While many families sought out the services of the Bureau in an effort to keep their breadwinners at the home front, others—confronted with husbands, fathers, and sons already at the war front (or in training camp)—requested Bureau intervention with government and military authorities charged with overseeing pay allotments and family allowances. Repeated official public assurances of bureaucratic efficiency were well off the mark. Frequently, Fannie May Witherspoon and her coworkers found themselves serving as advocates of frantic clients who had not received their monthly stipends from the newly-created Military and Naval Division of the War Risk Insurance Bureau.

Upon entering the war, the U.S. government had moved quickly to boost the monthly pay of enlisted soldiers to $30, which made American soldiers among the highest paid in the world. Concomitantly, government investigators had set about devising a comprehensive benefits scheme comprising disability compensation, life insurance, pension, and family allowance provisions. As noted above, a War Risk Insurance bill passed Congress on October 6, 1917, effective November 1; officials scrambled to pull together personnel, equipment, and office space. At one point, the Military and Naval Division of the War Risk Insurance Bureau was accommodated in eleven different government buildings in the nation's capital.

By February 1918, the War Risk Insurance Bureau was sending out over one-half million checks per month. However, twelve thousand checks per month, on average, were returned undeliverable. Not infrequently, families failed to receive checks because of name mixups. Draft board agents were notoriously sloppy with recording names of immigrants, and the problem persisted in military records. (Towards the end of the war, serial numbers were assigned to soldiers, simplifying identification of enlisted men— especially those with common names.) In other cases, soldiers refused to admit dependency. Moreover, wives or other family members, entitled under the law, filed claims only to face a complicated investigation process. The War Risk Insurance Bureau's clerical staff of seven thousand people could not keep up with the paper work, and claims investigators fell woefully behind in their case work.

The chief aim of this new government initiative was to maintain the morale and combat-readiness of soldiers. During summer 1918, Lieutenant-Colonel S. H. Wolfe, detailed to the Bureau of War Risk Insurance by the secretary of war, reported enthusiastically that after only eight months in operation, the Bureau was meeting its prime objective. General John Pershing, commander-in-chief of the American Expeditionary Forces, declared unambiguously that soldiers were particularly keen to enroll in the voluntary life insurance scheme: "All ranks of the American Expeditionary Forces appreciate deeply the generous measure the government has taken to provide insurance for their families, in proof of which more than 90 per cent of the men have taken out insurance. Wisely to make provision for their loved ones heartens our men and strengthens the bonds that unite the army and people in our strong determination to triumph in our most righteous cause."[21]

A somewhat different point was made by Professor Samuel McCune Lindsay of Columbia University with regard to pay allotments and family allowances. He commented that Congress recognized the country's responsibility to supplement the soldier's regular pay "since the call to arms does not annul the moral and legal obligations of every man to support his family and those who have a blood-tie claim upon his earnings." Compulsory pay allotments and family allowances would prevent a "disproportionate sacrifice on the part of [the soldier's] dependents." However, Lindsay stressed that the overriding concern was that there not be an "undue lowering of [the soldier's] standard of living."[22] Hence, compulsory pay allotment (required of soldiers whose families received monthly allowances) could not exceed one half of an enlisted man's pay. Like the draft board official who rejected a dependency request on the grounds that it would require drafting yet another man to replace the exempted spouse, the architects of the War Risk Insurance Bill were focused primarily on the well-being of the soldier. Nonetheless, inculcating a "spirit of service" in the soldier necessitated solicitude for his "loved ones."

Significantly, government officials, notably those associated with the War Risk Insurance Bureau, identified the families of soldiers—many of them recent immigrants to the United States—as candidates for education in proper citizenship deportment during wartime. The antiwar attitudes and behavior of immigrant working-class families in places such as Brooklyn, as exhibited in the near riots during the mobilization phase of the war, had to be eradicated. The Civil Relief Commission of the American Red Cross was established with these concerns in mind. Mary Willcox Glenn, the chair of the Red Cross chapter in the Bronx, expressed her organization's wartime mandate by noting that one "duty of the patriotic home service worker" was "to help maintain army morale by assurance given that family life is safeguarded." Glenn then elaborated upon "a deeper claim:"

> The [home] service [of the Red Cross] is a trust. The trust is to deliver to the returning soldier not the fabric of the home he left, but a home which potentially, however housed, will *carry on*, refined by common sacrifice. If he fail to return, if he return

broken in mind and body, the demand of the trust is that there may abide in his home a quality which will perpetuate its value. If he return a stranger to his old responsibilities, his one-time affections, the trust is to try to revivify the attributes lost in the big demoralization of war.[23]

Civilians, not just soldiers, experienced war-engendered demoralization. As noted earlier, Witherspoon and other Bureau workers were besieged from an early date with families in need of various kinds of legal "first aid." Many times such people were unaware of the services of the Red Cross, particularly its liaison role between families of servicemen and military and governmental officials in the War Risk Insurance Bureau. In some cases, however, families made the conscious choice to appeal to the Bureau of Legal Advice rather than to the Red Cross. Many immigrants distrusted organizations like the Red Cross; one Bureau client likened the Red Cross to the poorhouse. The paternalistic or maternalistic patina of "caring" that Red Cross officials and volunteers exhibited was not disinterested. Families who required Red Cross services to sort out bureaucratic problems or to supply temporary charitable aid often felt themselves to be patronized. Working-class people, especially immigrants, comprehended that there were strings attached to the help they received and were not convinced of the need to become "refined by common sacrifice." Because of these misgivings, families of soldiers found their way to Witherspoon and the Bureau of Legal Advice, where they felt assured of competent help.

Witherspoon, for her part, was somewhat stymied about what to do with War Risk Insurance cases. At first, she did not realize that the Red Cross could advise families of their rights and could intervene in some ways to smooth out the processes available for redress of grievances. By fall 1917, Witherspoon understood this aspect of the Red Cross's war work, and in correspondence to one official, she communicated her relief in knowing where to send clients who had problems with allotments and allowances. Somewhere along the line, however, Witherspoon must have had second thoughts, for allotment and allowance cases abound in Bureau records. Witherspoon and her coworkers took on the role of go-between, evidently concluding that the Red Cross was a compromising affair.

Over the course of the war, the Bureau of Legal Advice handled well over five thousand draft, dependency, and pay allotment and family allowance cases.[24] Bureau workers sought the reversal of illegal or unjust draft decisions. These endeavors led the women Bureau workers (who did most of the work in such cases) to identify the degrading, humiliating experiences of powerless people, notably immigrant women, who were buffeted about by impersonal structures and processes that had not been equitably established for their benefit. Bureau members, following Witherspoon's lead, were sincere in their commitment to help such clients and labored indefatigably on their behalf. The left-liberal or socialist, pacifist, and feminist perspectives of Bureau members provided them with explanations or analytical tools for assessing the impact of wartime conscription on specific groups. The social activist backgrounds of Bureau workers also encouraged certain strategies and discouraged others. Witherspoon, about whom we know the most, was eminently pragmatic and versatile in her approach to problem-solving. Her background in the suffrage and socialist movements helped her to organize her arguments with the proper audience in mind.

Fannie May Witherspoon and a majority of her coworkers, such as Tracy Mygatt and Joy Young, came from privileged backgrounds. Not surprisingly, an elitist, noblesse oblige sensibility is manifest from time to time in Bureau correspondence. When serving as advocate for immigrant working-class families, for instance, Witherspoon would sometimes refer to a client as "ignorant and uneducated" when writing to a government official or military commander. At another time, in a letter to a client, a tone of annoyance would surface if maternal care or firmness did not suffice, as Witherspoon or Young sought to convince someone that she knew best. Occasionally, Witherspoon's comments to an official could be construed as a betrayal of a client's integrity; in one such instance, Witherspoon, exasperated in her attempt to convince a woman to seek temporary funds from the Red Cross, referred to her client in a letter to a Red Cross official as "that sort of woman."

As noted at the beginning of this chapter, exemption-dependency claims constituted but one aspect of the Bureau of Legal Advice's work. Another group of clients were draft-age men who were not U.S. citizens and who sought exemption from military service on these grounds. The special problems of the alien and enemy alien with respect to the draft and other legal matters cannot be understood apart from the state's war mobilization strategies and the public's response to them. Before we turn to a consideration of the Bureau's efforts to protect the civil liberties of foreigners, therefore, we require a more comprehensive understanding of how and why aliens and enemy aliens, along with other outsider groups, became victims of intolerance and violence within the context of the militarized and ideologically regimented U.S. wartime culture.

No national unity stood behind the U.S. war declaration of April 6, 1917. However, "preparedness" and "armed neutrality" had served as powerful slogans of the preceding years and had helped to condition Americans to the possibility of U.S. participation in the world war. Once the United States had become a belligerent and the Selective Service Act had passed Congress on May 18, the Wilson administration placed high priority on defining the war's meaning for the American people. The preferred meaning of Wilson's "war to end all wars" centered around the notion that America was engaged in a monumental struggle pitting western democracies against German autocracy. High-ranking members of Wilson's administration such as Secretary of the Treasury William Gibbs McAdoo insisted that "any great war must necessarily be a popular movement. It is a kind of crusade; and, like all crusades, it sweeps along on a powerful stream of romanticism."[25] Thus, the conscription of a committed fighting force and the creation of a tractable, efficient workforce went hand-in-hand with plans to convince a reluctant citizenry to view the war as a heroic undertaking requiring unswerving loyalty to the state, unconditional patriotism, and ungrudging self-sacrifice.

Historian David Kennedy has shrewdly observed that the Wilson administration's approach to war mobilization was informed by a "deep-grained reluctance to exercise power in a straightforward, statutory, and necessarily coercive way." Wilson and his chief advisors wished to avoid "unilateral exercises of government power."[26] However, their solution—to rely on voluntarism and persuasion as much as possible—contributed in a fundamental way to wartime hysteria, as persuasion on the part of the Committee on Public Information (CPI) and other hastily established federal agencies and bureaus turned to crude propagandizing and deliberate mobilizing of emotions. Such self-conscious manipulation of patriotic feeling led to vigilantism on the part of nominally supervised citizen's groups such as the American Protective League, the American Defense Society, and the National Security League.[27] The mainstream press, with a tradition of sensationalism and distortion, was for the most part stridently and uncritically patriotic.[28]

Mobilization of a country's citizens for warmaking always necessitates the creation of a dreaded and despised enemy. The Wilson administration understood this axiom of war. Given that the United States was at war with Germany, the CPI and other government agencies and spokespersons, in concert with a shrill press and superpatriotic citizen groups, were soon spewing out invective against the Kaiser and his soldiers, "the Huns." President Wilson's assertion that America was at war with Germany's leaders, not its people, carried little weight as the crusade to bring all Americans to a fever pitch of war enthusiasm gained momentum. Over the summer months, in the wake of draft registration day on June 5, suspicion and contempt for all things German evolved into a fierce loathing of Germany and its people. President Wilson fostered the insidious spread of Germanophobia in his Flag Day speech on June 14 (which marked the end of the first Liberty Loan drive), when he intimated that all Germans (and by extension anyone of German extraction) were potential enemy agents: "The military masters of Germany [have] filled our unsuspecting communities with vicious spies and conspirators and [have] sought to corrupt the opinion of the people."[29]

In the meantime, CPI strategy included the cultivation of an intensely emotional patriotic discourse in a variety of popular forms including news stories, films, and poster displays.[30] The speeches of the thousands of volunteer "four-minute men" who spoke in communities across the nation for the CPI during summer 1917 became saturated with the notion of the terrifying and omnipresent internal enemy. The CPI—which had begun with a fact-based informational mission—had devolved, according to David Kennedy, into "a crude propaganda mill."[31]

The polyglot nature of American society in 1917, consisting as it did of millions of first-generation Americans or recent immigrants, represented a staggering challenge to the administration's wish to create a homogeneously loyal, actively patriotic populace.

Many immigrants from central, eastern, and southern Europe did not understand English. In the four years before U.S. entry into the war, over five million immigrants arrived; 22 percent of these individuals could not read or write in any language.[32] A significant proportion of immigrants from Germany, Austria-Hungary, and Russia, in particular, had come to the United States to avoid militarism and war service in their own countries. Some, like the German-speaking Mennonites, were nonresistant pacifists out of religious conviction.

Confounding the war administration's mission to mobilize a popular movement in support of the war effort was the existence of the respectable Socialist Party of America, which from its inception in 1901 had garnered strong immigrant support, especially in urban centers. The party persisted after the war declaration in its firm opposition to the war, and party stalwarts facilitated the establishment in May 1917 of the antimilitarist People's Council of America for Democracy and Terms of Peace. The boisterous and militant anarcho-syndicalist union, the Industrial Workers of the World (IWW)—also known as the Wobblies—was also defiantly antiwar. Since its founding in 1905, the "One Big Union" had attracted both native-born Americans and immigrants to its ranks. The Wilson administration and certain capitalist interests considered the IWW to be a dire threat to wartime production by virtue of its insistent demands for union recognition in lumbering and in key industries such as textiles.

As war fever mounted over the hot summer months, antiradicalism, Germanophobia, and a generalized nativist repugnance for all things foreign fused in the popular mind with the notion of the enemy within. Antiwar socialists, Wobblies, and pacifists, as well as enemy aliens and other assorted outsiders, became easy targets of a rising vigilante spirit in many communities.[33] Frank Little, a committed native-born IWW organizer in the West, was an early casualty. Historians H. C. Peterson and Gilbert Fite have described how in the early morning hours before daybreak on August 1, 1917, Little (who was lame) was hauled from his bed at a boardinghouse in Butte, Montana, tied to the back of an automobile, and "dragged through the streets until his kneecaps were scraped off."[34] He was then hanged from a railroad trestle outside of town. A few weeks later, Herbert Bigelow, a pacifist preacher and public speaker for the People's Council, was seized at a hall in

Newport, Kentucky, just as he arrived to make a speech. Bigelow was gagged, handcuffed, and taken in a car to a forest twenty miles away. A mob stripped off his shirt, and one of their number administered numerous lashes upon his back with a blacksnake whip. He was then released after being warned away from Cincinnati.[35] The established press made little fuss over such occurrences.

Eight months later, on April 4, 1918, Robert Prager, a young German-born man with socialist proclivities, was apprehended by a mob in the small town of Collinsville, just east of St. Louis, Missouri, and dragged barefoot through the streets. Prager was transported outside the town limits and, after much baiting, was told to write a farewell letter to his parents. The five-hundred-strong mob then lynched the defenseless young man. Prager's crime was that he was German and a socialist; in fact, he supported the war but had been turned down by the American Navy when he sought to enlist because he had one glass eye. In a spurious trial a few weeks later, a jury found those accused of murdering him not guilty. Wilson did not publicly condemn the lynching and miscarriage of justice until late July, although in this instance—unlike the murder of Little and the whipping of Bigelow—many large newspapers and a number of national leaders, including former president Theodore Roosevelt, quickly deplored the murder of Prager at the hands of the mob.[36]

Harassment and persecution came to specific groups as well as to individuals. Soon after the war declaration, militiamen descended on the women in charge of the Emergency Peace Federation office in Washington, D.C. They told the women to disband immediately and "'beat it,' or they would be 'raided and raped.'"[37] Mobs of citizens and soldiers took to invading Socialist Party and IWW headquarters across the country, destroying records and offices and intimidating individuals. In early September, the Department of Justice conducted widespread raids on IWW offices; over two hundred people were arrested (including Wobblie leaders Big Bill Haywood and Elizabeth Gurley Flynn) and held for three mass trials in Illinois, California, and Oklahoma. Speakers in halls or on the street were summarily arrested for "disorderly conduct" and sedition; individuals were imprisoned for violating the Selective Service Act and the Espionage Act. In the fall, the American Protective League, under the guise of its semi-official status with the Justice Department, conducted "slacker raids" across the country, netting six thousand nonregistrants, four thousand of whom faced legal charges. "Invariably," historian Joan Jensen states, "radicals found not to have registered were prosecuted to keep them from organizing strikes."[38] Radical publications and many foreign-language newspapers were banned from the mail. All of this transpired before October 1917.

By autumn, then, civil libertarians like Fannie May Witherspoon, Charles Recht, and Roger Baldwin comprehended that such troubles were bound to increase in intensity and in scale. They and their coworkers were well aware of the power of the official propaganda leveled against the war's dissenters as well as against those who chose to protest against the vilification and unreasoning hate of the outsider. By November 17, the *New York Times* identified even women's suffrage—which had been won in the November 7 statewide elections—as "a Socialist and pacifist vehicle."[39]

When writing his memoirs, Charles Recht remembered November 7, 1917, as particularly significant. On this day, New Yorkers turned out for a hotly contested, ideologically-charged election, which resulted in Socialist Party standard-bearer Morris Hillquit gleaning four times the usual socialist vote in a three-way mayoralty campaign. Hillquit came in second, only seven thousand votes behind the Tammany Hall candidate Judge John F. Hylan, and some of his socialist comrades were elected city aldermen and state assemblymen. Women's suffrage won the day, too. Moreover, unbeknownst to western countries for a few days, on November 7 the Bolsheviks took power in Russia. Within a very short time, most patriotic Americans no longer distinguished among leftists; historian Frederick Luebke has noted that after the Russian Revolution, all political dissidents were viewed as "extremists plotting to destroy the American way of life."[40] In particular, henceforth socialists were seen almost uniformly as dangerous pro-German radicals.

By autumn 1917, the power of the state's own propaganda had, willy-nilly, unleashed such a mob spirit that President Wilson was forced to speak out against what his own administration had created (to some extent unwittingly). In November, at a speech in Buffalo before the patriotic American Federation of Labor, Wilson warned that an individual who joined a mob was not "worthy of the free institutions of the United States."[41] However, in the same month, Wilson—taking his cue from the Alien and Sedition Act of 1798—issued new executive orders that compelled all German aliens fifteen years of age or older to register with the government. At the same time, German men and boys over the age of fourteen were barred from areas deemed to have military importance, including wharves, canals, and railroad depots. German aliens were expelled from the District of Columbia and had to request permission to travel within the country; they could not change their residence and were forbidden to travel on ships or boats, except for public ferries. The American Protective League citizen group, which was openly hostile to foreigners, political radicals, and pacifists, was authorized to investigate all applications for permits and handled over two hundred thousand such requests. By the end of the war, over six hundred thousand persons had been affected by these regulations, and several thousand Germans ended up in detainment camps for minor infractions of the rules.[42]

The press coverage in New York City of the establishment of "barred zones" provides an eerie, almost surreal backdrop to the harassment and persecution that enemy aliens endured for the rest of the war and in the Red Scare aftermath. As a child in Bohemia, Charles Recht had been witness to aspects of the discrimination, violent intimidation, and ghettoization that Jewish people had experienced for centuries in Europe. He understood that mass hysteria against any group occurred quite easily when state repression of free thought was linked to the manipulation of language for sensationalist purposes. Recht must have felt a sense of déja vu during this time as Germans, the state-defined "other," were forced from their homes, businesses, and places of employment with absolutely no recourse before the law or public opinion, which by November 1917 was very firmly set against aliens, especially German nationals.[43]

In the midst of such confusion and uncertainty in New York City and throughout the country, Fannie May Witherspoon was herself arrested. The only record we have of this rather bizarre event—one which actually might have provided a bit of giddy relief for Witherspoon and her coworkers from the oppressiveness of dark times—is from a *New York Herald* clipping found in the Bureau of Legal Advice scrapbook, sandwiched in among the alarming reports of barred zones and innocent displaced people. On Sunday evening, November 25, the People's Council held a peace benefit at the People's House of the Rand School of Social

14. *"Notice to Enemy Aliens." Enemy aliens are warned that they "must not under any circumstance pass WEST beyond the line." By order of U.S. Marshall Thomas D. McCarthy, November 28, 1917. Courtesy of UPI/Corbis-Bettmann.*

Science, 7 East Fifteenth Street. Two detectives from Inspector John Bolan's staff were sent to the People's House "to see if it were true that a dramatic performance was being given on Sunday under the guise of a benefit."[44] The detectives followed the crowd up the stairs to the second floor and purchased "invitations" for one dollar. They then arrested Witherspoon and two others, Lindley Gordan, a 23-year-old clergyman, and Dora Levett, of the Bronx. They were taken to the East Twenty-second Street police station and arraigned later that evening in the Men's Night Court on the charge of selling tickets for a theatrical performance on Sunday without a permit. Magistrate McQuade discharged them "because the complaint did not come within the statute they were charged with having violated."

Did Witherspoon and her comrades get back to the People's House in time to see the one-act skit by George Bernard Shaw, "Press Cuttings," which went ahead as planned? The reporter noted with some acerbity that in his opinion the "affair [was] a freeze out," for the hall was unheated. Members of the Arts Council of the People's Council, which was "said to have a large membership of artists, musicians and writers," performed the skit. The Star-Spangled Banner was not sung, much to the *Herald* reporter's disgruntlement, although an "extended musical programme" was part of the evening's entertainment.[45]

In this period, New York City was viewed by the popular press across the nation as a dramatic symbol of all that was suspect. According to the *Tacoma (Washington) Ledger,* the vibrant metropolis was "a hotbed of near-traitors" and of "pestilential pacifism."[46] In the popular imagination, the barred zones of waterfront areas were battle zones infested with potential enemies. In fact, despite what amounted to spy hysteria, government agencies and citizen groups failed to turn up even one enemy spy over the course of the war. However, the government-orchestrated popular movement to whip up enthusiasm and unquestioning loyalty to a narrowly-defined patriotism succeeded only too well: although no actual spies served time in jail, hundreds of labor radicals and political dissidents were incarcerated, and pacifists and civil libertarians were put under military and civilian surveillance. Some, like Witherspoon, faced legal harassment. If they were civil servants with independent minds, such as German-born high school teacher Gertrude Pignol, they were sometimes suspended or fired from their jobs.

Within six months of the U.S. war declaration, we can speak with absolutely no irony of a home front war against all those labeled "aliens" and "dissenters."[47] There is a dark irony, however, in the fact that local draft boards appeared eager to conscript the services of aliens, particularly Austro-Hungarians, whose country of origin was allied with Germany. Conventions of international law forbade a belligerent nation from drafting aliens and enemy aliens for war service. The Selective Service Act of 1917 automatically exempted enemy aliens and nondeclarants (aliens who had not secured their "first papers" for U.S. citizenship), but—in a departure from international law—aliens who had taken out their first papers were liable to conscription under the U.S. draft law. Moreover, in practice, even the legislated exemptions were not always granted.

Soon after Registration Day on June 5, distressed young men, mostly Austro-Hungarians, began to seek out the Bureau of Legal Advice office with complaints that local board officials were refusing to exempt them. The civilian volunteer appointees who constituted the personnel of local draft boards were working under a quota system, and in some districts, as many as 50 percent of draft-age men were neither citizens nor declarants.[48] Native-born residents in such locations set up a hue and cry against what they believed to be discriminatory draft law practice, and a nativist animus informed the thinking of many draft board officials. One member of a Brooklyn draft board furiously exclaimed that the Russian immigrants in his district "practically deny us, while many of them shrug their shoulders, laugh at us and say, 'What are you going to do about it?'"[49] In a revengeful spirit, some local draft boards simply refused outright all claims for exemption on the basis of alien status.

Fannie May Witherspoon sought redress for this breach of the Selective Service Act and of international law with chairs of local boards, with the head of the district board, and with draft director Martin Conboy, but she was usually put off or rebuffed. In an exasperated but unyielding mood, Witherspoon cabled New York governor Charles S. Whitman at the end of August; he refused to take action on the itemized list of illegal (sometimes physically abusive) actions of local draft board officials that the Bureau of Legal Advice forwarded to him. Instead, Whitman replied:

The work of the moment is to select and train an army, and our first consideration must be to prosecute that work to a successful termination. If, after the last quota to be furnished by the state of New York has been mobilized, you desire to make formal charges against specified local boards these charges will receive my careful consideration and recommendations will be made to the president, but at the present time such proceedings would practically stop the work of these boards in New York city, something which cannot be even considered until that result is accomplished.[50]

Whitman went further, declaring in apocryphal language that should the nation fail to raise an army immediately, "we may be forced to fight on American soil to defend our homes from the invasion of a relentless foreign power and neither you nor I can assume the responsibility of hindering in the slightest degree the work of selecting that army."[51]

By the end of the summer, conscripted aliens found themselves in training camps, and Witherspoon was forced to petition camp commanders, War Department officials, and the adjutant general's office for their release.[52] Occasionally, she was aided in this effort by representation made by embassy officials to the State Department, which received so many complaints that it was forced to send instructions to local draft boards to be more careful.[53] However, once a man was inducted, the bureaucratic and legal red tape standing in the way of reversing a decision was staggering.

Witherspoon and Joy Young refused to be deterred and tackled this many-headed monster for the Bureau. Case files bulging with correspondence to and from various government officials and military officers reveal that the Bureau achieved some limited successes on a case-by-case basis.[54] Still, thousands of aliens across the country were illegally drafted into the army against their wishes and forced to serve their term. This situation prevailed even for aliens whose countries were allied with Germany, despite the public announcement in November 1917 by Provost Marshal General Enoch Crowder that such individuals were to be taken off of draft lists or ousted from the army if already inducted.[55] Austrians, Hungarians, Turks, and Bulgarians continued to be drafted by recalcitrant local board officials in New York City and elsewhere, even after Crowder's ruling. Some of these men were shipped to Europe and forced to fight against their countrymen, including in some instances members of their own families.[56]

Such flagrant and often purposeful disregard for the law was anathema to the spirit of the Bureau of Legal Advice. As we have seen, many of the aliens affected by the draft law in New York City were recent arrivals to the United States who struggled at low-paying jobs to make ends meet. Often, these young men were responsible for the material well-being of their parents, siblings, wives, or children. Thus, a circle of suffering widened with each successive draft call (there were four all told).

In later years, Charles Recht recognized that the Bureau of Legal Advice came into being with "no ultimate purpose." As its initial name—the Bureau of Legal First Aid—implied, its members were there to help out wherever need for legal services to defend civil liberties in wartime arose. At the same time, the members of the Bureau, notably its prime movers Witherspoon and Recht, were well aware of the larger historical currents swirling around them. They understood that the state had been immeasurably strengthened as a result of its prosecution of the war; they also appreciated that the vaunted independence of the legal system was in shambles. In a biting and incisive essay, "Mobilizing the Judicia," Recht (with Witherspoon's input) penned a searing indictment of legal practice during the first months of the war. Much of the essay (which was published in pamphlet form in spring 1918) focused on the plight of aliens and enemy aliens, especially in relation to conscription. Its underlying theme was the usurpation of civilian law by military authority.

Well before "Mobilizing the Judicia" was written, Witherspoon and Recht had become disturbed by the tendency of civil courts to deny jurisdiction over any draft question. They decided to bring one case to court, that of John Angelus, an Austro-Hungarian who had been sent to Camp Upton on Long Island with the first 5 percent of conscripts called into service in September 1917. After a negative ruling made by the district draft board, Recht took Angelus's case before Judge Julius Mayer of the Federal District Court. Seeking an injunction, Recht argued that the draft law was unconstitutional and that the courts possessed jurisdiction to enjoin the board from certifying Angelus for service. Mayer refused the injunction and upheld the district draft board's decision. He ruled the draft law constitutional: "It is a military measure in time of war, and it would be most subversive of military control and the proper disposition of this extremely difficult problem if the courts should interfere in this situation."[57] Nevertheless, Mayer recognized the importance of this decision and at Recht's request arranged to have Angelus's case heard before the U.S. Circuit Court of Appeals. In its first ruling on a draft case, the appellate court sustained the lower court on technical grounds, noting that Recht should have applied for a writ of certiorari instead of an injunction.[58]

Angelus lost his bid to be released from military service, but the Bureau won on the main legal question. In October 1917, the court rendered a decision that sustained the Bureau's claim that civil courts had jurisdiction over draft cases: "We think a decision of the boards is final only where the board has proceeded in due form, and where the party involved is given a fair opportunity to be heard and to present his evidence. But if an opportunity to be heard should be denied there can be no doubt as to the right of the aggrieved party to come into the courts for the protection of his rights."[59] The Bureau *Yearbook* reported: "Thereafter in dozens of decisions throughout the United States the case of Angelus vs. Sullivan was cited and jurisdiction taken by the court. This decision therefore stands as the most frequently quoted authority in draft law cases."[60]

Another knotty legal problem concerned the status of aliens with first papers (declarants). As already noted, such individuals were identified as draft-eligible by the Selective Service Act of 1917. In February 1918, the executive committee of the Bureau agreed to challenge the constitutionality of this proviso in the draft law. Charles Recht secured a hearing before the Department of Justice in the case of Abraham Pfefer, a Russian declarant. Recht argued that the Selective Service Act was unconstitutional "in those provisions which include aliens who have filed declarations of intention to become citizens"; he asserted that the draft law had to be tested "by the Law of Nations" and that the Selective Service Act was expost facto (Pfefer had been admitted to the country under certain international law agreements, which would be violated by a change in his condition through acts of Congress). The ruling was to dismiss the writ and then to remand Pfefer to the military authorities. The language of the decision stated explicitly that international law did not "give to the courts of the United States any authority to set aside nor to restrain Congress from enacting a statute violating the *so-called* rule, if it sees fit to do so."[61] This precedent, once established, held firm throughout the war. For Recht, the implication was clear: "If we ourselves are taught that International Law is a thing to be invoked at will, and only when it is convenient to do so, how can we logically protest then against other countries who have so glaringly misinterpreted and neglected it?"[62]

The Angelus and Pfefer cases set legal precedents and raised the visibility of the Bureau's work in the legal profession and in the national civil liberties movement. Closer to home, the Bureau's consistent efforts on behalf of its numerous exemption and dependency clients earned it a respected reputation in immigrant and working-class communities. As the war dragged on and as hatred against aliens and dissenters grew in intensity, Witherspoon came to believe that the Bureau's championing of the legal rights of the outsider could be linked to socialist reconstruction aims in postwar America. Many of the Bureau's working-class clients, she believed, were potential recruits to socialism's ranks. The Bureau's spirit of service, planted during the war and nurtured by socialist ideals, could be harvested in peacetime.

Fannie May Witherspoon and her coworkers never doubted that they belonged to a larger and ongoing movement for progressive change (as their labors on behalf of victims of the postwar Red Scare will further illustrate). Before turning to the Bureau's history in the wake of the armistice, however, we need to consider the special relationship of the Bureau to another marginalized and maligned group within the nation during the war: the conscientious objectors.

4

Feminist Pacifists
and Conscientious Objectors

*All I expect and demand of you gentlemen sitting in
the court-martial is that you judge me as a Conscientious Objector to War and not as a soldier, and in so
judging me, be guided by the highest dictates of your
own sense of justice. I do not wish mercy, but justice.*
—Erling Lunde at military court,
Fort Riley, Kansas, 1918

War brings gender definitions into bold relief, and social constructions of manliness and of womanliness often have been central to
the process of warmaking. Jean Bethke Elshtain, Cynthia Enloe,
and Betty Reardon, among others, have argued convincingly that
during wartime, most men have found themselves identifying with
a composite ideal of the "just warrior" or brave hero, a combat-
ready man committed to the defense of the state and to the protection of civilians. Most women, in contrast, have identified with an
ideal of the patriotic, moral mother or "beautiful soul." They have
expressed gratitude for men's willingness to defend them and the
state; they have also become nurturers of the war effort on the
home front and have buoyed up men's resolve to fight and, if
necessary, to die.[1] Enloe, in her study of women's relation to the
military in contemporary societies, demonstrates that despite some
women's military participation in social revolutions and in war, the

gender constructions of man the warrior and woman the nurturer remain dominant cultural images.[2]

Some historians of World War I America are now beginning to document how gender definitions, the state, and warmaking are interconnected. For instance, Gerald Shenk has taken up the question of gender identity in relation to the state and to warmaking in his investigation of the U.S. Selective Service Act of 1917. Shenk argues that although white elite men had begun to voice a particular view of "true manhood" in the 1890s—one that linked masculinity, state power, militarism, and warmaking—it was by no means hegemonic in 1917. Rather, his examination of the responses of individuals and of groups to the wartime draft reveals a plentitude of contesting discourses on masculinity. Nonetheless, he questions whether "the state could have mobilized American manpower for war" without exploiting "deeply embedded ideologies of manhood."[3] Kathleen Kennedy has examined "how wartime repression reshaped the gender systems that assigned meaning to women's political activity";[4] her specific focus is the antiwar socialist women's response to wartime repression. Kennedy has discovered that "a political language" of the "disorderly woman," the antithesis of the patriotic moral mother construct, was employed to prosecute antiwar socialist women under the Espionage Act. In contrast, socialist women defined themselves as autonomous full-fledged citizens of the nation; for the most part, they avoided describing themselves as peace-loving mothers. In so doing, they alienated their antiwar male comrades in the Socialist Party, who preferred to define "the masculine citizen through his ability to protect and defend helpless women." According to Kennedy, "Women remained . . . the 'Other' through which the [antiwar socialist] male citizen defined himself."[5]

Taken together, these two nuanced historical studies bolster the claims of social theorists that war is a gendered process. The authors offer compelling evidence of resistance to the dominant gender constructions of the patriotic warrior and the moral mother favored by the wartime state. They show that in the midst of war, the men and women who questioned the legitimacy of any aspect of the wartime gender system challenged the foundational structures of warmaking. At the same time, Kennedy's study also reveals that unexamined assumptions of patriarchal superiority (in this case, manly "protection" of women) created a sexual politics within antiwar socialist ranks that undercut the effectiveness of this group in their fight against war. Nonetheless, the refusal of some men and women to accept either the warrior or the patriotic mother role and identity for themselves shored up the fortunes of a peace culture, which managed to survive on the margins of a dominant and threatening war culture.

The women and men of the Bureau of Legal Advice were part of this subversive peace culture. As we have seen, the Bureau was founded by pacifists, feminists, and socialists who recognized the need to protect civil liberties during wartime, especially the legal rights of those—such as conscientious objectors—who spoke out against or took a stand critical of the war. Soon after the commencement of the war, Fannie May Witherspoon voiced the concern of her coworkers in the Bureau when she noted that "the problem of the 'conscientious objector' is the center of all pacifist thought."[6] Witherspoon and others in the Bureau also seemed to recognize that the "problem" of the objector was at the center of the gendered war system; feminist pacifist women understood that state power, warmaking, and manliness were linked. Over the course of the war, as their work brought them into close contact with COs, Bureau women and other similarly inclined civil libertarian women in the broader national movement came to believe that it was possible and desirable to sever the identification of masculine identity with state and military power. They encouraged the objector in his resolve to reject soldiering as "unmanly." Bureau women were convinced that the creation of a new set of values about manliness, one that incorporated the ideal of a nonviolent "New Man," constituted important peace work. They hoped that the future ability of the state to prosecute war would be compromised by their disruptive voices and actions.

———

During World War I, an extreme masculine ideal of the intrepid combat-ready patriot, prepared not only to kill but to die for his country, held sway in the minds of many young men and in the population at large, despite pockets of resistance to this view. Those who volunteered and the vast majority of those who were drafted were trained in military camps to accept a militarist ethos that held that power and status came by subduing and controlling others. Of the 2.8 million men who were conscripted into the armed services, fewer than twenty-one thousand were listed as COs by their local draft boards; after some time at training camps, most of these men changed their minds and took up arms. Only about four thousand drafted men remained COs, maintaining their stand to define themselves outside the norm of the war-engendered manhood ideal.[7] Nearly 90 percent were religious objectors, finding a moral grounding for their CO stand in a nonresistant Christian ethos of love. Such men rejected for themselves the soldier's raison d'être: to kill on command. In contrast, several hundred COs were secular or political objectors, opposing participation in war on the basis of their humanitarian, ethical, or political beliefs.[8]

Fannie May Witherspoon and Roger Baldwin agreed that the Bureau of Legal Advice and the Civil Liberties Bureau (which in May and June 1917 was still a committee of the American Union Against Militarism) had to work together on behalf of conscientious objectors to war. They appreciated that the militarist mood and superpatriotism of the times put the CO at special risk, and members of their organizations set about to study the objector problem. In May, Norman Thomas authored an informative pamphlet under the auspices of the American Union entitled *Conscription and the "Conscientious Objector" to War.*[9] In the same month, it was decided that the Bureau of Legal Advice would handle CO draft advising and legal cases for New York City.[10] By July, agreement had been reached that the Civil Liberties Bureau would serve as national coordinator for the CO problem and would produce literature like Thomas's pamphlet on the objector position during wartime. The executive members of both organizations understood that lobbying efforts to protect the legal rights of objectors would be necessary, and the Civil Liberties Bureau assumed chief responsibility in this area.

President Wilson and Secretary of War Baker initially disliked the idea of a conscripted army. However, once conscription became law (with the passage of the Selective Service Act on May 15, 1917), the Committee on Public Information (CPI) and other agencies of the federal government used emotional appeals to convince young men and their families that the draft was not to be viewed as a "conscription of the unwilling." The draft law did recognize the right of one group—members of historically established peace churches such as the Friends (or Quakers), Mennonites, and Dukhobors—to claim conscientious objector status and

15. *Left to right: Roger Baldwin, Crystal Eastman, a conscientious objector, and Ruth Pickering in front of Eastman's studio at Croton, New York, June 1917. Courtesy of Joyce Fuller (Fuller Photo Collection).*

thereby to be exempt from combat duty.[11] If drafted, such individuals were to be sent to military training camps and inducted into the army, but the president would determine (at a later date) appropriate noncombatant service for this group of men. The law did not recognize conscientious objector status on any other basis.[12]

The first challenge that the Bureau of Legal Advice faced was the intransigence of local draft board officials who were often unwilling to permit draft registrants to note "CO" as a reason for exemption from military service. A deeper problem, however, lay in the law itself: all men claiming CO status who were drafted came under military authority once they had been sent to training camps.[13] The draft law did not provide camp commandants with guidelines for handling objectors. Thus, the Bureau elected to stay in close contact with their drafted CO clients once they had been sent to military training camps.

In late summer and early fall 1917, when young men began arriving at training camps, President Wilson still had not designated what constituted noncombatant duty for CO enlisted men. In mid-September, however, Baker notified camp commandants that individuals claiming CO status were to be treated with "kindly consideration" and to be segregated from the regular enlisted men. He noted that objectors were not to suffer "punitive hardships." In further memos and directives, it became clear that Baker hoped that most men claiming objector status would eventually accept a combatant role in the military. Thus, in the first months of the war, Baker and the war administration played a waiting game while Wilson prevaricated on the question of noncombatant service. In the meantime, objectors were, in effect, in the army and under military authority.[14]

From the start, the Bureau of Legal Advice enjoyed a special relationship with the conscientious objectors who became their clients. In one of its first flyers, Witherspoon praised the objector as a new kind of hero:

> Connected with an organization or struggling along in apparent isolation, he stands in urgent need of all the support which can be given him. He faces the most momentous test of convictions and principles, for of all those who work for the fulfilment of peace ideals, it is he who will be called upon to make the greatest personal sacrifice in their support. Often young and inexperienced, he is confronted with a problem which even the man of mature judgment and unalterable principle would find extremely difficult of solution and he is eagerly turning to every source from which advice or help may be secured.[15]

Charles Recht concurred with Witherspoon's view, commenting in later years: "Quite early in that period the conception of a different kind of heroism began to crystallize among those in contact with objectors to war that the more poignant courage was required from those who stood alone."[16] Both religious and political (or secular) COs sought Bureau assistance, but political COs in particular seem to have found the Bureau, with its pacifist and socialist philosophical orientation, appealing. Given the Bureau's fast-growing reputation, it took very little time for young men who traveled in politically or culturally radical circles to make contact with the organization.

By late summer, Bruno Grunzig, a young objector who opposed military service for himself on humanitarian and socialist
grounds, worked alongside Witherspoon in the office at the Ginn
Building as a referral agent for other objectors. When CO clients
of the Bureau were drafted and sent to nearby military training
camps, Witherspoon (occasionally accompanied by Grunzig) visited them. (On one occasion, she was courteously received by General J. Franklin Bell at Camp Upton on Long Island.) Back in the
office, Witherspoon maintained an active correspondence with
these CO's, some of whom had been in and out of Bureau headquarters before induction; in letters, they would send greetings to
Grunzig or to "the girls in the office." Later, in spring 1918,
Grunzig was himself drafted and joined some of the men he had
previously visited at Camp Dix, New Jersey. At this point, maybe
earlier, it appears that he and a few other COs in a number of
camps up and down the east coast served as Bureau "informants,"
writing detailed letters to Witherspoon on the treatment they and
other objectors received at the hands of the military. Even before
the informant system was created, Bureau members gleaned much
knowledge of the CO situation in the camps by virtue of their
personal contacts with objectors and, often, their families. Witherspoon passed such information on to Roger Baldwin, who utilized the material to good effect in his lobbying efforts with the
War Department.

Historian John Whiteclay Chambers II has asserted that the
war administration's policy towards the CO "vacillated between
concern and indifference."[17] As noted, Baker had cautioned camp
commandants in September to be considerate of objectors under
their charge until the president had determined the scope of noncombatant duty for such "soldiers." However, with no disposition
on what constituted noncombatant service, the commandants were
left with authority to keep order and to discipline the CO enlisted
men as they saw fit. The level of hostility of military officers towards objectors varied, but none of them were particularly sympathetic to the CO position in wartime.[18]

The news from the segregated CO quarters in military camps
was disturbing. Within the first seven months of the war, the Civil
Liberties Bureau received over forty reports of documented brutalities against objectors, some of which were supplied by the Bureau
of Legal Advice. In summarizing these reports, Chambers observes

that "military authorities starved the objectors on bread and water, hanged them by their wrists, forced them to exercise and then drenched them in icy showers, and beat them with belts and broom handles."[19] In the civilian world, as the concept of 100 percent Americanism gained ground in the wake of the state's campaign to create a unified war spirit across the nation, COs joined the category of the vilified other (which came to include suffragists, enemy aliens, and radicals of all persuasions). "Slacker raids"—mass roundups of draft delinquents and draft dodgers, conducted by Justice Department agents and American Protective League members beginning in March 1918—further exacerbated hateful feelings against objectors.[20] Although nearly 90 percent of the objectors were native born, in the "crowd-mind" they were dangerous foreigners or at least pro-German.[21] There is ample evidence in support of Chambers's contention that "conscientious objectors became in general the most despised group of men in the war."[22]

President Wilson and his administration were partly responsible for the inhuman treatment many COs experienced in military camps. The indeterminate status of the objector helped to seal his unenviable fate in the first phase of the war. Finally, on March 20, 1918, the president issued an executive order designating assignments to the engineering, quartermaster, or medical corps as noncombatant service for which COs were eligible. Later, overseas Quaker relief work was also permitted to a small number of objectors. Most of the fourteen hundred men who accepted noncombatant military duty were religious COs who found it within their moral code or denominational creed to accept such alternative service.[23] However, some religious objectors found it impossible to accept noncombatant assignments; they were joined in this stand by several hundred other objectors who possessed either personal scruples or political convictions that prevented them from engaging in noncombatant military service. In subsequent months, these objectors faced further suffering and reprisals, including physical and mental torture.

On April 18 and 27, 1918, Baker sent out two additional directives to military authorities, the first of which requested that hardships against COs be mitigated. Donald Johnson, in his study of the wartime Civil Liberties Bureau, conjectures that the civil liberties movement's protests against the cruel treatment of the objectors in the army influenced Baker to take such a step. Perhaps this is so; Baker's second April memo, however, did not mention harsh treatment. Rather, he informed camp commandants that COs should be "brought promptly to trial by court-martial" if they were "sullen or defiant," insincere, or "active in propaganda."[24] Military authorities considered Baker's second memo to be a blank check, and a rash of courts-martial ensued; for instance, twenty-one of the twenty-three objectors located at Camp Devens in Ayer, Massachusetts, were summarily court-martialed within a few days of the issuance of the April 27 memo.[25]

Tragically, for one young idealistic socialist man, Baker's April 18 memo urging forbearance in the treatment of objectors came too late. In a letter to President Wilson dated April 16, Walter Nelles, counsel for the Civil Liberties Bureau, wrote: "At Fort Hancock, New Jersey, April 8, 1918, Ernest Gellert put his left breast against the mouth of a loaded rifle and pulled the trigger with a stick." Nelles then quoted from Gellert's suicide letter: "I fear I have not succeeded in convincing the authorities of the sincerity of my scruples against participation in the war. I feel that only by my death will I be able to save others from the mental tortures I have gone through. If I succeed I give my life willingly."[26] Nelles appended a ten-page single-spaced report detailing Gellert's persecution (which included drastic physical punishments and mental torture) and requested a full investigation of his suicide. An in-house military investigation exonerated the military officers who had held authority over Gellert. Many years later, Charles Recht wrote with bitterness that Gellert's death "made no change in the way the army treated their fellow-Americans."[27]

In response to reported atrocities committed against objectors, the government made one last attempt to clarify the situation of COs under military authority. A board of inquiry was set up on June 1, 1918, to establish uniform rulings for objectors who had refused noncombatant military duty. Composed of Major Walter G. Kellogg, U.S. Circuit Court Judge Julian W. Mack, and Dean Harlan F. Stone of the Columbia University Law School, the board traveled from camp to camp, reviewing cases of COs who had already been court-martialed and interviewing all other objectors to determine whether they were "sincere" or "insincere." The board's overall pattern was to judge religious objectors sincere and political objectors insincere. Sincere objectors who had scruples against noncombatant military service were offered farm furloughs, and twelve hundred men eventually accepted this offer. However, a man assessed as sincere by the board who refused farm work was reclassified insincere and turned over to the military along with other objectors who had been judged insincere. Objectors who found themselves under military authority in the aftermath of board deliberations were often placed in situations where they felt compelled to disobey an order. These "absolutists," so named because they refused to follow any military commands, were quickly court-martialed under the articles of war and given extremely severe punishments.[28] Sentences were reduced after the war ended, but the ruthlessness of the court-martial decisions for over five hundred objectors bears consideration here. As historian Lillian Schlissel has pointed out, War Department records reveal that "there were seventeen death sentences, 142 life terms, and 345 sentences where the average term was sixteen and one-half years. None of the death penalties was carried out."[29]

Because of their personal decision to reject soldiering, many World War I objectors experienced extraordinarily brutal conditions under military authority. A number of memoirs attest to the strength of purpose that most objectors exemplified in light of such savage treatment and reveal the high price they paid for their stand.[30] Historians of the home front war and of the wartime civil liberties movement have incorporated this aspect of the CO story into their studies.[31] However, there is more to the history of the objector in wartime; Bureau of Legal Advice records permit us to examine the objector from a more personal or intimate perspective.

The objectors who became Bureau clients varied in their reasons for their stand against military service, but the majority were political objectors who defined themselves as socialists or internationalists. Virtually all were white, and the majority were native born and fairly well educated.[32] The members of the Bureau of Legal Advice (unlike their counterparts in the Civil Liberties Bureau) knew their clients as individuals; objectors visited the Bureau office, Bureau workers visited the objectors in training camps and, later, in military prisons, and they maintained a voluminous correspondence with objectors and their families. Letters and other documents provide a wealth of information on conditions in military

camps and prisons, and as already indicated, much of this information was passed on to the Civil Liberties Bureau or used by Witherspoon herself when dealing with government or military authorities.
The correspondence imparts a sense of the character and values of
the authors. Letters of objectors show that in the process of writing
to Bureau sympathizers about their experiences in camp, individuals came to know themselves better. Few letters written to these
young men from Witherspoon and others in the Bureau office have
survived, but we can infer from many letters composed by the COs
that Bureau members encouraged their clients to maintain their
integrity of purpose and to believe in the political and historical
significance of their stand.

The feminist pacifists of the Bureau and the conscientious objectors they helped grappled as individuals and in relation to one
another with the polarized wartime gender system. Objectors
sought to move away from the warrior ideal—the particular form
of manliness favored by the state in the context of war—while the
feminist-pacifist civil libertarians attempted to distance themselves
from the contradictory ideal of the wartime woman as an actively
loyal patriotic mother-citizen as well as a passive and defenseless
creature in need of male (warrior) protection. Objectors and feminist pacifists struggled to invent new identities for themselves as
they resisted societal pressures to conform. This project to decon-
struct and then reconstruct gender identity outside of the wartime
norm was not always (or perhaps even usually) a fully self-conscious act on the part of objectors and feminist pacifists. However,
out of the conflicts and tensions involved in the attempt to become
more self-directed people emerged some fresh understandings of
the personal dimension of war resistance. It was through the
dynamic dialogue between objectors and feminist-pacifist civil libertarians (and among the objectors themselves) that new peace-
culture attitudes and commitments began to take shape.

As one example, the letters of Bruno Grunzig to Fannie May
Witherspoon provide a rich source for understanding the kinds of
relationships that developed among objectors and feminist pacifist
women of the Bureau. This correspondence also reveals how difficult it was for young men such as Grunzig to resist imbibing
aspects of the ultramasculine soldier ideal. Grunzig was in some
important ways representative of the young absolutist political CO
of World War I America. His parents were immigrants, but they

were also established middle-class people. Grunzig, 21 years old in 1917, was a thoughtful person (he had not attended college) who earned his living as a poultry farmer in Scotch Plains, a suburb of Westfield, New Jersey. He was a member of the Socialist Party and, therefore, might have become acquainted with Witherspoon and Tracy Mygatt before the war. Witherspoon and Grunzig became good friends during the time he worked for the Bureau, from fall 1917 until spring 1918 (when he was sent to training camp). Grunzig's letters to the Bureau were usually addressed to Witherspoon and reveal a deep attachment to her. Witherspoon, ten years older than Grunzig, was a serious and passionate person, and he admired her qualities of persistence and her dedication to "the cause." He was drawn to the somewhat Victorian Witherspoon— who also possessed a streak of the bohemian New Woman in her makeup—and seems to have related to her as a comrade, a mother, and a sister. It is also possible that Grunzig was in love with Fannie May Witherspoon.[33]

As we have seen, Witherspoon felt a special calling to help the objector. In part, she expressed her concern in maternal language and did not completely reject a self-image as a pacifist moral mother. She and other feminist pacifists who worked at the Bureau or in the national civil liberties movement spoke in terms of protecting and nurturing "their boys." However, these same women (including Witherspoon) also saw themselves as comrades of the objectors and identified personally with their struggles and sufferings. They knew themselves to be outsiders, too, and believed that they could, in cooperation with these young men, create a new world after the war, one in which men would reject the "mastery over" aspect of masculine identity so crucial to militarism and to warmaking. Anna Davis, a Quaker and a socialist engaged in civil liberties work in Boston and a frequent correspondent of Witherspoon's, put it well for all of them: "In our time our men will prove to be the heroes and prophets of a better day."[34]

Witherspoon, in writing for the public, idealized the CO and set him apart from other men: "The true objector throughout all his trials seems never to lose his confidence in the justice of his cause and its perfect vindication in the future. For this reason his spirits are always high. . . . He is not a self-absorbed egotist, but is full of care and affection for the family and friends who are suffering vicariously with him."[35] Presuming that her readers "believe physical endurance the supreme test of courage," she elaborated on the response of objectors to the hardships that they endured as reviled outcasts under military authority: "To visit objectors in camp was to realize that they were 'strangers in a strange land'— no one spoke their language; they were hated, bullied and . . . frequently subjected to outrageous brutalities. Usually the petty officers and guards who had these men in charge were in no way capable of understanding intellectual convictions or religious ardor. . . . Here was a creature obviously different from themselves; and not understanding him, they hated and goaded him."[36]

Bruno Grunzig and many of his comrades basked in the attention of women such as Witherspoon and Davis, whom they recognized to be politically sagacious individuals with a sure sense of the historic moment and with a capacity to influence public opinion in their favor. They also counted on the visits, letters, and packages that they received from mothers, sisters, and lovers, individuals who were frequently in close touch with Bureau women.

When COs entered military camps, they came under immediate suspicion. If they were absolutists like Grunzig, they would refuse noncombatant service, civilian farm furloughs, and most camp assignments and military orders. Courts-martial and long prison terms often ensued, and mental and physical abuse became a fact of daily life. In such circumstances, it was crucial for objectors to possess and to maintain high self-esteem; in this, outside support was crucial, but so too was a strong belief in the integrity of one's stand. Grunzig, for example, respected himself and possessed strength of purpose, including a sense of responsibility to other objectors in his role as informant for the Bureau. He carefully observed the behavior of individuals and was conscious of the degrees of power and of status within the ranks of the men with whom he shared special, segregated CO quarters. Grunzig believed rather dogmatically in the socialist creed and found security in assuming that he and his socialist comrades were in some ways superior to religious objectors, as well as to army officers and enlisted men. However, paradoxically, he at times identified strongly with a military manly ideal and seemed to shun a pacifist one, which he associated with religion and with effeminacy.

Gerald Shenk, in his study of conscription and manliness during World War I, identifies a particular language of gender ridicule that authorities of the state employed to coerce men into participating as soldiers in the war. He argues that men who refused to accept the warrior role for themselves nonetheless often held certain assumptions about manliness that accorded with the wartime soldier ideal employed by government officials and military officers. Such individuals often utilized gender ridicule against others. For example, one political objector, Frederick Stehr, ridiculed government officials in the language often employed against men who refused military service for conscience sake: state authorities, in Stehr's mind, were perverts who were guilty of "'predatory conquest' and . . . 'unadulterated behavior.'" Shenk argues that such language "involved subconscious negative sexual innuendo to impugn the manhood of men who make war."[37]

Bruno Grunzig wrote to Witherspoon about the hazing—often including gender ridicule—that all objectors experienced in the army. Not long after arriving at Camp Dix in New Jersey, Grunzig recounted: "The guards took keen delight in telling all willing to listen, that we were slackers, deserters, cowards, etc., etc. . . . [We were marched] all thru camp again, with the whole camp shouting 'slacker,' now will you be good, you will run will yez, you'll like it alright, just like we do."[38] Several weeks later, Grunzig criticized CO groups with whom he chose not to identify. He noted that all the objectors at Camp Dix had been assigned to Company 48, which "receives all of the 'scum of the camp,' mostly . . . draft dodgers, in the most awful state of personal filth (bodily & mentally & morally)."[39]

Grunzig disliked the fact that the regular army people saw him and other political objectors as similar to the religious objectors, in this case mostly Mennonites and members of the International Bible Students Association. His gorge rose at such a comparison, and he did not shrink from employing the language of gender ridicule to distance himself from what he viewed as the unmanly character traits and behavior of the religious objectors: "Would that I could speak to them [soldiers] for just ten minutes and I venture to say that they would go away with a different impression; if not approval at least respect. I am quite sure that this attitude has been caused mainly by the religious nutts [*sic*] and their effeminate ways, not to speak of their perpetual howling of puerile ditties."[40] In the same letter, Grunzig recognized that he had somehow offended "Miss Mygatt," who was most sympathetic to the nonresistant pacifist stand of the religious objectors; he asked penitently for an explanation of his wrongdoing. Grunzig must have received feedback on this point, because his subsequent letters contain no direct criticism of religious COs.

Nonetheless, nine months later, Grunzig found himself once more out of favor with Mygatt, his "dear friend." His remarks on her published play *The Good Friday: A Passion Play for Now* (which concerned the torture and death of a religious objector in military prison) reveal an ongoing and unresolved dialogue between them:

> Was I a bit scrappy in my rash criticism of The Good Friday?
> . . . This is in great measure due to my dislike for rose tints;
> they are so unreal in a world of flaming red and overpowering,
> deadly blacks. My preference runs to the strong and viril [*sic*] in
> literature. . . . It is with regret that I must admit, the too ready
> acceptance by many people of what you have pleased to term
> "slush." For this very reason I shall encourage the little "Red
> Cock" in his crowing for if he keeps it up long enough we shall
> win out, are bound to by all the laws of nature.[41]

Grunzig believed in the desirability of what he perceived as a tough-minded, combative male world of stark realities. The "slushy" or sentimental female world of softened or muted realities—rose as opposed to red and black—held little appeal. The "little 'Red Cock'" is none other than the socialist conscientious objector. Grunzig set "us the Reds" apart from and against other objectors; this attitude extended to Wobblies who refused service, despite their radical credentials and the IWW slogan "Don't be a soldier, be a man."[42] For instance, Grunzig disparagingly described one "I-Double-Double" at Camp Dix as "a rough and tumble sort of a fellow . . . typical, I think, of the average."[43] On two occasions, however, Grunzig mentioned approvingly the last names of two African Americans, Morgan and Clayton—whom he identified as "negro" and "colored," respectively—in the context of "our boys," an apparent reference to the political objector group in the camp.[44]

When his socialist confrere John Grass seemed to be considering noncombatant service because of worries that he could not endure a long penitentiary term, Grunzig's strategy to set Grass straight paralleled the gender ridicule approach employed by some military officers. He and Elsie Knepper, Grass's "girl" and "a brick," met for several hours with Grass: "The two of us surely did go at him in grand style. Joking, bulldozing and threatening were

16. Left to right: Bruno Grunzig, Clarence Hotson, Elsie Knepper, Leo Robbins, and Ronald Hotson, Camp Dix, July 21, 1918. Courtesy of the Tamiment Institute Library, New York University.

alternately brought into play and as a result he is now in fine shape, both mentally and physically. He won't even take farm service now if given the opportunity. This however is no fault of mine since my efforts were directed principally to the general attack on his weak-kneed appearance and stand."[45]

Elsie Knepper played a significant role in this ritual of gender ridicule, and Grunzig acknowledged his admiration for this young woman. Nonetheless, it is also apparent that a traditional chivalric code often influenced Grunzig to counterpoint the "Red Cock" against vulnerable womanhood. For example, in one letter to Witherspoon, Grunzig cautioned her against an action that might put her own freedom at risk:

I am quite sure that all of the Absolutists whom you might be able to relieve of physical discomforts . . . would join me in asking that you do your little bit for human progress on the outside and leave us to fight our way on the inside. You can be of infinitely more benefit to a struggling ideal where you are, than by getting yourself into trouble for a couple of hardened

Reds who could not be downed anyhow, even though they may be for a time.[46]

Three months later, the theme of "hardened Reds" going it alone had become almost an obsession for Grunzig: "I have sort of an instinctive feeling that we should fight for recognition and decent conditions all alone and prove to the authorities that we are big enough in ourselves. . . . If we complain about every little thing and ask outsiders to communicate with [Washington] D. C. how on earth can we expect the authorities to respect us as men?"[47] Grunzig wished to avoid what he viewed as feminine strategies to aid objectors; the true CO man could accomplish his redemption "all alone." Ten days later (the day following the armistice), Grunzig continued: "If we waver now, regret our present position after peace has been declared, even if it is only a mental condition, then we are open to serious charges. It is just at this time that we must go forth willingly to another battle in the great moral fight. . . . We must take our medicine like men and precisely because the natural reaction is *expected* to be the very reverse."[48] Grunzig's marked desire to project a tough, manly self-image in the context of the ultramasculine world of the army barracks paralleled his need to affirm that women found objectors such as himself sexually attractive and worthy of respect.[49] In the same letter, Grunzig remarked that one of the "boys" had written to him en route to Fort Douglas, Utah (the military prison where many conscientious objectors were incarcerated) that a "Red Cross girl" had offered them (the CO prisoners) a basket of fruit, cake, candy, and cigarettes. The men had initially refused, but the young woman had insisted: "Well, if you are conscientious objectors you are *men* anyway." Grunzig's next sentence was: "Censor & *all other officers* please note." He then described "the keen interest" that a waitress at the St. Louis Terminal Restaurant had taken "in the boys." When she heard that they were COs, she promised to visit them if they ended up at Fort Leavenworth, as Leavenworth was her hometown.[50]

There is no record of this woman visiting objectors at Fort Leavenworth, but Bureau records do contain reports and letters from several sweethearts and wives of objectors and from two Bureau correspondents, Mabel Higgins and Ella Reeve Bloor, who visited a number of military prisons. The documents demonstrate that "visiting" sometimes camouflaged a rather ingenious informant or spy system, orchestrated by Witherspoon. When several militant young women decided to travel to Fort Riley to be near "their boys," Witherspoon facilitated communication between Higgins and Bloor and these young women.

On August 15, 1918, Alice Navard and Frieda Ledermann arrived in Junction City, Kansas, near Fort Riley. Ledermann's fiancé, William Jasmagy, had managed to get a pass into town and was waiting for them at the train station; he and Carl Maier, Navard's fiancé, were socialists from Brooklyn and residents of the "tent colony" established at Fort Riley for conscientious objectors. Ledermann and Navard settled into Junction City quickly. They found accommodations in a private home, procured employment, and spent every opportunity they could at Fort Riley visiting all the objectors, not just Jasmagy and Maier. For several weeks, they secured visiting passes both for the tent colony and for the guard house with an ease that surprised both of them. As Alice Navard explained, "[O]ur youth and supposed interest in only the boys whom we asked to see—has made it possible for us to get along so well." Moving around the fort easily, Navard was able not only to collect information on the condition of COs but also "to convey existing conditions and the news from one place to the other." When transfers from Fort Riley to neighboring Camp Funston occurred, Navard visited objectors at the second location. However, both women were repeatedly questioned by officers about their views, and the conscientious objectors were always (according to Navard) "denounced as cowards, unmanly, good-for-nothings."[51]

Trouble surfaced when an intelligence officer, Captain Jolliffe, took an interest in Ledermann and Navard. He questioned them minutely about their backgrounds, parents, and occupations; when he decided to investigate their private lives himself, Ledermann retorted: "You are welcome at any time."[52] Navard later recounted the visit that he paid to their lodgings:

On Tuesday, Sept. 17, Capt. Joll. called at our residence here, and in a very military fashion insisted on seeing the lady with whom we live. . . . After speaking with her, Capt. J. was thoroughly convinced that we were perfect ladies, and he then asked for an interview with me personally.

Very majestically, drawing himself up to his 6'3" height, he told me he believed the best thing we girls could do would be to go home where we belonged—that Junction City is a soldier town, and a very bad place for unmarried girls.[53]

The next day, Navard and Ledermann visited Jolliffe, informing him that they would not leave town. The captain responded with a not very subtle sexual threat: "Don't you realize that I could make it so uncomfortable for you that you would have to leave, and possibly in disgrace[?]. I, as the Intelligence Officer, have the right to go into any house, anytime I want, and demand what I want. You girls are all right. I know it, but don't you realize you can be framed up[?]. You know, too, there are men who take advantage of their position to get what they desire, and they wouldn't hesitate to insult even you." Retelling the story, Navard commented that "he made it appear so bad, that we decided it might be best to leave."[54] However, they remained in Junction City, and Frieda Ledermann decided to marry William Jasmagy, who by this time (mid-September) was in the guard house at Fort Riley. At one point, Ledermann, accompanied by a minister, arrived at the guard house prepared to get married then and there, but permission was denied. A few days later, Jasmagy was granted a day pass and he and Ledermann were married after all. According to Ledermann, "[T]he officials gave him this day just to see if we were both sincere and honestly meant to fulfil what we aimed for—which was marriage."[55]

In the midst of these occurrences, Navard was forced to debate Lieutenant Woodward, the camp adjutant, on the subject of manliness. Armed with her convictions, with the memory of Captain Jolliffe's menacing "advice," and with her own unassailable logic, Alice Navard got the better of the officer. Woodward began by deprecating the value of a man who would not "defend" his mother, sister, or sweetheart. Navard recalled:

> Dramatically he outlined all the horrible German atrocities to Belgian and French women—and concluded by asking, "Is it fair to stand back and refuse to fight for such a noble cause as the defense, protection of womankind?" I made known to him that it was not my belief to right a wrong with a wrong—and I did not believe one army to be better than another. They are all alike, and the same indecencies could be reported about our own army. What right would I have to expect an enemy soldier to be

decent to me, when I am told by good authority here, that boys will take advantage of their uniform to get what they desire[?]. If my protectors make it impossible for me to live without being insulted and degraded—what am I to expect from others?"[56]

According to Navard, Woodward responded lamely that "he didn't believe it was very manly to do the reverse from what the majority believed to be right."[57]

At the end of September 1918, ten days after the marriage of Frieda Ledermann and William Jasmagy, Sadie Brandon—the wife of socialist CO Joseph Brandon—joined Alice Navard and Frieda Ledermann Jasmagy in Junction City. She took a room at the New Rush Hotel and was visiting with her husband within the hour. A short time later, she found herself fending off the sexual advances of Captain Washburn, who had offered her a drive into town in his car because he did not "like to see a young girl like you around here when it's dark." Brandon, in her report to the Bureau, chastised herself for failing to ascertain the motives behind Washburn's initial chivalry. At one point, Brandon threatened to jump out of "the machine" if Washburn did not leave her alone; after telling her that he was her "protector," he finally acquiesced and dropped Brandon off at her hotel. Another time, a Lieutenant Pike pestered her to take a buggy ride: "We could spend a pleasant afternoon and he'd [the husband] be none the wiser." Brandon gave him a tongue lashing, and Pike left her alone after that.

Less than three weeks after arriving in Junction City, Brandon faced another form of intimidation: she lost her job at the Army Bank because she was the wife of a conscientious objector. A Major Spiller told Brandon that she could have her fare paid back to New York and even receive money to divorce her husband because "a man who wouldn't fight for his country wouldn't defend his wife."[58] Brandon recalled her exchange with Spiller on this topic:

> "Your husband is such a scoundrel he isn't worth having such a fine woman for his wife." I said, "In my estimation there is nobody really good enough for him." "You foolish girl, you ought to go back to N.Y. and get a divorce. You'd have absolutely no trouble either, I'd help you fight your case right thru." "No, sir, just at present I don't think I care to consider your kind offer." He even offers [*sic*] to give me money if I'm out of work.[59]

The perceptive observations of Alice Navard, Frieda Ledermann Jasmagy, and Sadie Brandon underscore the centrality of
gender constructions to the war system. In this era, if men refused
to become warriors, they became targets for gender ridicule and for
more formalized punishments; women who shared the views of
such men faced gender ridicule and also became potential "bad"
women and outcasts who could not depend upon the patriarchal,
militaristic code of chivalry to protect them.[60] Like the men whom
they respected, loved, and perhaps glamorized, Navard, Jasmagy,
and Brandon challenged the gendered war system in fundamental
ways. They, and the feminist-pacifist civil libertarian women with
whom they made common cause, consciously rejected a compliant,
patriotic role for themselves—a rejection that confounded military
men and led some officers, as we have seen, to become verbally and
physically aggressive and abusive towards them. In a letter to
Frieda Ledermann Jasmagy, Witherspoon praised Jasmagy and her
comrades for their courageous efforts and promised: "Some day I
mean to see to it that the story of the feminine Conscientious
Objectors is told also."[61]

Mabel Higgins and Ella Reeve Bloor were also "feminine
COs," but they represented the generation of women activists who
were in their middle years of life during World War I. Higgins
and Bloor were both committed to the civil liberties cause, but
they were otherwise quite different. We know very little about
Higgins's background except that she was married and an artist
and lived in New York City. In contrast, Bloor was a seasoned
labor activist with a national reputation, who was respected by
socialists and Wobblies alike; she and Witherspoon had already
worked together in defense of the legal rights of radical workers in
wartime. Bloor consented to include visits to military camps where
COs were housed in her western speaking tour (which was sponsored by the Workers Liberty Defense Union).

There is no extant correspondence between Higgins and Bloor,
but letters between them and Witherspoon and between Bloor and
Frieda Ledermann Jasmagy demonstrate that Witherspoon had to
deal with a broad range of perspectives as coordinator of some
aspects of national civil liberties work among women. For instance,
Higgins's letter to Witherspoon of October 21, 1918, in which she
described the work of the young CO women Navard and Ledermann (Jasmagy), demonstrates that she admired these young

women but also that she held them in disdain because they were young, foreign-born, and Jewish. Higgins criticized a number of officers for their crude "cajolery and seduction" intimidation techniques but then added condescendingly that "of course little girls may get this sort of thing a bit twisted and exaggerated, but I daresay their story is more than two thirds straight. It does make one a little 'hot under the collar' doesn't it?" In the same letter, Higgins noted that she and "the girls" had decided to meet "on the quiet" so that her freedom to visit the objectors at Fort Riley would not be hampered by her association with Navard and Ledermann Jasmagy, who had already been asked by officers if they were associated with "70 Fifth Avenue" (the Bureau's Manhattan address). Higgins continued: "Their little Russian Jewish minds are just as shrewd as can be—and I love the girls very much."

Witherspoon responded to Higgins quickly, and her tone was entirely respectful of the young women. She requested that Navard and Ledermann Jasmagy be asked to send her their own reports, and she also urged Higgins to investigate all incidents of sexually aggressive behavior towards the young women on the part of officers. "This sort of thing is very hard to run to ground," Witherspoon remarked, "but I think you would be doing a real service if you could secure well authenticated reports of this kind of intimidation. . . . See everything you can and report it as fully and promptly as possible."[62] Then, she wrote to Frieda Ledermann Jasmagy's mother-in-law and informed her that "Mrs. Higgins" had praised Frieda as "a lovely girl . . . plucky and resourceful."[63] Witherspoon understood the power of language, and she doubtless chose her words carefully to avoid the anti-Semitic cast of Higgins's comments. Nonetheless, it is probable that Witherspoon shared some of Higgins's prejudices with regard to Jewish people; on one occasion, for instance, she described a young imprisoned political dissident as "the emotional Jewish type [who] suffers so keenly when deprived of affection and companionship."[64]

For her part, Ella Reeve Bloor was already becoming a legend in her own time; after the war's end, she would join the Communist Party and become the "Mother" of the postwar communist wing of the labor movement.[65] Even at this time, however, young women like Frieda Ledermann Jasmagy called her Mother Bloor. In January 1919, after Jasmagy had moved to Leavenworth, Kansas, to be near her husband (who had been transferred to Fort

Leavenworth from Fort Riley), she wrote a warm, newsy, and intimate letter to "Dearest Mother Bloor," in which she acknowledged receipt of Bloor's "welcome and sweet" letter to her: "It sure did give me new courage, and I will do all in my power to keep the boys happy and couragious [*sic*], as heretofore." Jasmagy recounted the visit of "brave little me" to Judge Mack of the board of inquiry and commented that she was looking forward to meeting Winthrop Lane of the Civil Liberties Bureau in Leavenworth and to sharing what information she had with him. She added that she corresponded regularly with another CO wife, Canadian-born Woman's Peace Party activist Laura Hughes Lunde of Chicago, and relayed greetings from "Gussie," who appears to have been a sweetheart or wife of another objector. Jasmagy closed effusively; "[I]f I have more news I will write again, so hope & trust as ever in me, Yours with love, Mrs. Wm. Jasmagy or plain 'Fritzie.'"[66] A few days before this letter was written, Bloor had informed her comrade Anna Davis that the latter could write to her in care of Mrs. William Jasmagy, stating that "she is the brave wife of a CO; went to Fort Riley and married him, so as to be near him. Trust her."[67]

Two other feminine COs journeyed to Kansas in August 1918 to visit their lovers: Lottie Fishbein, whose fiancé, Ben Breger, was a Brooklyn-born dentist and an objector on humanitarian grounds, and Elsie Knepper, who (as noted above) was romantically involved with political objector John Grass. Fishbein had been Roger Baldwin's secretary for a time and was well acquainted with Witherspoon and her coworkers at 70 Fifth Avenue, and Knepper as well had worked for the Civil Liberties Bureau and had close ties with the Bureau of Legal Advice.

These women, in concert with Ledermann Jasmagy, Navard, and Brandon, managed to collect from objectors in Camps Riley and Funston a wealth of damning evidence concerning savage tortures perpetrated upon many COs between July 5 and October 21, 1918. These tortures included bayonetting, forced cold showers under fire hoses for up to fifteen minutes at a time (sometimes repeatedly) in the middle of the night, vicious blows, and hanging by the thumbs. Manacling of the wrists to prison bars for nine hours a day for fourteen days in a row—which was a legal military punishment for recalcitrant soldiers—was also frequently employed. As Norman Thomas noted in his history of the objector during World War I, "some of the worst brutalities occurred in the last months of the war when there was no longer the excuse of the confusion of establishing new camps and the difficulty of installing proper machinery for dealing with objectors."[68] The tortures suffered at Camp Funston, especially, were given publicity by the civil liberties movement in fall 1918. The public outcry against the "Camp Funston Outrages," also known as the "Reign of Terror," forced the War Department to insist on a military investigation. However, against the recommendation of the investigating officer that the two officers responsible be summarily dismissed, Secretary of War Baker gave in to protestations from the newly-established American Legion and the two men were merely censured for neglect of duty and granted honorable discharges in December 1918.[69]

While the feminine COs were engaged in their informant work and helping to stir up a national campaign against the torture of objectors, the men themselves stolidly endured the long days and nights in disciplinary barracks at several different military camps. High profile women—including Jane Addams and Emily Greene Balch—visited the camps, as did prominent pacifist and civil libertarian men, mostly lawyers. When we read the latter's reports and note the language that they used to express themselves, we see that these men shared many common assumptions with the women of the movement: both men and women spoke not only as civil libertarians on behalf of American first amendment freedoms but also as nurturing parent figures who could not abide the mindless violence and nihilism of a military system that sought to break the wills of idealistic young men.[70]

The imprisoned objectors with whom the Bureau of Legal Advice had most contact successfully resisted the manifold pressures to conform to a warrior role. To be sure, there were casualties even within this group, including the suicide of Ernest Gellert and the deaths of at least seventeen objectors as a result of torture and medical neglect.[71] Nonetheless, Howard Moore, a comrade of Bruno Grunzig's, probably articulated the sentiment of most objectors when he spoke of an area of freedom that existed for him even under military authority: "Though brutally confined, I can still fight for the ideals in which I believe."[72] Like Grunzig, Moore believed his identity as a man to be inextricably bound to his position on liberty of conscience. He also acknowledged a partnership of sentiment and of commitment between himself and Witherspoon:

> I am ever mindful of the contribution you are making to the cause of a saner world and the splendid courage which you have manifested in a time of such painful conformity has been an inspiration [and] a solace. I wish aside from the appreciation I feel for the benefits I am now enjoying, largely as a result of your efforts in behalf of the C.O.s, [you to] know that I am grateful to you all for the work you are doing toward the restoration of civil liberties and against the reactionary measures that would sterilize the civic manhood of the country.[73]

Moore was confident that he and other like-minded men were the standard bearers for male citizenship in the nation. At the same time, he was convinced that women deserved to be accorded equal citizenship status with men; for Moore and for many other political objectors (including Bruno Grunzig), woman's suffrage was an unquestioned goal. He approved of militant feminist activism, and before the outbreak of war, he had written to the New York City branch of the Woman's Peace Party to congratulate them on their peace efforts. However, unlike Grunzig, the thirty-year-old Moore felt no need to boost his ego or to validate his identity at the expense of other powerless groups.

Frieda Ledermann Jasmagy's husband, William Jasmagy, who was an objector on humanitarian and socialist grounds, believed (like Moore) that his principled stand against war was a feature of his manhood. He and other political objectors thought that a new and better day was at hand; in his court-martial proceedings, the twenty-six-year-old musician declared:

> The present temporary lapse into hatred, viciousness and passionate intolerance, festered by a subjugation of the people and stimulated thru a perversion of truth and ideals, may cause my position to be misjudged, but in this I will experience no feelings of resentment; instead I will rest content in that inward compensation, knowing I retained my manhood and had lived to help and promote among mankind the kingdom of love and good will, and that in time, my stand will be vindicated by posterity.[74]

The same individuals who thought in terms of a visionary future also took risks while imprisoned to make their ideals manifest. One such individual was Evan Thomas, a theology student before the war and the brother of Norman Thomas. Evan Thomas, a political objector, arrived at Fort Leavenworth Disciplinary Barracks on September 20, 1918, and was at first willing to do work assignments around the camp. He changed his mind, however, when he learned of the brutal punishment that several Molokans were receiving because of their conscientious refusal to perform work for the military.[75] In a letter to the commandant of Leavenworth, Colonel Sedgwick Rice, dated November 5, 1918, Thomas announced his resolve to join the three Russian religious objectors in solitary confinement:

> I have known these men for several months and am convinced of the absolute sincerity of [their] religious objections to working here. Their punishment is in my opinion a plain case of the government's refusal to respect the individual conscience and an effort to coerce men against their conscience. . . . Under these circumstances, I have come to the decision to refuse to work so long as the principle of freedom for which I have taken my stand as a conscientious objector continues to be violated.[76]

The Civil Liberties Bureau publicized Thomas's stand, revealing that nine objectors were in solitary confinement for their refusal to engage in prison labor: "These nine men are handcuffed and chained by their wrists to the bars of the door, for nine hours a day in darkened cells. The solitary cells here are in the sub-basement of the prison. Prisoners in such confinement are rationed on bread and water. Most of these executive sentences are for fourteen days, but some of the objectors have been in solitary thirty, forty, or even, in one case fifty days."[77]

Howard Moore endured the same punishment at Leavenworth during this period. He commented in his autobiography that he was ordered to the prison pathology laboratory one day, where a sample of his sputum was taken. Two days later, he was told the result was positive for tuberculosis, but after being given some cough syrup and an extra blanket, he was sent back to "the hole." Moore, who at this point weighed ninety pounds (down from 150 pounds), saw Evan Thomas at the hospital. He noted that his friend looked "pale, weary, and thinner than ever. When I rushed forward to greet him the guard threatened to beat me with his club, but we managed to shake hands before I was pushed into a corner."[78]

During fall 1918, when Thomas, Moore, and others were undergoing solitary confinement and the punishment of manacling, Witherspoon and Baldwin were publicizing such treatment widely. Then, on October 30, Baldwin himself began a one-year sentence in civil prison for failing to obey his draft board's instruction to appear for a physical examination. His statement to the court at his trial represented an eloquent plea for liberty of conscience in wartime. In contrast, Judge Julius Mayer noted in passing sentence that the state's ability to exist depended "upon obedience of the law." He continued; "It may often be that a man or woman has greater foresight than the masses of the people. And it may be that in the history of things, he, who seems to be wrong today, may be right tomorrow. But with those possible idealistic and academic speculations a Court has nothing to do."[79]

Baldwin's position and Mayer's denial of its legal validity spoke to the fundamental challenge to nationhood that absolutist objectors as a group represented. Repeatedly, in letters and in statements before court-martial hearings and before board of inquiry proceedings, absolutists—whether religious or political objectors—declined to recognize the right of the state to conscript them into military service. Their refusal to fight underscored their rejection of the ultramasculine soldier-citizen ideal. Erling Lunde, a comrade of Moore, Evans, and Grunzig, put it clearly when he stated at his court-martial trial that he wished to be judged "as a Conscientious Objector to War not as a soldier."[80] This the state's representatives could not do. Similarly, Fannie May Witherspoon recognized that "the government, having instituted conscription, the ultimate expression of state supremacy, could not with logic admit the principle of complete refusal of service under military authority—not because it feared the loss of the men to the army, but because this principle involved the whole question of relationship between the individual and the state. Hence the deadlock between the absolutist and the government."[81]

Regardless of the logic of the case against absolutists, a number of them attempted to convince the state to expand the concept of male citizenship in time of war to include the conscientious objector. For instance, on August 21, 1918, four Fort Riley objec-

17. Left to right: conscientious objectors Bruno Grunzig, Howard Moore, Ben Breger, and Erling Lunde at Fort Douglas, Utah, October 18, 1919. Courtesy of the Swarthmore College Peace Collection.

tors—Evan Thomas, Howard Moore, Erling Lunde, and Harold Gray—wrote to Secretary of War Baker that they were "unalterably opposed to the principle of conscription and believe it to be un-American as well as the very backbone of militarism and war." They were determined not to cooperate with the military authorities and to refuse all assignments and duties expected of them under the Selective Service Act. Rather, the four COs informed Baker that "we are ready and eager to work for society as private citizens, nor do we desire to engage in propaganda against the state, but to live useful, constructive lives in society." Accordingly, they gave notice that they were beginning a hunger strike, which they intended to continue "as long as we are kept from following the pursuits we feel called upon to follow in life."[82] They were joined by twenty other men, and many of them were hospitalized after they became weak and were force fed to keep them alive. Visits from family members—including Norman Thomas and Moore's mother and sister—convinced the men to halt the strike.

Not long thereafter, the board of inquiry establishing sentences for objectors interviewed Moore at Fort Riley. At one point, Harlan Stone argued that Moore was an inconsistent absolutist because he bought postage stamps. Fellow board member Judge Mack turned to Stone and said sharply: "Why quibble? The fact is that if everyone believed as Moore does, there couldn't be any war. Our job is to decide what to do with him."[83] Not long after this, Moore volunteered as a hospital worker during an outbreak of influenza among the solders at the camp (the worldwide influenza epidemic resulted in the deaths of many soldiers and civilians in the United States and in Europe). Moore described his role in his autobiography:

> Some nurses and corpsmen were assigned to me, I was given a stethoscope, and I took charge of a ward in which most of the patients were delirious. Nobody there knew I wasn't a doctor. Although I did not wear a mask, which was required of everyone else, and slept in the ward with men dying all around me until space was made for my cot in the linen room, I was never ill. . . . Statistically, our section had the fewest deaths, but in the whole hospital men were dying so fast they could not get corpsmen enough, or guards to station around the bodies that were piled up like cordwood on the parade grounds.[84]

Moore was transfered to nearby Fort Funston on October 21, 1918 (a day that marked the end of the Funston Outrages). He was court-martialed for refusing to obey a military order and sent to Fort Leavenworth to begin a five-year prison sentence. The captain who was the medical doctor at Fort Riley at the time that Moore worked in the hospital had told Moore that he feared that he would not live more than six months if sent to Leavenworth Disciplinary Barracks.

Meanwhile, as we have seen, the Bureau of Legal Advice and the National Civil Liberties Bureau were publishing exposés of prison conditions. In one article, written after Moore and Thomas had been transferred to Leavenworth and entitled "If This Hap-

18. *The conscientious objector barracks at Fort Douglas, Utah, November 12, 1919. Courtesy of the Swarthmore College Peace Collection.*

pened in Russia," Witherspoon denounced as barbaric the punishment of manacling military prisoners. Witherspoon, with an eye to her readership, spoke in traditional language as she cited physical bravery and chivalry as aspects of the objector's character; taking up the question of cowardice, Witherspoon exploited a conventional view of manliness when she pointed out that Howard Moore was the recipient of the Carnegie Hero Award "for the gallant rescue of a woman at the risk of his own life." She recounted that Moore resided in a solitary cell at Leavenworth, "with his hands manacled high about his head nine hours a day. He sleeps on a cement floor between foul blankets, is forbidden to read or write or talk, is fed on bread and water—and all this for the sake of loyalty to conviction."[85] Like Moore, Evan Thomas "voluntarily gave up congenial work and unflinchingly accepted confinement in one of these chambers of torture in order to make his protest against the coercion of his comrades."[86] As of November 15, 1918, there were twenty-nine others in "the hole:"

> Some of these prisoners had been cruelly beaten; they had been in solitary confinement for more than 50 days. But they had all remained loyal to conscience. These are the men the *Baltimore Evening Sun* calls "cowards." In their ranks are Russian and Mennonite farmers, Socialist workmen, college professors, social

workers, differing widely, but brothers in courage and in loyalty
to their ideals. Has America come to such a pass that she must
break such men spiritually, mentally and physically in order to
feel secure?[87]

Witherspoon quoted excerpts of a letter from an objector at Leavenworth to his mother that explained why he felt compelled to
"show solidarity" with his brothers of conscience. She then concluded her argument with a challenge to all "decent [men] for the
sake of the honor of America" not to rest content until manacling
of prisoners to cell bars had been abolished.

Witherspoon's article accomplished two goals. She alerted the
readers of *The World Tomorrow* (the journal of the Fellowship of
Reconciliation) of the existence of a protest movement demanding
the end of manacling as a military punishment. At the same time,
by focusing on Moore and Thomas in particular, she described a
novel masculine ideal, one that incorporated older views of physical courage (even martyrdom) with a new ideal of pacifist comradeship and solidarity among men who might otherwise be quite
different. In an extended essay, published a few months later in
pamphlet form, Witherspoon sought to dispel the representation
of the objector "in the columns of the daily press" as a man possessed of "every kind of skulking cowardice, pro-Germanism, or
'bad-boy' insubordination."[88] She borrowed from the title of a
pamphlet written by Norman Thomas to insist that the "war's
heretics" had proved by their sufferings the strength of their principles, and she stressed the commitment of men like Erling Lunde
to be defined not as soldier citizens but as pacifist citizens.[89] Witherspoon quoted a number of objectors who articulated their belief
that their pacifism would help to usher in "that better day," including an excerpt from Bruno Grunzig's court-martial at Camp
Meade, Maryland, on October 1, 1918: "A new order is about to
dawn. . . . We are now in the transition stage, and it needs big
men morally (big in the sense of the daring) to bring this newer
and better stage into blossom."[90]

Individuals such as Fannie May Witherspoon and Bruno Grunzig believed in the possibilities of the future, but they also recognized the importance of setting immediate goals and persisting
until they were accomplished. One concrete outcome of the protests against the inhumane treatment of objectors under military

authority during the war was Secretary of War Baker's public announcement of December 6, 1918 (several weeks after the armistice had been declared) that "fastening of prisoners to the bars of cells will no more be used as a mode of punishment."[91]

Thus, in varied ways, the state's aim to create a particular sense of what constituted manliness and womanliness in wartime was resisted by specific groups of men and women of the World War I pacifist movement, most notably the absolutist objectors and their feminist CO counterparts. This struggle occurred at a personal level, as individuals challenged themselves to think beyond the just warrior and the beautiful soul constructs as well as (albeit less clearly) beyond the tough Red or pacifist moral mother ideals. Here, we can identify the beginnings of a collective attempt to refashion men and women into nonviolent, autonomous citizens of the nation and recognize that the feminist pacifists and objectors with whom we have been concerned appreciated that a warless world required both new men and new women. Unfortunately, however, "that better day" seemed to recede rather than to draw closer with the ending of the ruinous "war to end all wars."

❧ 5 ❧

The Push for Amnesty

—History creates our clients.

—ACLU maxim

In July 1918, Fannie May Witherspoon and Tracy Mygatt journeyed to Ogunquit, Maine, for a much-needed rest and a reprieve from Manhattan's sweltering heat. Joy Young, their capable associate, was left in charge of the office at 70 Fifth Avenue until Witherspoon returned in mid-September. In one letter to Witherspoon, Young anticipated the war's end and worried about what lay ahead: "We all talk of the 'Reconstruction period after the War' and the 'Repeal of Wartime Laws,' but in our hearts we know it will be more than a generation before there is any appreciable change. The lid is on too tight now, there would be such an explosion of wrath and condemnation against the government the moment it is off that that government knows perfectly well it would be their death."[1] On August 31 (as noted earlier), eight Department of Justice officials barged into the Bureau office, questioned Young closely, and made off with all of the association's records. A *New York Times* headline the next day referred to this incident as a raid, and the caption stated that the "action is part of nation-wide movement to put an end to anti-war agitation."[2]

When Witherspoon arrived back in the city, she had to cope with running the office without records in a climate increasingly hostile to civil libertarians like herself. In fact, the Justice Department waited many months to return the files, and the index card records of Bureau clients were never relinquished. This was the time of the Funston Outrages, and Witherspoon and her associates were extremely busy. Moreover, the Bureau's finances, always precarious, were in disarray. Witherspoon had to raise about $600 per month to keep the office running and to pay for her salary, Charles Recht's retainer, and the stenographers' wages. Small monthly pledges from a few left-wing labor groups, comrades in the movement, and grateful families of conscientious objectors were supplemented by donations of fifty cents or one dollar from the many working-class people who came to the Bureau requesting various legal services. Young, however, had not written many "begging letters" (Witherspoon's term) over the summer, and after the raid, clients stayed away from the Bureau for a while and pledge payments fell off.

Once before, in May 1918, the Bureau had faced a similar funding crisis and had been saved by the generosity of executive committee member Jessie Ashley. Ashley had been born into luxury and privilege; her father was the president of the Wabash Railroad. She became a lawyer and an indefatigable movement activist for suffrage, birth control, radical labor (IWW), socialism, and pacifism. In October, however, when Witherspoon importuned Ashley once more for a substantial donation, her comrade was practically without funds herself. In 1917, she had put up $10,000 in cash for Emma Goldman's bail; although this money was returned to her, she gave away most of it over the course of the war. Indeed, by fall 1918, she was borrowing money at seven percent interest "to answer worthy causes." Nonetheless, on October 22, Ashley came through one more time with $175 to cover office rent and Witherspoon's salary ($35 per week): "Dear F.M.W. Here it is then, my last gasp. And *how* are we going to be able to go on? But let's hope on, hope ever that the Lord will provide for his rather naked little lambs. Here's to courage! JA." Witherspoon responded with a lighthearted quip: "As you say, let us hope that the Lord will provide. I am trying my best to assist him."

In the opening days of 1919, Witherspoon informed Ashley that the Bureau was, for once, in sound financial shape. "I have certainly not forgotten," Witherspoon wrote, "that it was you coming to the scratch in our most dismal hour that kept the committee together and made it possible for us to go on and do what we are now doing."[3] Tragically, eleven days later Jessie Ashley was dead, the victim of pneumonia. Ashley's death was felt keenly in

radical circles, and Witherspoon would doubtless have agreed with
Goldman's characterization of Ashley as "a valiant rebel"; according to Goldman, "[N]o other American woman of her position had
allied herself so completely with the revolutionary movement as
Jessie."[4]

Fall 1918 was a time of stock-taking and of worry for individuals such as Joy Young, Fannie May Witherspoon, and, before her
untimely passing, Jessie Ashley. Charles Recht, many years after
the armistice, recalled how jaded and empty he felt on November
9, when the war's end was announced (two days before the actual
cessation of hostilities): "I was immeasurably weary. Weary of reading of the slaughter of millions of human beings, weary of carrying
on the fight—a fight of a tiny group pitting itself against the
juggernaught of the war machine." When the streets became
thronged with celebrating crowds, Recht made his way to the Hotel Brevoort in Greenwich Village and spent a few hours with
friends. Recht and his comrades did not feel great joy, however;
instead, "in a mood of sober calm," he and the "tiny little group"
with whom he associated observed unfolding events with unquiet
hearts.

On November 29, the War Department issued its first demo-
bilization order. Soldiers returned home, and as civilians, they began to compete with others in a labor market unadjusted to
peacetime industry. Business interests saw in the demobilizations a
ready tool for lowering wage schedules. Everywhere workers became impatient and fought employer plans, in the aftermath of
war, to weaken or to destroy even the established bread-and-butter
unions of the American Federation of Labor (AFL). A wave of
strikes—beginning with the AFL-sponsored Seattle general strike
in January 1919—pushed across the country, enveloping in its
turn the lumber, coal, steel, and textile industries. Recht anticipated the unrest; on November 9, 1918, he noted, "the sentiment
. . . was that everything was going to be settled; this seemed to be
the feeling throughout the entire world. . . . As a matter of fact,
however, everything was only becoming unsettled."[5]

In November, the Bureau of Legal Advice executive committee
grappled with the question of what course to set for the association
in the immediate postwar era. In peacetime America, the ordinary
citizen remained wedded to intolerance of dissent. A miasma of
fear and hate appeared to be spreading quickly across the nation.

Expecting the worst but rejecting defeat, Witherspoon, in her capacity as executive secretary of the Bureau, took the lead in exploring her organization's postwar options. She corresponded with members of the executive committee, asking them to consider the future direction of their organization. Witherspoon worried about the threat of "permanent militarism" and toyed with the idea of the Bureau becoming more closely aligned with the labor movement; she suggested to a number of people, including Elizabeth Gurley Flynn, that their association serve the legal needs of small unions with weak treasuries. Charles Recht was more interested in developing a critique of the kind of justice (or injustice) represented by the magistrates courts and wanted to push for a public defender's office in New York.

Despite her anxiety about the future, Witherspoon was refreshed by her two-month summer rest and labored energetically to pull things together at the Bureau. She pushed (badgered) Recht into finishing his part of the report for the *Yearbook* and saw to it that this publication was distributed widely to sympathetic Bureau backers. Witherspoon also worked with the Civil Liberties Bureau to expose the reign of terror at Camp Funston and to lobby for the end of manacling as a military punishment. Roger Baldwin was in prison, and so after October 1918, Witherspoon's counterpart in the Civil Liberties Bureau was another man about her own age, Albert De Silver. A congenial, wealthy lawyer, he was a liberal and staunch civil libertarian; on a number of occasions, he donated generously to the Bureau of Legal Advice's always lean coffers.

In a revealing letter of October 1918 to a member of the Bureau executive committee, Anna Brenner, Witherspoon referred to their organization as "my child."[6] One month later (and a week after Armistice Day), the nurturing, maternal language surfaced again. Writing to Laura Hughes Lunde, the wife of objector and Leavenworth hunger-striker Erling Lunde and a pacifist activist in her own right, Witherspoon referred to "this little bureau of care." She admitted that when she considered all the work that the Bureau did, what was "most dear to my own heart" were the conscientious objectors. In further correspondence with Laura Lunde a few days later, Witherspoon reported that she had initiated a new scheme to aid the many objectors (including Lunde's husband) who were still behind bars, with little hope of immediate release from their long prison terms.[7]

On November 22, fifty people met at Witherspoon and Mygatt's flat to establish the Friends and Relatives of Conscientious
Objectors. Jules Wortsmann, the brother of court-martialed political objectors Jacob and Gus Wortsmann (who were themselves Bureau informants), assented to head the association, and his parents
agreed that their home in Brooklyn would serve as the group's
official address. Lottie Fishbein, one of the "feminine COs" and the
fiancée of objector Ben Breger, became secretary; Sadie Brandon,
the wife of political objector Joseph Brandon, and Helen Fleischer,
who would later marry Jacob Wortsmann, joined up as well.

Witherspoon made it clear to Laura Lunde (and to a few others
to whom she wrote in the same vein) that the Bureau of Legal
Advice was not to be linked publicly in any way with the Friends
of COs. In language that suggested both a joy of intrigue and
utter seriousness, Witherspoon explained:

> We wanted to look like a spontaneous protest of separate men
> and women who do not propose to let these atrocities go on if
> they can help it. They are today beginning a distribution of a
> petition to be in by December 14th, addressed to Baker, and
> asking for nothing less than immediate discharge. Also they are
> going to stimulate a letter campaign to the press; to follow up
> the press publicity on the Leavenworth situation, already begun
> by the Civil Liberties Bureau, in their open letter to Secretary
> Baker last week, and to be followed up by a pamphlet to be
> distributed the early part of this week.[8]

Witherspoon added that the Friends of COs wished to create a
national organization and were counting on Laura Lunde to establish a "distribution center" in Chicago. To this end, Witherspoon
had that very day posted a batch of petition forms to Lunde.

Witherspoon already had a sense of Laura Hughes Lunde's
views and abilities when she contacted her in October 1918. The
two women had become acquainted at the office of the New York
City branch of the Woman's Peace Party at the beginning of the
war. Lunde was a journalist, the daughter of the well-known Canadian educators and social reformers James L. Hughes and Ada Ma-
rean Hughes and the niece of Sir Sam Hughes, Canada's Minister
of Militia. In 1915, she had traveled aboard the *Noordam* to Hol-
land to attend the Women's International Congress at The Hague;
upon her return from Europe, she helped to establish a woman's

peace party in Canada, which later affiliated with the Women's International League for Peace and Freedom.[9] By November 1918, Laura Hughes Lunde was a new mother and was living in Chicago, her husband Erling's hometown. She had already seen to it that a number of protests against CO prison treatment had reached Secretary of War Baker from different locations in Canada. She suggested that Witherspoon write to feminist pacifist Gertrude Richardson of Swan River, Manitoba, asking her to forward information to "English Sympathizers," as Canadian mail to England was not censored as U.S. mail was.[10] Lunde also recommended that information on the torture that many U.S. objectors endured in military camps and prisons should be made public in other Commonwealth countries, particularly Australia and New Zealand.

Laura Lunde's enthusiasm and support for the Friends of COs was matched if not exceeded by that of her father-in-law, Theodore Lunde, who was a prominent Chicago businessman and owner of a large piano hardware manufacturing company. A dynamic and somewhat irascible rugged individualist, Lunde had little respect for the mindless spirit of superpatriotism, intolerance, and violence in the mass of Americans; he had even less regard for government officials such as Secretary of War Baker and for high-ranking military officers who turned a blind eye to abuses and tortures in military prisons. Generous-hearted, Lunde gave willingly of his time and money to publicize the ill-treatment of military prisoners and to secure general amnesty for political prisoners. He absorbed the expense of printing and distributing several pamphlets on prison conditions, with much of the content being supplied by letters from his son and from other CO informants to the "outside." By late 1918, the movement of information out of the prisons and into the hands of the Civil Liberties Bureau, the Bureau of Legal Advice, and the Friends of COs was referred to as "undergrounding."

On the very day that Witherspoon held the founding meeting of the Friends of COs, William Simpson, the associate director of the Civil Liberties Bureau, wrote to her to suggest that she spearhead a publicity campaign for amnesty for objectors. It seems likely that by this time, Simpson and others in the Civil Liberties Bureau recognized Witherspoon's political acumen and her ability to bring individuals and groups together in innovative ways and to stay a course as long as necessary. Witherspoon must have enjoyed answering Simpson's letter. She had become somewhat defensive in her attitude towards the Civil Liberties Bureau: although she often sought approval from this organization and attempted, mostly successfully, to work cooperatively with its predominantly male leadership, she resented the tendency of the press to give credit to the Civil Liberties Bureau for work done by the Bureau of Legal Advice. In her response, Witherspoon informed Simpson of the formation of the Friends of COs at her home and described its purpose. She mentioned matter-of-factly that "this Bureau [of Legal Advice] is to be kept absolutely out of the affair in order that it may have the appearance of spontaneousness." She added that she would be contacting individual members of the Women's International League—the new name for the New York branch of the Woman's Peace Party—and other groups to garner a wider membership for the Friends of COs.[11]

Witherspoon was as good as her word. In the next few weeks, she spent most of her time networking with family members and friends of COs. She drew people such as Laura Hughes Lunde and Theodore Lunde into the amnesty campaign and sought support for the petition to Baker from two other civil liberties associations, the League for Democratic Control in Boston and the American Liberty Defense League in Chicago. Both groups had been established in April 1917, and like the Bureau of Legal Advice, their executive committees possessed committed feminist pacifists.[12] Lola Maverick Lloyd, a delegate to the 1915 Women's International Congress and a staunch Woman's Peace Party member, and her colleague in the women's peace movement, Lenetta Cooper, were Witherspoon's main contacts in Chicago.[13] In Boston, Witherspoon turned to Anna Davis—a writer, social worker, socialist, and Quaker. Davis, like Witherspoon, had established close personal contact with many objectors, including Bruno Grunzig.

By early December, Witherspoon had secured agreement from the Friends of COs to send a delegation to Washington, D.C., to present the amnesty petition to Secretary of War Baker in person. An appointment was set up with Baker for December 24. She then set to work arranging for a politically appropriate blend of relatives, prominent national figures, and civil libertarians. It was agreed that Dr. John L. Elliot, the chair of the Bureau of Legal Advice and a member of the Civil Liberties Bureau directing committee who also headed the Hudson Guild Settlement House and was a founding member of the Ethical Culture Society, would serve as spokesperson. Witherspoon secured Fanny Garrison Villard's participation, as well as that of the Reverend Richard Hogue of Baltimore, chair of the Maryland Prison Association. She received letters of endorsement from Dr. Percy Stickney Grant, minister of the Church of the Ascension in New York; Mary Simkovitch, head of the Greenwich Settlement House; John F. Sinclair, president of the John F. Sinclair Banking Company, of Minneapolis; Sarah M. Cleghorn, a poet residing in Vermont; and others. Additional delegates included Mabel Higgins, Elsie Knepper, Anna Davis, and a number of relatives of imprisoned COs, including Theodore Lunde and Mrs. W. E. Thomas, the mother of Evan Thomas. Howard Moore's parents could not make the trip but insisted on paying for Witherspoon's travel expenses.

While arrangements for the delegation were being made, the Civil Liberties Bureau sponsored a mass meeting on December 5, in protest against the treatment of political prisoners in federal military prisons. The meeting was held in the Church of the Ascension on Fifth Avenue and Tenth Street, with Mary Simkovitch presiding; speakers included John Elliot, Norman Thomas, and the Reverend Dr. Grant. At particular issue was the punishment of manacling men to the bars of their cells in solitary confinement in the dark for nine hours a day. As noted above, Secretary of War Baker issued a directive abolishing manacling as a military punishment the next day, December 6.

Meanwhile, Witherspoon and the "spontaneous uprising" of the Friends of COs continued their efforts in circulating the petition. By the mid-December deadline, fifteen thousand people had signed. On the morning of December 24, the Friends of COs issued a press release that has all the markings of Witherspoon's writing style. The release explained the purpose of the petition and the makeup of the delegation and mentioned that following the formal statement by John Elliot (the group's chair), Fanny Villard, Anna Davis, and Richard Hogue would speak. The language of the release was indignant, emphasizing cruel treatment, but also reassuring: some of the delegates were "pretty girls engaged to Leavenworth prisoners" who were attending to "plead for them." These conventionally defined women would be accompanied by "several men in uniform" who, despite their own acceptance of soldiering, were sympathetic to the objector position. The principled stand of the objectors and the worth of their personal character were stressed in order to underline the "manliness" of individuals who had been vilified in the popular mind as unmanly cowards and slackers.[14]

The delegation met with Baker for almost two hours on Christmas Eve day, as planned. No one in the group was surprised that Baker rejected the petition's request for general amnesty, although Witherspoon was pleased that press coverage was "much fairer than usual." A few days after the meeting, Witherspoon wrote to Howard Moore's mother that Baker had "showed himself small and disingenuous."[15] She was more specific in her letter to Lenetta Cooper, written on the same day:

> [Baker] heckled all our speakers with the same questions that every military man has put to every Conscientious Objector with whom he has come in contact. I felt that Baker had compromised with the military more than people are aware of, and learned their cheap tricks. . . . He was also absolutely unyielding on my point of immediate abolition of solitary confinement, bread and water diet, and the return of mailing privileges, etc. He told us that solitary confinement was not bad and that he would endure it without complaint if he were a Conscientious Objector. . . . Perhaps the hardest thing to bear was his categorical denial of any abuses in Leavenworth. He either really does not know the situation, or as I suspect connives at his own ignorance.[16]

Almost fifty years later, what remained vivid for Witherspoon was Fanny Villard's incisive and vigorous exchange with Baker during the interview:

> Mr. Baker was very gracious and wanted to play up to Mrs. Villard, but Mrs. Villard was a very spirited old lady. She had come on a serious mission. She didn't want just pleasantries, you know. He said he was delighted to see us and had always honored her father and so on and so forth. But Mrs. Villard would have none of this small talk. She had come on a serious errand, and she pled for the freeing of the conscientious objectors. She said, "How would you, Mr. Baker, like to be in prison on Christmas Day under a sentence of twenty years because you had done what you thought was the right thing, the patriotic thing?" She made a very spirited little speech of course. Well, he

said he knew it was very hard for people to stand up for what they thought was right, but this was the law and we had to pursue the war, etc., etc. And the interview ended inconclusively of course. There was no promise of amnesty.[17]

Despite Baker's out-of-hand rejection of general amnesty for objectors and his insistence that solitary confinement was appropriate punishment for military prisoners, some amelioration of their treatment was achieved by the fall protests and by the Christmas delegation's demands. In addition to the ending of manacling on December 6, after the Christmas holidays military commandants agreed in principle to discontinue the punishment of indefinite (or repeated) solitary confinement for absolutists (objectors who refused to perform military duties). The War Department and military authorities came to accept that severe punishments would not succeed in breaking the wills of the approximately three hundred objectors still incarcerated in military prisons at the end of 1918.[18]

In the new year, "working" objectors and objectors awaiting farm furlough assignments were released quickly. At a much slower pace, War Department officials began to commute sentences and to release other objectors on a one-by-one basis. Nonetheless, many absolutists remained in military prisons during 1919 and for part of 1920: Fort Leavenworth, in Kansas; Fort Douglas, near Salt Lake City, Utah; or Fort Alcatraz, on Alcatraz Island in San Francisco Bay, California. The last thirty-three objectors (one of whom was Howard Moore) were not released until November 23, 1920. In the meantime, although conditions improved for the absolutists—especially at Fort Douglas, where they were segregated into their own stockade and by summer 1919 permitted to take day-long hikes into the Wasatch Mountains unaccompanied by guards—incidents of severe abuse and torture still occurred sporadically, even at Douglas.[19]

The fort on Alcatraz Island was a much less attractive place to be held than either Leavenworth or Douglas. For the thirty objectors incarcerated there in 1919 and 1920, solitary confinement in "the hole" was still employed as punishment for those who refused to work, despite the War Department's directive to commandants that solitary confinement be discontinued for absolutists.[20] In January 1920, two men at Fort Alcatraz—Phillip Grosser, a Jew-

19. *Cartoon by conscientious objector Fred Jerger, incarcerated at Fort Douglas, Utah, 1919–20. Courtesy of the Swarthmore College Peace Collection.*

ish absolutist political objector, and an African American religious objector named Simmons—were placed in cages that were constructed so that a confined individual could not lie down, sit down, or even turn around. Californians protested; Simmons was released, but Grosser was kept a prisoner. He agreed to work when he felt himself going insane, but was not released from prison until November 1920.[21]

In his study of the CO in World War I, Norman Thomas noted that objectors had very few "friends" outside of radical circles to plead their case to the American public in 1919 and 1920. Liberal support of civil liberties in general and the CO and political prisoner in particular was minimal, and religious support (except for members of the pacifist Fellowship of Reconciliation and the Quakers) was almost nonexistent. Those who "bore the brunt of the agitation for the objectors" were Anna Davis in Brookline, Massachusetts, whom Witherspoon called "the mother of the conscientious objectors"; Theodore Lunde in Chicago; the Friends of COs in New York; the Bureau of Legal Advice; the Civil Liberties Bureau; liberal magazines such as *The Survey, The Nation, The World Tomorrow,* and *The New Republic;* and a few progressive labor newspapers.[22]

Because of the persistent publicity and lobbying of this small group of determined protesters, two reports of tortures and atrocities were read into the *Congressional Record* by Representatives Charles H. Dillon in January 1919 and William E. Mason in March 1919.[23] As objectors were released, they contacted groups such as the Friends of COs or the Bureau of Legal Advice to offer their services on behalf of their comrades still behind bars. By December 1918, Frederick Eckes, a socialist political objector, was working in the Bureau office on the Baker delegation project. Evan Thomas, released in early 1919 on a "technicality," immediately wrote an exposé for *The Survey* entitled "Disciplinary Barracks: The Experience of a Military Prisoner at Fort Leavenworth."[24] Thereafter, he worked closely with his brother Norman of the Civil Liberties Bureau and with the Fellowship of Reconciliation and gave public lectures in major cities for the amnesty cause. At the end of January, Theodore Lunde received a letter from Witherspoon informing him of the release of several objectors who had returned to New York City: Clarence Jasmagy, the brother of William Jasmagy; Carl Maier, Alice Navard's fiancé; and Ulysses da Rosa. "As soon as they come," Witherspoon exulted, "they go right to work helping us get out the others."[25] The Friends of COs remained active in propaganda, with Witherspoon writing up a pamphlet that was printed and distributed by the Friends, *Who Are the Conscientious Objectors?*

By spring 1919, the Friends of COs had raised and spent about $1,800. All the work was done by volunteers. In a circular letter of June 1919, Witherspoon reported:

> We have secured hundreds of protests in every instance of cruelty, of which there have been shamefully many, in camp or prison, and finally forced the press to take notice. We have distributed thousands of pieces of literature all over the country. At Christmas we took 15,000 names to Secretary Baker urging amnesty and are now planning to carry 100,000 names to President Wilson as soon as he returns and we can secure an interview. We are also sending down a little lobby to Washington to open up the Senatorial mind.[26]

The meeting with Wilson never materialized, but the Friends of COs (and thus the Bureau of Legal Advice, as the Friends and the Bureau were finely meshed in purpose and personnel if not in name) kept up their pressure on the government for a general amnesty rather than individual pardons and continued to insist that the public acknowledge the principle of liberty of conscience and the right to dissent, even in wartime. Roger Baldwin wrote on this theme from his prison cell. He rejected the plan of some of his friends to seek for him a presidential pardon, insisting that he had to stand with the other absolutists who were demanding a general amnesty: "It is an amnesty to vindicate a traditional principle, to declare anew after the exigencies of the great war, the sanctity of individual conscience as the basis of any really free society."[27]

In July and August 1919, an interesting exchange of letters occurred between Jules Wortsmann, Fannie May Witherspoon, and Joseph Kantor of Williamsburg, West Virginia (the brother of William Kantor, an absolutist objector who had been transferred from Leavenworth to Alcatraz in June). Joseph Kantor had served in the Army for fourteen months and had been honorably discharged at the rank of sergeant. He and his cousin, "a most liberal, kindly man," wished to help secure the speedy release of objectors such as William Kantor: "While I did not take the stand that William pursued, I hold that the men were thoroughly justified in following the dictates of their conscience, and now that the war is over, they should be released at once." Witherspoon responded, asking Kantor to circulate an amnesty petition and to collect funds to facilitate the spread of Friends of COs literature. She also requested that Kantor and his friends write individual letters to the president and to members of Congress: "Don't fail to mention in your letters that you have been in the service. Fortunately there are a good many men who have been in the service who are willing to secure the release of the conscientious objectors." Kantor wrote back that he had already written such letters but was disappointed with the "stereotyped manner" in which they were answered. He also mentioned that the "sentiment in this part of the country, as far as I can determine, is hostile towards the C.O.s, but [that] a liberal minded person is encountered here and there." Kantor promised to send Witherspoon lists of men who supported amnesty. In her pragmatic way, Witherspoon wrote back that their work was not in vain: "I note what you say about the stereotyped replies to the letters you sent regarding conscientious objectors. That, I think, is only to be expected, but does not to my mind prove that such letters are not worth writing. The more we annoy these people, the sooner we shall obtain our end."[28]

At the same time that Witherspoon was initiating the so-called spontaneous uprising of the indignant friends and relatives of COs, she was also maintaining the involvement of the Bureau of Legal Advice in the national movement for the release of all political prisoners, COs as well as those who had been prosecuted under the wartime espionage and sedition acts.[29] As noted above, Witherspoon had helped Elizabeth Gurley Flynn (of Wobblie fame) to found the Liberty Defense Union in March 1918.[30] As business interests and the state had teamed up in the name of patriotism to destroy the IWW and other manifestations of radical labor activity during the war, Flynn, Witherspoon, and other socialist women such as Ella Reeve Bloor, Elizabeth Freeman, and Helen Phelps Stokes (along with their socialist male counterparts) had geared up to defend the civil liberties of workers, native-born Americans as well as aliens.

By August 1918, the Workers Liberty Defense Union had been established, which focused on securing the release of labor people who had been imprisoned under war legislation, ostensibly for disloyal behavior and utterances but in reality because of their union activities. Flynn and Bloor were the main field organizers for the Workers Liberty Defense Union, and they crisscrossed the country speaking before worker assemblies to raise funds for the amnesty cause. Witherspoon, never one to miss an opportunity, secured both Bloor's and Flynn's help as information gatherers on CO conditions in military prisons. In July, on one of her trips west, Bloor—who had to raise money to finance her trips as she traveled—found herself penniless and wired Witherspoon for emergency funds, which were readily supplied.[31]

The concern for the plight of imprisoned political prisoners developed into a full-blown amnesty campaign well before the armistice. The Workers Liberty Defense Union, the Bureau of Legal Advice, the Civil Liberties Bureau, and (on a less grand scale) the Socialist Party and the remnant branches of the People's Council of America each played a role. The driving force behind the amnesty movement in 1918 and 1919, however, was the anarchist activist M. Eleanor Fitzgerald, an intimate friend and associate of Emma Goldman and Alexander Berkman and a founding member of the short-lived No-Conscription League.

Fitzgerald, an arresting-looking woman with fair skin and thick auburn hair, was idealistic, warmhearted, and a proficient administrator. On February 3, 1918, she became secretary of the Political Prisoners' Amnesty League, founded in the Greenwich Village studio of Emma Goldman's niece, Stella Ballantine, at Goldman's insistence, on the day before she and Berkman began serving their two-year prison sentences. Also present were the civil libertarian lawyer Harry Weinberger; Leonard D. Abbott, an anarchist editor and educator; Lucy Robins, a young labor organizer and a protegé of Goldman's; Max Pine and Morris Finestone, of the United Hebrew Trades; Carlo Tresca, anarcho-syndicalist editor, labor organizer, and Elizabeth Gurley Flynn's lover; and Pryns Hopkins, a wealthy contributor and associate of the libertarian Modern School for Children in Stelton, New Jersey. Hopkins became the chair of the newly-struck League.[32]

Hopkins and Fitzgerald began their work immediately, and within a few weeks, Hopkins reported in person to Goldman at the Missouri State Penitentiary in Jefferson City that branches of the League were being established as he toured the country raising funds. In April, a hostile *New York Tribune* reporter noted that the League had active branches in New York, Rochester, Detroit, Chicago, Cleveland, Ann Arbor, St. Louis, San Francisco, and Los Angeles.[33] In May, Eleanor Fitzgerald and Lucy Robins reorganized the group somewhat, renaming it the League for the Amnesty of Political Prisoners (or the Amnesty League).

In accordance with Goldman's wish, the Amnesty League was pledged to arouse the public and the labor movement to the problem of political prisoners—"those who have been convicted for holding and advocating social and political opinions contrary or believed to be injurious to the country's war activities." Members of the Amnesty League—which included on its board Jessie Ashley, Harry Weinberger, and Roger Baldwin—hoped to secure recognition of political prisoners as a discrete group within federal penitentiaries and then win a general amnesty for them when peace was declared.[34] Hopkins remained as chair, Fitzgerald continued as secretary, and Leonard Abbott and Jessie Ashley became a finance committee of two. Hilda Kovner, the young anarchist Russian emigré who was a stenographer for the Bureau of Legal Advice, served in the same capacity for the Amnesty League.

With the exception of the *New York Tribune*'s announcement of the Amnesty League's founding, press coverage on the group was minimal up to the armistice. On November 27, 1918, however, the *Tribune* announced that a national movement to seek amnesty for political prisoners had been launched by two "local radical societies, the League for the Amnesty of Political Prisoners and the Bureau of Legal Advice." The article noted that Fitzgerald had written to President Wilson and to Secretary of War Baker requesting general amnesty by Thanksgiving Day and quoted Fitzgerald to the effect that meetings were to be held across the country to "crystallize public sentiment in this matter so that it can be made a subject for representation at the general peace conference." Fannie May Witherspoon's letter pleading for funds to fight for the release of objectors imprisoned at Fort Leavenworth was also mentioned. The article ended on an alarmist note, contending that such an amnesty would mean the release of some two thousand socialists, anarchists, Bolshevists, and IWWs.[35]

The *Tribune*'s attribution of leadership in the amnesty movement to the Amnesty League and the Bureau of Legal Advice proved accurate. In 1919, Witherspoon's Bureau and the Friends of COs, in cooperation with the Civil Liberties Bureau, the League for Democratic Control, and the American Liberty Defense League, labored to build up a strong network of support for amnesty of political prisoners, especially COs. At the same time, Fitzgerald's Amnesty League worked to build a left-liberal and radical coalition in support of a general amnesty for political prisoners, stressing the working-class victims of wartime espionage and sedition laws. Witherspoon's networking brought together left-liberals, pacifists, middle-class feminists, and socialist and culturally radical political activists, as well as politically moderate civil libertarians and relatives and friends of COs. Fitzgerald shared Witherspoon's integrative activist style; she was also the inheritor of Emma Goldman's nationwide network of radical comrades, which facilitated her effectiveness in amnesty work. Lucy Robins, Fitzgerald's associate, was strong-minded, ambitious, and a capable organizer; by summer 1919, she had succeeded almost singlehandedly in drawing AFL unions into the amnesty movement.[36]

It is difficult to track the history of the amnesty movement in 1919, a year punctuated by terrorist bombings, numerous and prolonged strikes by militant workers (and a fierce employer counteroffensive), urban race riots, numerous lynchings of African

Americans in the South, and vicious mob attacks on foreigners and radicals. The splintering of the Socialist Party into left-wing and right-wing factions in the wake of the Bolshevik Revolution exacerbated generalized public fears of "reds." Still, even in these reactionary, tumultuous times—which we now refer to as the Red Scare—the civil liberties and prodemocracy movement did not falter. Activists focused on amnesty, although as we shall see, the defense of radical aliens who were threatened with deportation also occupied the time of movement people during 1919 and 1920.

Left-wing women, crucial to civil liberties and prodemocracy work during the war, assumed an even larger role in these areas immediately afterwards. While many of their male comrades struggled over ideological and structural issues within and outside of the Socialist Party, a significant proportion of socialist women (as well as anarchist and left-liberal women), excluded from such power brokering, chose to stay focused on civil liberties work. A key justice issue for Fitzgerald, Bloor, Witherspoon, and others was the speedy release of COs and political prisoners: at war's end, an estimated three hundred objectors and fifteen hundred other political prisoners were serving long sentences in military prisons and in federal penitentiaries. Radical women, many of whom were the wives, lovers, mothers, and sisters of political prisoners, worked at local levels to build up amnesty support. At the same time, they maintained the interregional civil liberties coalition of the war era that some of them had done so much to promote. Local leaders also evolved a practical strategy to ensure a coordinated national voice. Because they could not count on the bickering male leaders of the Socialist Party for much sustained help, they effected an alliance of left-leaning, grassroots, woman-directed amnesty groups with the politically liberal male-led Civil Liberties Bureau.

The Civil Liberties Bureau was well situated to coordinate a national fight for amnesty. Its directing committee boasted a number of influential male members who had not been absolutely labeled as dangerous Reds in the public mind and who were eager to defend first amendment freedoms and the democratic right to dissent from majority opinion. Members of the Civil Liberties Bureau such as Norman Thomas and John Haynes Holmes wrote and spoke forcefully on behalf of amnesty; others, such as Albert De Silver, possessed a class and educational background that facilitated communication with Washington politicians and high-ranking civil servants. Moreover, Elizabeth Gurley Flynn sat on the directing committee, which helped the Civil Liberties Bureau establish solid ties with left-wing labor groups. However, the association had no bona fide chapters or branches, and although nationally well-known, it possessed no mass base from which to launch a popular movement. Indeed, when women's amnesty associations first approached the Civil Liberties Bureau, its male leadership was uneasy with the swell of enthusiasm for mass direct action that such groups represented.

Director Albert De Silver responded cautiously at first to the ebullient demands of radical women across the country that the Civil Liberties Bureau assume the role of national coordinator of the amnesty movement. Within a short time, however, De Silver shed much of his wariness, and a mutually respectful cooperative relationship evolved between the naturally diffident De Silver and the less reserved and more effusive radical women of the far-flung amnesty movement.[37]

As early as December 13, 1918, socialist Dorothy Clark of Toledo, Ohio, wrote to the Civil Liberties Bureau to inform its members that she had succeeded in organizing two general amnesty leagues, one in Toledo (which was "poor," with about twenty-five members) and the other in Detroit (which had "several wealthy people who are willing to let their dollars serve"). Clark continued: "I want to get those leagues in touch with you and let you work through them or let them work through you as the case may be." She was going on to Chicago to "organize another League and from there to Kansas City and possibly to the south and west." Clark hoped for mass meetings and "monster parades" across the country and suggested that workers might be mobilized to conduct a general strike to protest the government's refusal to release all political prisoners.[38]

Another relentless amnesty worker was Agnes Inglis, a member of a wealthy and conservative Ann Arbor family who became secretary of the Detroit General Amnesty League. She was also a loyal friend to Emma Goldman, who relied on Inglis's financial and emotional support during the war era. Goldman described Agnes Inglis as a person of "rare spiritual courage" who had overcome "the middle-class morality and traditions of her environment" to become an independent and original thinker. For her part, Inglis loved and admired Goldman but, in time, also found her to be egocentric and demanding.[39]

Inglis wrote to the Civil Liberties Bureau on the same day that Dorothy Clark did, December 13, 1918. She informed the Bureau that she expected it to be taking action with regard to political prisoners and mentioned that she had heard recently from Eleanor Fitzgerald. Inglis's report on her activities points to the existence of a vibrant political culture of radical women with varied class backgrounds, which was cemented by bonds of affection and common purpose. Such women were also members of a larger mixed-gender movement.[40]

De Silver responded circumspectly both to Inglis and to Clark. He wrote a brief, general letter to Inglis, promising to keep in touch, and an equally short letter to Clark, asking her if her group would be interested in a new Civil Liberties Bureau leaflet on amnesty. Not to be deterred, Inglis wrote back to De Silver on February 20, 1919, from the House of the Masses in Detroit, informing him that her group was sponsoring a mass meeting on March 2. In a rather disjointed epistle, Inglis asked for amnesty literature and commented that she would be writing Theodore Lunde for materials to sell at their meeting. She seemed disenchanted with petition drives, declaring "big business is franker than we are. It says the war is on—not off. Every paper we read admits it. I think we shall have to give up our bourgeois psychology and face the facts. Don't you think so?"[41]

In his response, De Silver informed Inglis that he would send her one hundred copies of a pamphlet on political prisoners and thanked her for informing him of the meeting, but he ignored Inglis's other points. As was the case with Dorothy Clark, De Silver avoided discussion of a mass organization of workers against employers. In April, Inglis alluded to a controversy regarding COs and the Amnesty League and declared that "a good many [objectors] will stand as counter-revolutionists with the issue being industrial control by the workers"; she was evidently under the misapprehension that a fundamentalist religious creed and antiunion attitude informed the thought of most objectors. She also noted that the political climate in Detroit was getting "worse and worse. Many are held for deportation—many secretly & incommunicado."[42]

De Silver's response was quite sympathetic and supportive, a changed perspective from his earlier communications with Inglis and Clark. He acknowledged that a certain number of COs would not be interested "in the struggle to secure better and fundamentally democratic conditions in industry," particularly members of mystical religious sects such as the Molokans and the Hutterite Brethren. Nonetheless, he sought to enlarge Inglis's understanding of the objector:

> I am quite sure, and this includes both the religious and others, they will be quite as vitally interested in the problems of American industrial life as any of us. There is nothing in the world which will make a man realize the injustices and inequalities of our existing social and economic order, as for once in his life finding himself in a small and persecuted minority. Whatever may have been the opinion of most conscientious objectors before they went through their experience of the last two years, I am pretty well prepared to bet on what their opinions are now.[43]

Albert De Silver also corresponded with Elizabeth Thomas of the Milwaukee Committee of Amnesty for Political Prisoners, a group that was associated with the local branch of the Socialist Party and that included Meta Berger, the wife of the imprisoned socialist leader Victor Berger.[44] From her first letter of February 18, 1919, Thomas was adamant that she expected the Civil Liberties Bureau to take bold leadership in the amnesty drive. Over the course of their correspondence between February and July, Thomas recounted to De Silver her group's activities in hosting meetings, sponsoring petition drives, and distributing literature (much of which was supplied by Theodore Lunde of the Friends of COs). In March 1919, De Silver informed Thomas that his group had Lunde's publications on hand and was always ready to fill orders for them. This pleased Thomas, who had specifically requested that the Civil Liberties Bureau serve as a distribution and production center for all amnesty literature. It also represented an exception to Civil Liberties Bureau policy: De Silver informed Thomas that because the Bureau did not list literature "by others," Margaret Hatfield of the Amnesty Committee of Chicago had agreed to establish a distribution center at her group's headquarters for all amnesty literature. De Silver was at pains to state his support of this venture: "We are giving her our best co-operation, and I know you will want to do the same."[45]

A recurrent refrain in Thomas's letters to De Silver was the need for united action. By spring 1919—a time of heightened discord within the Socialist Party—her letters possessed a desperate, pleading tone: "Mrs. Berger will be in New York about the time this letter will reach you. I very much wish that she could meet you. It is of the utmost importance that all who are working for amnesty shall get into touch and work out a plan for united action of some sort. I feel that we are all not doing what we might, just because we are not working together. Will you not try to see her and talk things over with her?"[46]

De Silver admitted he had become dispirited too. The Civil Liberties Bureau had been accepting signed amnesty petitions that were intended for President Wilson (Witherspoon's suggestion); however, as he explained to Thomas, the president repeatedly refused an interview with amnesty petitioners. De Silver added dryly: "I haven't as much confidence in the gentleman as I used to have." However, De Silver had had a "long talk" in person with Mrs. Berger. In July, Thomas wrote again, urging De Silver to see Mrs. Berger "without fail" when he went to Washington: "She has some very good suggestions to make in regard to our work which should be carried out at once, as soon as the President returns [from Paris peace talks]. We must work most diligently just now to get every force into line."[47]

In Thomas's mind, getting "every force into line" included the sustained involvement of the Socialist Party. By July, however, those socialists in favor of education and electoral politics (the right wingers) had excluded the pro-Communist, permanent-revolution members (the left wingers). This expulsion of socialist revolutionists led to the formation of the Communist Party; membership in the Socialist Party plummeted, from 109,589 in January 1919 to 39,750 six months later.[48] Witherspoon and Lenetta Cooper of the Chicago amnesty committee decried the factionalism within the party, Witherspoon writing to Cooper that the "Party Branches" were not helping with the second amnesty petition "because of this awful left and right tug of war."[49] Cooper concurred: "The fight between the right and left wing Socialists is handicapping all of our work for Amnesty. To my great disappointment, the right wingers decided to postpone the amnesty convention which was to be held July 3rd and 4th to September 25th."[50]

Despite disappointment with the Socialist Party and the pariah status of social critics in Red Scare America, the amnesty movement forged ahead. The Civil Liberties Bureau had assumed, willy-nilly, the mantle of national coordinator of the irrepressible grassroots movement. It arranged mass meetings across the country on specific dates (such as Lincoln's Birthday) and aided the Bureau of Legal Advice with the ultimately doomed second petition drive. The Civil Liberties Bureau also sponsored lectures by released COs in a number of cities. On the suggestion of Fannie May Witherspoon, the Civil Liberties Bureau attempted to procure the signatures of "weighty persons" for a special petition to the president, on the model of the famous British petition of notables developed for the same purpose. The directing committee accepted Witherspoon's plan, but in the end, the venture failed. At the top of a two-page draft letter to President Wilson on Civil Liberties Bureau stationery was inscribed: "Proposed letter to be signed by pro-war liberals—but they never could be found."[51]

By summer 1919, a variety of women's groups had sought to align themselves, via the Civil Liberties Bureau, with the amnesty movement. For instance, in June, the secretary-treasurer of the National Women's Trade Union League, on the suggestion of the militant New York City labor leader Rose Schneiderman, wrote to the Civil Liberties Bureau to inform it that the League had passed an amnesty resolution at its Seventh Biennial Convention in Philadelphia.[52] In July, Louise Hunt of Newark, New Jersey, notified De Silver that she was traveling to St. Louis to attend a conference to form a federation of business and professional women. She wished to be of service. What, she inquired, could she do? De Silver suggested that she try to get the conference to adopt an amnesty resolution.[53]

During this time, Lucy Robins's pertinacious wooing of labor paid off: in July, the mainstream labor movement of New York City embraced amnesty. The Amnesty Committee of the Central Federated Union of Greater New York and Vicinity published a four-page pamphlet entitled *Labor Free Your Prisoners*. The author of the pamphlet argued that various states were passing criminal syndicalist bills, ostensibly to control groups like the IWW but with the actual intent of fighting all organized labor. Workers were adjured to support immediate amnesty for "all political and labor prisoners whose religious, political or economic beliefs formed the basis of their prosecution." The Central Federated Union, representing 350,000 AFL workers, had passed its own resolution for amnesty on July 25, 1919. The pamphlet concluded: "See that similar resolutions are passed in your labor organizations and send copies to the President of the United States, the Attorney General of the United States, and the Secretary of War." Labor groups were also urged to send copies of their resolutions to M. E. Fitzgerald, 857 Broadway, New York City, so that records could be kept on file. In small print at the bottom of the last page, it was mentioned that one could write to Fitzgerald for literature or "for information regarding work of creating sentiment for immediate amnesty to labor and political prisoners."[54]

This AFL involvement heralded a new departure for the amnesty movement, and in 1920, Lucy Robins chose to renounce erstwhile radical comrades such as Eleanor Fitzgerald and to lead the AFL-directed amnesty campaign. This decision by Robins was perhaps not too much of a shock to those who, like Emma Goldman, knew her well. According to Goldman,

> [Lucy] understood *Realpolitik* long before the term had become a vogue. She would grow impatient with our idea that neither love nor war justifies all means. We, on the other hand, were anything but sympathetic with her tendency to get results even if the goal were lost in the process. We scrapped a great deal, but it did not lessen our regard for Lucy as a good worker and friend. She was a vital creature with unlimited energy, whom no one could escape.[55]

The work of individuals such as Robins and a revulsion against Red Scare excesses led, in the early twenties, to a widened amnesty movement. War veterans, members of Congress, community leaders, and ordinary citizens joined the amnesty bandwagon. Nevertheless, the process of securing pardons or commutations of sentences was agonizingly slow, especially for those languishing in federal penitentiaries; the final thirty-one political prisoners were not released until December 15, 1923, well after the last war-era political prisoner in England and on the continent had achieved liberty.[56]

In 1919, however, the amnesty movement was still a left-wing women's initiative. Historian Kathleen Kennedy, in her fine study of socialist women's opposition to wartime repression, argues persuasively that "the most effective work" in the amnesty field came from coalitions devised by socialist and liberal women.[57] Radicals

Eleanor Fitzgerald, Fannie May Witherspoon, and Elizabeth Gurley Flynn assumed the lead, while the national headquarters of the Socialist Party gave support when it could. By mid-1919, the Civil Liberties Bureau had fallen (somewhat timorously) into line behind the woman-directed grassroots movement.

Witherspoon and Flynn had been associates since the founding of the Liberty Defense Union. They had common goals with regard to COs, and Flynn had helped to gather information about imprisoned objectors for the Bureau of Legal Advice and for the Civil Liberties Bureau even before the armistice. Moreover, Witherspoon and Fitzgerald developed a productive relationship as well. For over a year, the two shared donors lists, served together on committees, and organized meetings and conferences; cordiality and mutual respect grew into a warm, trusting partnership. Documenting their resulting friendship helps us to appreciate how pleasure and pain, hope and despair mingled in the everyday lives of movement women such as these.

Fitzgerald was under a special kind of stress at the time because Alexander Berkman, her lover as well as comrade, was serving a two-year sentence in Atlanta Penitentiary. Witherspoon was sensitive to Fitzgerald's suffering and wrote to her in May: "I hope you are rested from your long trip South, and the depression which I know it must have caused. I hope Mr. Berkman is out of isolation, and that your last news from him is good."[58] Two months later, Witherspoon sought to alleviate some of Fitzgerald's distress over Berkman's confinement:

> I hope your work is going well. Ella Reeve Bloor, at a meeting for political prisoners the other night, told a story which I know would interest you. She said that a certain I.W.W. boy, whose name I cannot recall, was for eight months in a basement solitary cell in Atlanta Prison. There was a little window high up at the top of his cell. He told me that about once in two weeks the routine of the factory in which Mr. Berkman worked would bring his head into the line of his vision—not all of his head, but the bald spot, and enough of the shape for him to recognize its owner. He said the fact that he could see Berkman's bald spot, and know that a comrade was up there, also doing time for the cause, was the thing that kept him going. A wonderful story, I thought.[59]

20. *M. Eleanor Fitzgerald and Alexander Berkman on Mount Tamalpais in California, ca. 1916. Courtesy of M. Eleanor Fitzgerald Papers, Golda Meir Library, University of Wisconsin at Milwaukee.*

Telling wonderful stories such as this one helped activist women validate their work and maintain hope. Labeling some situations absurd or at least ironic provided opportunity to create some emotional distance and perspective on specific events. For example, in one instance, Witherspoon and Fitzgerald exchanged comments on a War Department order that drafted COs (legally considered "soldiers" by the state, despite their refusal to fight) would not be awarded victory medals. 'Dear Fannie Witherspoon," jested Fitzgerald, "Our C.O.'s will feel badly about this!" Witherspoon, who had little respect for War Department officialdom, responded: "Is it not terrible about the war buttons? Fools or knaves, or merely a splendid combination of the two!"[60]

Mostly, however, organizing public opinion in favor of amnesty in the turbulent days of the Red Scare left little time for sardonic chit-chat. "People are too scared to come to see or hear a Radical," Ella Reeve Bloor wrote Witherspoon, while on a western speaking tour. "It is getting like Russia, we will have to make the personal appeal more and more. . . . I had a small 'Conference' in Kansas City with a few brave ones but the papers are full of threatening lies classing all Radicals as a peril to American Institutions."[61]

Fortunately for amnesty workers, the pressure lessened on their organizations somewhat when the beleaguered Socialist Party managed to organize an impressive conference on behalf of political prisoners. As early as March 1919, the national Socialist Party headquarters in Chicago had begun plans for an "American Freedom Convention." Despite its postponement from July until the fall—an action bemoaned by Witherspoon and Lenetta Cooper, among others—the three-day conference was endorsed by over three hundred organizations, including the Bureau of Legal Advice, the League for the Amnesty of Political Prisoners, the Civil Liberties Bureau, and the Workers Liberty Defense Union, all of which sent representatives to preconference planning meetings in Chicago. Ella Reeve Bloor served as the Bureau of Legal Advice delegate, and she and Charles Recht attended at least one of the planning meetings.

In early September, three weeks before the conference convened, Elizabeth Thomas of the Milwaukee amnesty committee entreated Witherspoon to attend, explaining that Meta Berger was especially keen for her to be present in order to procure Witherspoon's advice on how to organize a press bureau. Witherspoon did not make it to the three-day conference but Bloor was there, as were Roger Baldwin (recently released from prison) and Albert De Silver; a number of other released objectors were on hand, accompanied by Theodore Lunde. Indeed, the delegates represented all of the groups associated with the civil liberties and peace movements, and the strong presence of organized labor betokened that another shift towards popularization of the amnesty cause had taken place.

Working for the release of COs and of other political prisoners absorbed much of the Bureau of Legal Advice's resources in the immediate postwar period. In early 1919, however, it became clear to Witherspoon and Recht that a new threat—the deportation of radical aliens—also required their attention. In fall 1918, Recht had prepared a pamphlet entitled *American Deportation and Exclusion Laws,* which was ready for distribution by the new year. On January 15, Witherspoon wrote to Lenetta Cooper, informing her of the immediacy of the "deportation question." In somber language, Witherspoon related that what "is concerning me most after the Conscientious Objector problem, which is always nearest my own heart, is this deportation question. The New York papers are full of scareheads about the blacklist the Department of Justice is compiling for the deportations, and our Bureau has already several deportation cases." Witherspoon explained that the Workers Liberty Defense Union and the Civil Liberties Bureau were planning to reprint and distribute Recht's pamphlet. The Bureau of Legal Advice had acquired a fresh purpose: "Our pamphlet is pretty technical, as we are after all a legal aid bureau. We find very few people know anything about these laws, and we thought we should render real service by digging up the law and letting other groups popularize the information we give them."[62]

One month later, the measured quality of Witherspoon's thinking about deportation had vanished. In an engaged, combative spirit, she explained to Theodore Lunde that "everything here in New York has had to give way to the deportation situation, which as you know is the latest and perhaps most exaggerated of all the high-handed things this country has perpetrated in the name of law and order. Our office has been altogether tied up with, first, a series of Chinese deportation cases, and now that of the fifty-four I.W.W.s brought from the West and held at Ellis Island."[63]

Meanwhile, another cause in the civil liberties field was emerging in 1919: an increasingly clamorous demand on the part of African American leaders and some white allies for a federal anti-lynching law. Since Reconstruction days, but especially from the 1890s, African Americans had been terrorized into submitting to a white supremacist "southern way of life" by the threat of brutal torture and lynching at the hands of vicious mobs. Between 1889 and 1922, over one hundred blacks—including women and children—were lynched annually in the United States. Rape of African American women by lynch mobs also occurred. From 1918 to 1922, twenty-eight African Americans were publicly burned at the stake.[64]

U.S. white society was so saturated with racist notions of African American character—particularly, as southern-bred Fannie May Witherspoon noted, of the purported overweening "sexual instinct" of the black man—that politicians and leading citizens found it easy to acquiesce to the white South's insistence that the African American was "their" problem. Despite the ground-breaking antilynching organizational work of Ida B. Wells-Barnett (beginning in the 1890s among both African American and white women), in 1919 lynch law was uncontested in the land that had just fought a war to make the world "safe for democracy."[65]

During the war, African American leaders championed the fighting man, hoping that an enthusiastic response to the call to arms would help black people find acceptance when peace was declared.[66] The wartime reality was that African American men volunteered for the U.S. Army in large numbers and endured insults and cruel treatment as enlisted men for the chance to fight and die for their country, while on the home front African Americans were exploited as field hands on southern plantations (state-defined "necessary" farm work) and used as temporary workers in wartime industries, often as strikebreakers.[67] In July 1917, a race riot broke out in East St. Louis, Illinois, brought on by white workers' resentment of African American strikebreakers in a labor dispute. Eight whites died, as did at least thirty-eight African Americans, often after being horribly beaten; the true mortality figure will never be known, but may have run into the hundreds. Some black victims were lynched. Historians H. C. Peterson and Gilbert Fite point out that not all of the hideous brutality was confined to African Americans resident in the city: "A Negro man and his wife and son were passing through that city when a mob grabbed them at Collinsville and Illinois Avenues, beat the man to death, shot the 14-year-old boy, and scalped the woman."[68] Lynchings of African Americans in other regions, mostly in the South, continued unabated.

Southern-born President Wilson refused at first to denounce

21. Silent parade down Fifth Avenue in New York, sponsored by the NAACP in protest against lynching and other forms of racist violence, June 28, 1917. Courtesy of the NAACP.

the heinous crimes perpetrated upon African Americans. On August 15, in a rare public statement on the topic, he finally issued a statement condemning such behavior. Wilson was deeply steeped in white supremacist thought, as were many of his advisors, but his refusal to accept African Americans as full citizens of the United States was not just a southern prejudice. The vast majority of white Americans in all geographic regions did not question racist prescriptions with regard to African Americans. This was true of progressive and left-wing individuals as well.

In general, African Americans did not figure prominently in the thinking and work of the wartime civil libertarian pacifists, although Martha Gruening's investigative journalism work for the NAACP represents a notable exception.[69] Why not? First, the African American community was still not large in New York City on the eve of the Great War.[70] Furthermore, among African American men who were drafted from the available pool of qualified men, the prevalent attitude was to accept the rulings of their local draft boards. Pressure by the African American community to serve and the fact that an enlisted man's pay with family allowance was more than the average African American man could earn in the labor market translated into few demands for exemption. Thus, there was little reason for African Americans to seek out associations such as the Bureau of Legal Advice for assistance with draft issues. Second, very few enlisted African American men defined themselves as conscientious objectors, cutting off another possible reason for contact with civil liberties organizations. Once the war ended and amnesty became the issue of the hour, the workers for this cause became preoccupied with freeing political prisoners who were mostly white.

The priorities that African Americans set themselves during the war did not dovetail in an obvious way with those established by the leaders of the civil liberties movement. Still, it is instructive to think about the physical spaces that African American and white activists shared. Before the war, Witherspoon marched with an African American woman in a suffrage parade in New York City and was much distressed when she and her suffragist comrade were denied service in a good restaurant. They ended up at a small coffee shop and were compelled to sit at the back of the room. (Witherspoon recounted this experience in her seventies in a published open letter to a young white southern woman who had denied a Nigerian diplomat the right to eat in the restaurant at which she was employed, in Charlottesville, Virginia.)[71] The Ginn Building housed not only the Bureau of Legal Advice, the Civil Liberties Bureau, the Woman's Peace Party, and the Church Peace Union but also the NAACP; we can imagine Gruening moving back and forth between the Bureau of Legal Advice and NAACP offices. Oswald Garrison Villard, grandson of the famous abolitionist and nonresistant William Lloyd Garrison, was active in the Civil Liberties Bureau and was a founding member of the NAACP. He, then, like Gruening, served as a link between civil liberties work and civil rights advocacy for African Americans. In later years, Fannie May Witherspoon and Tracy Mygatt became members of the NAACP. Did personal contacts made in the halls and offices of the Ginn Building influence them to join this organization?

As already noted, a number of African American COs appear

fleetingly in the Bureau of Legal Advice records and occasional mention of a "colored" or "Negro" objector is found in letters that objectors wrote to Witherspoon. Military training camps and prisons were sites where white and African American men shared somewhat similar fates, especially if they were COs. Scattered sources indicate that the comradely spirit among white objectors extended in some instances to the African American CO, as was the case when Bruno Grunzig referred to a black CO as one of "our boys."[72]

Black soldiers who were not objectors sometimes identified in explicit ways with the marginalized, ill-treated COs. For instance, at Leavenworth, a black soldier took pity on absolutist Howard Moore, who was enduring one of his many periods in solitary on bread and water. In his autobiography, Moore captured the moment vividly: "Some kind of sympathy apparently stirred a black man, who concealed a raw onion in his shirt and, at the risk of being put in solitary himself, threw it into my cell as he passed. It was a kindness I would never forget.[73]

Despite some evidence of an interracial cooperative spirit in military prisons, prevailing race relations among most ordinary military prisoners appear to have mirrored those of society at large. A strike by Leavenworth military prisoners in late January 1919 provides a case in point. The unrest began when white non-CO prisoners expressed dissatisfaction with poor prison conditions and long court-martial sentences, still in effect in peacetime. Some of the white soldiers involved in the early stages of the strike expressed outrage that African American prisoners were treated as well as they were. When leadership of the strike was assumed by a nonabsolutist objector, W. Oral James, he quickly buried the race relations issue. Some amelioration of conditions occurred as a result of the strike, in large part because of the sympathetic views of the camp commandant, Colonel Sedgwick Rice, who intervened personally with the War Department and secured better food and greatly reduced prison sentences for Leavenworth inmates. The civil liberties movement publicized the strike in the best possible light and ignored the racial tensions underlying the onset of the prison revolt.[74]

Although Bureau of Legal Advice records reveal little concern for African American civil liberties in or out of prison, the reprehensible treatment of black people by white society was a topic frequently discussed in private between Fannie May Witherspoon—

a daughter of southern "gentility" and white supremacist culture—and her Yankee-bred companion Tracy Mygatt. Witherspoon had begun to move self-consciously away from the racist precepts of the "Magnolia South" at college; at that time, Mygatt had visited Witherspoon's home in Meridian, Mississippi, providing her with first-hand experience of southern race relations. During the war era, while her beloved friend was taken up with the civil liberties movement, Mygatt used her talents as a writer to become a playwright for both the pacifist and the antilynching causes.

Mygatt's plays provided a means for her to express her abhorrence of society's intolerance for marginalized groups and her outrage against male violence. In 1919, she wrote two dramas, *The Good Friday* and *The Noose.* The hero in the former play represented Mygatt's version of the New Man, a self-abnegating, gentle warrior of the spirit. In the latter play, a searing indictment of the "best people" of white southern society who condoned, encouraged, and often led lynch mobs, the hero is a self-respecting, principled young wife and mother with a probing intelligence who is able to expose the hypocrisy of southern white male chivalry in the context of the unrelenting barbarism of a white supremacist patriarchal culture.[75] In 1919, *The Good Friday* was performed at the Peabody Playhouse in Boston and in the Central Music Hall in Chicago, and *The Noose* was produced by the Neighborhood Theater on Grand Street in lower Manhattan—the first antilynching play to be performed in the United States.

Mygatt had made her stand, and her critique of a malevolent patriarchal racist culture found favor in local liberal and radical circles.[76] In the meantime, however, the Red Scare mentality against "bolsheviks"—meaning all radicals and dissenters—had inflamed the omnipresent and virulent racism of white society. African Americans, regardless of age, gender, class, or political belief, became "fair game." A revived Ku Klux Klan sponsored more than two hundred public meetings in twenty-seven states; in many communities, members of the Klan pressured candidates for political office to maintain a pro-Klan attitude or face defeat at the polls. Such activity on the part of the white supremacist terrorist organization, contend historians John Hope Franklin and Alfred A. Moss, "stimulated the lawlessness and violence that characterized the postwar period in the United States."[77]

In the opening months of 1919, a number of returning African American soldiers, some of them still in the uniform of the U.S.

Army, became victims of lynch mobs in Mississippi, Georgia, Arkansas, Florida, and Alabama. All told, more than seventy blacks were lynched in 1919, eleven of whom were burned alive. The most severe interracial conflict the United States had ever experienced occurred in mid-year, a period that the African American writer James Weldon Johnson called the "Red Summer." From June until the end of the year, at least twenty-five riots took place. The explosion of violence was aggravated by job competition in industrial areas between whites and African Americans and "egged on" by organizations like the Ku Klux Klan.[78] Mobs composed mainly of white sailors, soldiers, and marines terrorized black neighborhoods in the nation's capital for three days in July. African American men fought back, and a number of whites as well as blacks were killed; many more individuals were wounded. Not long thereafter, in late July, a virtual race war erupted in the streets of Chicago. Rioting rocked the Windy City for several days and much blood was spilled, mostly African American.[79]

The emotional hatred and violence against the nonconformist "other" that was whipped to a hot frenzy during the war spilled over into the postwar era and threatened—sometimes to death—black Americans as well as white native-born dissenters of war and radicals, especially alien radicals. No longer were the mass of Americans united in what they believed to be a just war. Instead, "the patriotism complex," defined by literary critic Lewis Mumford as "the blind habit of running with the pack and following the leader on predatory expeditions," stalked the land.[80] A nation supposedly "at peace" was divided against itself. Nonetheless, maligned groups such as African Americans and their few white supporters fought back in organizations such as the NAACP. The Workers Liberty Defense Union mounted a campaign of protest and propaganda against the Ku Klux Klan.[81] Associations of people in what had become a rather sprawling and multifaceted civil liberties movement defied the reaction and repression of their times and pushed insistently for amnesty of political prisoners; at the same time, civil libertarians defended the right of minority dissent in a democracy. Further, as we shall see, civil libertarians Charles Recht of the Bureau of Legal Advice and Caroline Lowe, a legal representative for the Wobblies, sought to stem the tide of deportation proceedings against alien freethinkers and radicals.

⊰ 6 ⊱

The Ellis Island Deportees

At present there are signs of an overthrow of our government as a free government. It is going on under cover of a vigorous "drive" against "anarchists," an "anarchist" being almost anybody who objects to government of the people by tories and for financial interests.

—Louis Post, assistant secretary of labor,
Journal entry, 1920

On a cold winter evening, February 10, 1919, the People's Council held its first fundraising dinner of the year at the Central Opera House in Manhattan. Restoration of civil liberties, amnesty for political and industrial prisoners, disarmament, and opposition to military training and conscription were the main concerns of those attending the dinner. Among the evening's speakers and their subjects were Evan Thomas ("Democracy and Dungeons"), IWW counsel Caroline Lowe ("The Disillusions of Democracy"), and Charles Recht ("Deportation").

During the dinner, after the speeches had been given, a messenger from the local office of the IWW arrived with a telegram for Recht and Lowe, who were attending the event together. Scores of Wobblie aliens, the telegram stated, were being transported from Seattle, Washington, to Ellis Island, in the Port of New York, for immediate deportation. In consternation, Lowe and Recht departed for the latter's office to decide on a plan of action.

Recht had been associated with the unhappy fate of Wobblies since fall 1917, when a nationwide raid of IWW locals by Department of Justice officials and American Protective League volunteers resulted in mass arrests and subsequent espionage trials of IWW members. According to historian Joan Jensen, the fall raids "crushed" the IWW and provided "the first major victory" of the home front war against enemy aliens, free speech dissenters, conscientious objectors, and labor radicals.[1] In the months following the raids, Recht—whose name was almost daily in the news defending "undesirables"—came to represent a number of the eastern Wobblie locals.

In January 1919, the national headquarters of the IWW in Chicago sent their midwestern attorney, Socialist Party member Caroline Lowe, to New York to assist Recht in defending Wobblies. Canadian-born Lowe was 44 years old in 1919 having grown up in Oskaloosa, Iowa, before moving to Kansas City, Missouri, when she was sixteen. She taught school for a number of years and became president of the Teachers' Association in Kansas City. Lowe joined the Socialist Party in 1903 and from 1908 worked extensively in Nebraska coal towns with miners and their families as a Socialist Party field worker. By 1909, she had acquired regional fame as a popular speaker for the Socialist Party; in the immediate prewar years, she served with distinction as chairwoman of the party's Woman's National Committee. She was admitted to the bar in 1918, and from April to August, Lowe worked as one of the counsels at the mass trial of Wobblies (which included Big Bill Haywood) in Chicago.[2]

Ensconced in Recht's office on February 10, the two civil libertarian lawyers considered their options. The telegram from the IWW national office had given Lowe and Recht authority to handle the deportation cases. The obvious plan, from the lawyers' perspective, was to sue out writs of habeas corpus for the individuals headed for Ellis Island.[3] The difficulty, however, was that the authorities had kept the arrested men incommunicado and neither the IWW headquarters nor Lowe and Recht had the name of a single individual on the convoyed, armed train (which the press had dubbed the "Red Special"). Moreover, the detained men, as aliens, came under the authority of the Bureau of Immigration (an administrative arm of the Department of Labor) and were subject to congressional immigration law. Neither they nor their lawyers could count on the constitutional safeguards guaranteed U.S. citizens.

22. *Speakers at a Socialist Party Encampment near Hugo, Okla-homa, fall 1912. Left to right: Caroline Lowe, Oscar Ameringer, Eugene V. Debs, and Walter Thomas Mills. Courtesy of the Caroline Lowe Papers, Haldeman-Julius Collection, Pittsburg {Kansas} State University.*

It is important to appreciate the situation that led to the de-portation proceedings against these individuals. The state, with the eager assistance of the mainstream press, had encouraged a unified spirit among Americans during the war by insisting on absolute uniformity of opinion and unquestioning compliance with all aspects of the war effort. Because the "enemy" was several thou-sand miles away, it became expedient from the state's point of view—and in the context of pockets of resistance to the war from pacifists, labor radicals, socialists, and certain immigrant groups—to permit the concept of enemy to become associated with internal subversion. Thus, as we have seen, over the course of the war, enemy aliens, conscientious objectors, free speech advocates, socialists and other political and labor radicals, and urban, working-class African Americans all came to be painted with the same brush as the collective "enemy within." This simple-minded conceptualization of patriot and enemy facilitated the prosecution of the war, but it also proved difficult to dislodge after hostilities ceased. Historian John Higham, among others, has noted that the overwrought patriotic emotionalism of the war era spawned a nativist torrent of vituperation and violence against enemy aliens. An omnipresent, unreasoning abhorrence of dissent from any source overlapped dramatically with the antiradical, antilabor spirit that sprang up immediately following the war.[4]

During the war, organized mainstream labor had benefited from the needs of the state to maintain a mobilized, efficient workforce. Union memberships grew and paychecks increased for workers in industries where war-engendered profits were high. Once the war was over, however, the state backed away from its wartime watchdog regulation of productivity and worker-management industrial relations. At the same time, the U.S. economy reeled with the stress of adjusting to peacetime conditions; retail prices rose, wages fell, and war veterans flooded the labor market. Organized labor under AFL leadership saw its hard-won and fragile wartime security crumble as employers began to attack union legitimacy on a number of fronts. While some workers turned against their fellows—as horribly revealed in the mass of race riots during Red Summer (1919)—others sought solidarity with victims of wartime oppression such as political prisoners.

Not long after the Armistice, the nonradical labor movement began to appreciate its vulnerability in the weakly regulated postwar capitalist system. The year 1919 witnessed an unprecedented number of strikes, including America's first general strike in Seattle. Over four million workers participated in mass protests across the country, to the consternation of employers, civic leaders, and government officials. Although the vast majority of workers who went out on strike in 1919 were neither labor radicals nor aliens, they were identified as such in the overheated xenophobic popular mind.

The Seattle general strike has been brilliantly analysed by William Preston Jr. in the context of the antilabor animus fueling the actions of leading capitalist interests during and after the war. His study demonstrates how a mood of wartime superpatriotism among civic leaders merged with the perceived needs of lumber and shipping industrialists to seal the fate of radical labor on the northwestern coast (notably the IWW) over a year before the general strike occurred. Preston makes the very telling point that the episode of the Red Special deportees in early 1919 "took a nearly forgotten antiradical drive out of its northwoods setting and focused nationwide attention to it. . . . The Wobblies were an exciting curtain-raiser for the thrills of the red scare to follow."[5]

In fall 1917, at the same time as the dragnet raids of IWW offices occurred across the nation, Seattle immigration officials, in league with patriotic citizens and capitalists, rounded up every Wobblie alien they could find, detaining most (in accordance with Bureau of Immigration practice) without immediate right of counsel. Most of those who traveled on the Red Special en route to Ellis Island had been incarcerated for over a year in Seattle jails before being shipped east.[6]

Although release seemed a pipe dream on February 10, 1919, Recht and Lowe were determined to secure freedom for the fifty-three men and one woman who had been sent to Ellis Island. As noted above, Fannie May Witherspoon and Charles Recht had predicted that the postwar climate would be hostile to aliens and radicals. Their expectation was confirmed when Congress passed the Immigration Act of October 1918, which made it a deportable offense to propound anarchy (defined in the law as a disbelief in organized government) or to belong to an organization that advocated and taught the unlawful destruction of property, the overthrow by force of the U.S. government, or the assassination of government officers.

Recht's pamphlet publication, *American Exclusion and Deportation Laws,* distributed widely in January 1919, reviewed the legal history of immigration. His study provided much evidence of the precarious legal position of all aliens within U.S. borders under the wartime immigration legislation. Recht argued that the 1918 law was being interpreted by immigration officials in such a manner that mere belief in a radical political philosophy constituted ground for deportation. Such a perspective, he averred, reinforced the public's view that anarchists, socialists, and bolsheviks were all one: bomb-throwing assassins bent on the destruction of the country. The popular hue and cry to rid the country of the unwanted and dangerous revolutionary "other" lent support to the determined effort of government officials to deport alien radicals as fast as possible once the 1918 law was in place.

Nevertheless, when the Red Special arrived on the east coast three months after the ending of the war, the prodemocracy civil liberties movement was galvanized and ready to fight back. In the struggle to defend the rights of dissenters and of other victims of wartime repression, civil libertarians and their supporters had become a force with which to reckon. As we have seen, well before the cessation of hostilities, a coalition of radical and liberal groups—such as the League for the Amnesty of Political Prisoners, the Workers Liberty Defense Union, the Bureau of Legal Advice (in concert with the Friends of COs), the National Civil Liberties Bureau, and the League for Democratic Control—had developed an esprit de corps and a strong sense of legitimacy in the campaign for the release of political prisoners (which included many Wobblies) and of conscientious objectors to war. By the beginning of 1919, the IWW itself had recovered somewhat from the state's wartime prosecution of its leaders and had joined others in the demand for amnesty of political prisoners. In addition, its national officers had succeeded in bringing together bright and eloquent lawyers such as Lowe and Recht who were plugged into the vigorous civil liberties defense movement. Significantly, even before the armistice was declared, the IWW's chief attorney, George F. Vanderveer, was on the scene in Seattle and had developed some strategies for frustrating the attempts of immigration officials to deport alien Wobblies.

As noted, aliens came under immigration law. The Bureau of Immigration had created a set of administrative legal procedures for dealing with "undesirables," but its officers were not compelled to abide by due process constitutional provisions when dealing with aliens. Thus, with regard to alien Wobblies and other alien radicals, the custom was to discourage those detained from seeking legal counsel, at least until they had given testimony to an immigration inspector—who was frequently the stenographer, the cross-examiner, and the judge. The inspector also decided upon questions of fact and ruled on what constituted evidence. Such an official could supplement the charge against an alien by mere clippings from newspapers over which the accused had no control.[7]

Once Vanderveer arrived in Seattle, he began to sue out writs of habeas corpus in order to test the legality of his clients' detention. He also advised Wobblie detainees to refuse to testify without counsel and convinced Wobblie aliens not yet in prison to stop distributing IWW educational material. Over one hundred and twenty writs of habeas corpus were issued over a period of months leading up to the end of the war, providing credence to Vanderveer's assertion that Wobblies were being held on insufficient evidence. Wobblie aliens who were already incarcerated fought back with prison strikes. Released Wobblies publicly criticized the procedures that had led to their detainment.[8]

In light of these developments and in the face of a pending general strike of workers in the Seattle area, embarrassed and frustrated immigration officials, worried about the revolutionary potential of a unified labor protest, decided upon a dramatic action: the wholesale removal of imprisoned alien radicals to the east coast for immediate deportation. However, unbeknownst to the immigration architects of the Red Special, Vanderveer's counterparts in the East, Caroline Lowe and Charles Recht, were prepared to stymie their highly irregular plans to rid the country of so-called undesirables. It was civil libertarian lawyers such as Lowe and Recht to whom William Preston refers when he comments: "From the moment Vanderveer began to put pressure on the government with habeas corpus suits until the red scare had passed, deportation procedures were under the withering scrutiny of talented defense lawyers. Nothing like it has ever happened before or since."[9]

On the morning of February 11, Lowe and Recht presented themselves before Ellis Island officials and requested permission to meet with the Red Special prisoners. When such permission was denied, Lowe and Recht decided that their only alternative was to apply for a writ of habeas corpus. According to Recht's recollection, "By every rule our writ did not have a legal leg to stand on and should never have been issued and should have been dismissed. The rules prescribed that the application for the writ should be signed by the person imprisoned, or his relative or his next friend." Nonetheless, Caroline Lowe wrote in her name as the "next friend" on a writ application that contained the name of one of the men on Ellis Island. "Our irregularity," Recht noted dryly, "consisted in the fact that we got the name from the public newspapers."[10]

When the writ came to be argued before Judge John Knox of

the Southern District Court of New York, he told Recht and Lowe that they had done "a very reprehensible thing in getting the name of the relator from the newspapers." Recht freely admitted in court that none of the statements and allegations about the immigration inspector's hearings were based upon an examination of the records. As Recht put it, "How could they be, since we did not know even the names of the men, and if we had gone to Washington to inspect the records it would have taken perhaps weeks to do so and meanwhile the men would have been long since deported. We consoled ourselves in all our improprieties that justice was on our side." In the end, Recht's appeal "to mercy and to fair play" won the day. Recht and Lowe were given permission to study the immigration records in Washington, D.C., and to present their findings before Commissioner General of Immigration Anthony Caminetti and William B. Wilson, the Secretary of Labor. The state agreed not to deport any of the individuals in this group until the lawyers had presented their findings before the appropriate officials. For their part, Recht and Lowe "consented" to have the writ dismissed.[11]

The examination of the records in Washington, undertaken jointly by Lowe and Recht, uncovered that of the fifty-four individuals on the Red Special, thirty-nine had been arrested in relation to IWW activities; the other fifteen were not members of any radical organization. The Wobblies, upon whom Recht and Lowe concentrated their efforts, were of varied ethnic backgrounds: Scandinavian (13), British (9), Russian (7), Finnish (4), Polish (1), Dutch (1), German (1), Austrian (1), and Czech (1).[12] Most of them had been arrested in winter 1917–18, and their cases had been closed. Warrants for their deportation accompanied them to Ellis Island. Almost all of the deportees had been found to be undesirables under the anarchy provisions of the Immigration Act of October 1918.

Recht and Lowe were able to determine that the Wobblies and others who were brought east on the Red Special were treated first and last with shocking disregard for due process and for basic human decency. The poverty of the aliens provided another roadblock. A sense of the helplessness and the pathos of individuals caught in the grip of hostile forces emerges poignantly from the records of some of the hearings. One detained alien, for instance, pleaded with the immigration authorities to provide him with legal counsel; he had only three dollars in his possession, however, and the immigration inspector demanded: "How can you get a lawyer for three dollars?" The man continued to persist with his request, and the inspector continued to remind him of his poverty and powerlessness. Finally, the record states, the "alien puts his hand to his head and begins to cry," and "alien waives his right to an attorney."[13]

After inspecting all of the records, Recht and Lowe submitted a two-hundred-page brief to Secretary of Labor Wilson. Recht was the principal writer, and the brief was comprehensive. Recht not only berated Wilson for failing in his mandate to represent "labor" but also wrote an analysis of the economic conditions in the Northwest that had led to IWW activism in the region. In the second part of the brief, Recht summarized individual cases and provided a positive (and sentimental) portrayal of his Wobblie clients as dignified, high-minded, but long-suffering individuals of "manly" character:

> It may not be amiss to comment on the high standard of intelligence of these men, on their uniformly excellent morale and their splendid devotion to the cause which they advocated. Deprived of home, of the love of a woman, cast out into a hostile world, their emotions found sole outlet in their loyalty to the cause of labor. No offer of parole, even after long imprisonment, no banishment from the country where they were rooted, could effect its compromise.[14]

Recht and Lowe presented their arguments before immigration commissioner Caminetti and Assistant Secretary of Labor Louis Post. Shortly thereafter, on March 17, the Department of Labor canceled the deportation warrants against twelve of the Wobblies; one week later, two more men were released on their own recognizance. Six others preferred not to make appeals and were eventually deported. For most of the remaining nineteen Wobblies whose fate was still to be determined, Recht and Lowe secured writs of habeas corpus, which were argued before Judge Augustus N. Hand on April 10 and 15. Hand sustained one writ on April 10 (the deportee was discharged), and on April 15, eleven of the writs were withdrawn with no prejudice (mutual consent) and returned to the Department of Labor for reconsideration. Of these, warrants for deportation were canceled for three and three others were released on parole.[15]

Thus, in the thirty-three cases that received a second hearing, twenty-one were not deported. Of the remaining twelve still held for deportation, five left voluntarily and seven were released on bond because of the difficulty arranging for their deportation to their native land. A Dutch man, Marin De Wal, was the last deportee to be released in March 1920.[16]

One year earlier, however, in February and March 1919, the outcome was far from certain. Three days after the prisoners on the Red Special had been shifted over to Ellis Island, Fannie May Witherspoon produced the first press release on the deportees. The five hundred-word statement indicates that a great deal had already been learned about the cases. Although Witherspoon insisted that the Bureau of Legal Advice was "an organization whose function is that of defense rather than propaganda," she wrote wrathfully about the Department of Labor's attitude on the question of deportation of aliens, declaring it to be "in direct contradiction of a tradition which has always been one of the finest of our country, namely, that America is and should always remain an asylum for the earth's oppressed and for those persecuted by the autocracies of the old world." Witherspoon encouraged "all radical and particularly all liberal bodies" to register "vigorous protests" with Secretary of Labor Wilson.[17] One day later, on February 14, Witherspoon released another statement, in which she articulated the Bureau of Legal Advice's position that the Departments of Labor and of Justice were colluding in "a most sinister attack not only upon the workers of this country but also upon those traditions of justice and fair play which have always been America's pride."[18]

Legal defense funds were, as always, in short supply; Witherspoon wasted no time in alerting the Civil Liberties Bureau of the deportation crisis. Before long, De Silver offered his bureau's assistance, and a plea for defense funds entitled "Under the Shadow of Liberty" was distributed under the joint sponsorship of the two associations.[19] Witherspoon also cooperated with Caroline Lowe in an effort to unify the liberal and radical communities in a concerted effort to stop the Ellis Island deportations. Lowe penned an uncompromising indictment of the deportation proceedings, urging "members and friends of organized labor" to send in money in care of the Bureau of Legal Advice. Her month of research into the immigration records gave Lowe the confidence to declare unambiguously that "these men are being deported *solely because of membership and activity in a labor union—the Industrial Workers of the World.*"[20]

A groundswell of protest accompanied the agitation instigated by the IWW and by the Bureau of Legal Advice on behalf of the Ellis Island deportees. The press reported a spate of meetings within a few days of the Red Special's arrival in the East, sponsored by Socialist Party locals, AFL unions, the African American community in Harlem, and the Women's International League (WIL), formerly the New York City branch of the Woman's Peace Party.[21] In early March, the Central Federated Union of Greater New York City and vicinity took advantage of a White House conference of state governors and city mayors to attack the administration's alien deportation policy. In a prepared statement, the union accused the Department of Labor of using the purported threat of alien revolutionists as a pretext for controlling union and strike activities. Secretary Wilson was forced to reply defensively that "no one is being deported for strike or union activities but only those who have advocated or are advocating the overthrow of our Government by force."[22] Within a week of Wilson making this remark, however, the first twelve Wobblies were released, followed in fairly quick succession by most of the rest.

Not all of the aliens earmarked for deportation in early 1919 were men. Only one of the original fifty-four Red Special deportees was a woman, but other women undesirables were on the state's deportation list in this same period. The WIL was the first organization to come to their aid. On February 9, while the Red Special was speeding its way eastward, the WIL sponsored a protest rally in the ballroom of Manhattan's Hotel McAlpin for five women deportees. Else Williamson Merta, a Finn, was being deported because she was the wife of a deportee, Peter Merta (also Finnish). Jeanette and Margaret Roy were sisters who had emigrated from Scotland in 1911 and had become active in the IWW, first in the 1912 Lawrence strike, then in Chicago, and finally, just before their arrests, on the west coast. Molly Steimer was a twenty-two-year-old Russian anarchist who had been sentenced to fifteen years imprisonment, to be followed by deportation, because she had helped to distribute leaflets protesting U.S. intervention in Russia. She and Hilda Kovner, one of the stenographers for the

Bureau of Legal Advice, were comrades in the youthful Jewish anarchist group Frayhayt.[23] Jennie Matyos had emigrated to the United States from Riume (now Rijeka in present-day north-western Croatia) as a child; she was an active member of the International Ladies Garment Workers Union and of the Socialist Party at the time she was apprehended.

Several days after the WIL rally, the socialist *New York Call* ran a lead article entitled "Radical Women Denounce Deportation Scheme." By this time, thanks to Recht, Lowe, and Witherspoon, the radical community knew all about the Red Special. The views of several well-known Socialist Party women—Rose Pastor Stokes, Elizabeth Gurley Flynn, Ella Reeve Bloor, Theresa Malkiel, and Jessie Wallace Hughan—were quoted at some length. Stokes challenged "our college men and women socialists" to take up the class struggle if the deportations were successful. Flynn called the deportation attempt a blatant "act of intimidation" and laid the blame at Secretary of Labor Wilson's feet. Bloor pointed out that William Wilson had been a miner himself and claimed that he was now betraying his own class. Malkiel discussed the problems and possible dangers that would await the deportees in their native homes. Hughan, in line with statements issued by Lowe and Witherspoon and by the Civil Liberties Bureau, spoke of America's tradition as "the refuge of the discontented of all lands" and distinguished between actions and words: "Men of every sect and 'ism,' however mistaken, may find protection, provided they keep from deeds of violence. If the 54 men have committed crimes, let them be tried by a jury, and, if guilty, suffer the penalties of American law. If their offense is in speech and opinion only, then let them learn that America is, indeed, a republic, a republic with 'liberty and justice for all,' even for the I.W.W. Deportation of agitators will certainly not infuse patriotism."[24]

Intertwined, then, with the Red Special cases were the related cases of other individuals—some of them women—who by virtue of their own activities (or in the case of some wives, their husbands' activities) were destined for deportation. Lowe and Recht defended a number of these individuals, as did other civil liberties lawyers such as Harry Weinberger. The Bureau of Legal Advice also helped out by coordinating communication among counsel and deportees. Witherspoon organized visits (when possible) of "friends" of deportees and developed means for supplying Ellis Island internees with supplementary food and other small material comforts.

The WIL maintained its commitment to the Ellis Island women and held another mass meeting in support of them on April 9. Before the event, WIL member Elinor Byrns—who, as noted above, was a lawyer and a member of the Bureau of Legal Advice's executive committee—asked for Fannie May Witherspoon's help in drawing up resolutions to present to the rally. Witherspoon, also a member of WIL, complied. Nonetheless, she stressed the complexity of the gender issue in relation to the deportations. Although Witherspoon had been willing to argue that overseas alien wives of servicemen should receive wartime family allowances by virtue of their married status, her perspective was quite different in this instance:

> I could not frame a resolution on the deportation of women alone. I am sure you do not feel it is worse to deport women than men. Nor do I see in the deportation of these five women any specific sex point to be made. If we protest the deportation of the Roy girl on the ground that she is now a citizen, having acquired it by marriage, we should be upholding the very law which we really wish to protest, namely, that the citizenship of a woman is altered by her marriage. I think we are perfectly just in supposing that American born women who become too radical and objectionable, will be deported if they have lost citizenship through marriage, but none of these 5 cases illustrate this. The deportation of Jennie Matyos would be a most inhuman thing. She came to this country as a child and has her family and friends here. Again that is a human matter and not a sex one.[25]

Witherspoon had been a member of the National Woman's Party (NWP) since 1917, and she embraced its commitment to equal citizenship for women. However, in common with other feminists in this era, she wrestled with the dilemma of how best to represent the needs of all women in a patriarchal society. The NWP egalitarians sought equality before the law in all instances (as exemplified in their demand for an Equal Rights Amendment), but many other feminists who were not members of the NWP insisted that the myriad structures of gender inequality within a male-dominated state necessitated woman-specific protections before the law.[26] Witherspoon moved back and forth on this issue somewhat, especially when she was confronted with the suffering and powerlessness of immigrant women in relation to the wartime state, but intellectually she felt more comfortable with the egalitarian stand.

Witherspoon monitored and consciously struggled against her patrician, southern white supremacist upbringing, but deep-seated prejudices surfaced from time to time in her work for the "unfortunates" who sought Bureau assistance. For instance, in the same letter to Byrns, Witherspoon betrayed a conventional middle-class view of the sexual double standard, reinforced by racist expectations with regard to African American women. She mentioned the one "immoral woman case" with which the Bureau had been involved:

> It is of course obvious hypocrisy and cruelty to deport immoral women—who have become immoral through social and economic conditions in this country, and particularly is it absurd to the point of laughter, that we should send prostitutes out of this country when the after-match [*sic*] of the war in Europe has probably disarranged the marriage institution violently, and has as we know, actually resulted in the legitimizing of children born out of marriage, in a number of countries.
>
> The one immoral woman case that we had was that of a colored woman who had a child three years ago and was just on the point of being married by the man, and therefore being reinstated into respectable society, when someone got excited and had her arrested. Her case goes to illustrate the impropriety of deportation practice. She was deported one week after her arrest and while they knew Mr. Recht was trying to get at her on the Island with a writ.[27]

Witherspoon's concluding words for Byrns were somewhat patronizing, as she referred back to the five deportation cases: "Of course I realize that you are making a woman's point because you are a women's organization, and that you will soon pass out of a woman for woman stage into the broader field."[28]

A "broader field" might be beckoning on a distant horizon, but in the meantime, Witherspoon and Recht came to the aid of some of the WIL-sponsored women deportees. For example, Else Merta and her husband Peter Merta (one of the Red Special Wobblies) benefitted from Recht's intervention on their behalf. Although they were ultimately deported, Recht saw to it that the Mertas were permitted to choose Sweden instead of Finland—their native land—as their final destination.

The Roy sisters, Jeanette and Margaret, also chose deportation over remaining in the United States. They had been tried in Seattle before an immigration inspector and ordered deported, despite legal action to prevent this while they were still in the West. They were brought east in February to join their Red Special comrades, at which time they immediately declared their intention of making no further attempts to secure justice from the courts. On July 23, 1919, Margaret and Jeanette Roy sailed on the *Carmania* to Liverpool and thence to Glasgow.[29]

Unlike the other women deportees on Ellis Island, Molly Steimer had not been apprehended under the Immigration Act of 1918. Rather, she and four comrades—all in their twenties—had been arrested in August 1918 under the Sedition Act for distributing leaflets that criticized U.S. intervention in Russia. For this offense, she and three other young Russian radicals (Jacob Abrams, Samuel Lipman, and Hyman Lachowsky) had been convicted and sentenced to lengthy prison terms, to be followed by deportation to Russia.[30] (One of their number, Jacob Schwartz, had been so savagely beaten by the police in the Tombs Prison after his arrest that he died before the trial began against the other four.) Harry Weinberger represented the young people, all of whom were anarchists except Lipman, a socialist.

In early 1919, Steimer was temporarily free on bond awaiting an appeal of her case. She was picked up by Department of Justice officials in March and imprisoned at Ellis Island for five days. Weinberger secured her release, although Steimer was forced back to Ellis Island again in October. She eventually served time in the Missouri State Penitentiary in Jefferson City. Finally, in 1921, Weinberger's efforts led to the government's decision to commute the prison sentences of Steimer and of her three comrades in exchange for their agreement to be deported immediately to Russia. The diminutive and uncompromising Steimer never faltered in her tenacious commitment to anarchist ideals, and her indomitable will won her a beloved status among radicals. Shortly before her deportation at the end of 1919, Emma Goldman—who was a staunch supporter of Steimer and of her comrades—spoke glowingly of the "heroic young rebels," especially Molly Steimer, "whose courage and revolutionary integrity put many a man to shame."[31]

———

In his memoirs, Charles Recht wrote proudly that he won 90 percent of the eighty deportation cases that came his way in 1919; this impressive figure included the thirty-odd Wobblie cases that he and Caroline Lowe handled together. He also noted that he and Lowe were successful in part because of the persuasiveness of their arguments and their ability to convince public servants, including judges, of the inequities in alien deportation law. When the Red Scare got underway in earnest, however, their talents and commitment could not stay the tide of antiradical hysteria.

Historians find it difficult to locate the actual start of the Red Scare. Individuals such as Fannie May Witherspoon and Charles Recht expected a postwar reaction, particularly in relation to aliens and radicals, but the speed of the onset of the antiradical backlash—egged on by patriotic citizen's groups, antilabor capitalist interests, and the Ku Klux Klan—surprised even them. As Recht noted, "The early months of 1919 wove the manifold hostility to the new Soviet government into a pattern: All of our troubles were due to foreigners—the cry for social equality is inspired by agitators—all agitators are foreigners—all radicals are agitators—the Bolsheviks are the most radical—every radical is a Bolshevik."[32]

As noted above, historian William Preston refers to the Red Special deportation cases as the "curtain raiser" to the Red Scare. With hindsight, we can identify the essential ingredients of the witchhunt against aliens and dissenters in this little-known chapter of civil liberties history. For most Americans, however, it was dynamite, not the detention center at Ellis Island, that symbolized the times.

At the end of April 1919, just as the Red Special cases were being resolved (mostly in favor of Recht's and Lowe's clients), someone attempted to send bombs through the mail to a number of leading public officials. Most of the bomb packets did not reach their destination, thanks to the quick thinking of a New York City postal worker. However, the maid of a former Senator, Thomas Hardwick of Atlanta, Georgia, lost both her hands when she attempted to open the package addressed to her employer, and Mrs. Hardwick was badly burned about the face and arms. Then, on

June 2, a series of simultaneously-timed bombs exploded in several different cities; on the same day, the home of Attorney General A. Mitchell Palmer was severely damaged by a bomb. The unidentified dynamiter was blown up as he or she tripped on the steps of Palmer's residence.

No one ever claimed responsibility for any of these incidents, and authorities failed to apprehend a single suspect. Historians have puzzled over this failure of the state to determine the agents of the bombings. Scholars have surmised that they were probably the acts of isolated individuals, supported perhaps by a coterie of self-styled Bolsheviks or anarchists who had been inspired by the Soviet state's open commitment by 1919 to world revolution. Voices from established radical circles in the United States disclaimed all responsibility for the terrorism. Some radicals, such as Elizabeth Gurley Flynn, suggested that the bombings might have been the acts of agents provocateurs. Flynn also contended that "the despicable accusations" against radicals were serving the "dastardly purpose" of "creating an atmosphere of general fear. It is in such an atmosphere that blind mob fury does its work."[33]

Regardless of who was actually responsible, there is no gainsaying that the Soviet-identified left in the United States was in ferment at the close of the war. An exuberant hopefulness and idealism concerning the prospects for revolutionary change in the world informed left-wing groups, notably those (such as the Socialist Party foreign-language federations) whose members were recent immigrants. For a time, native-born socialists active in Socialist Party electoral politics kept faith with the Soviet experiment, too. Further, by early 1919, a number of small anarchist groups (some of which published newspapers such as the *Frayhayt*), were actively proselytizing their version of revolutionary theory and practice. All things considered, then, it is not surprising that when the bombs exploded, aliens and radicals would be blamed. Many citizens, including prominent public officials such as Attorney General Palmer, were convinced that a well-organized revolutionary movement threatened U.S. internal security.

According to Robert Murray, the chronicler of the Red Scare, it was at this point that the state, with concentrated help from zealous patriotic citizen groups, initiated a sweeping campaign against radicals. What had been (before the terrorist bombings occurred) a somewhat desultory roundup of radical aliens for deportation became a mass attack against all nonconformist thinkers, notably those who, like radical aliens, could be identified easily by virtue of language and culture as "other."[34]

In 1919, New York City became a microcosm of this modern-day witchcraze. International Labor Day (or May Day) came two days after the April bomb scare, and in New York City, as in other large urban centers with significant immigrant populations, socialists and prolabor people attempted to celebrate this traditional workers' holiday. However, incensed mobs, consisting of soldiers, sailors, and other patriots, attacked parade participants and broke into Socialist Party offices and those of the bureaus of various immigrant groups, including the Russian People's House at 133 East Fifteenth Street. The office of the *New York Call* on Fourth Street was also raided by an unruly mob that managed to break up a reception attended by over seven hundred people, destroying office furniture, books, and files in the process. The mainstream press failed to report this violence the next day, but the *Call* spoke out, calling the raids "orgies of brutality" and accusing the police of collusion with the mobs.[35]

In the meantime, the New York state senate's Judiciary Committee had approved, in March, the appropriation of $30,000 to support the deliberations of a committee headed by Senator Clayton R. Lusk, which was "to investigate the scope, tendencies, and ramifications of . . . seditious activities and report the result of its investigations to the Legislature."[36] In June, as the committee began its work, Lusk hired former American Protective Leaguers to help New York City police and state constabulary conduct daylight raids of the Russian Soviet Bureau, the Rand School, the offices of the Socialist Party, and IWW locals. The aim of the raids was the documentation of radical and subversive activities. Citing the seized materials as evidence, the Lusk committee provided the press with what Murray terms "the most astounding revelations," including the allegation that the Soviet Bureau, headed by L. C. A. K. Martens, aimed "to bring about a complete bolshevizing of American labor." Lusk called Martens the "American Lenin" and claimed that he had been provided with huge funds to foment an American equivalent of the Bolshevik Revolution. Archibald Stevenson, a prominent New York attorney who in January 1919 had written a report on radicalism in the city that had inspired the formation of the Lusk committee, was quoted in the press as insisting that

Rand School radicals were propagandizing among African Americans, helping them to establish their own radical newspapers and exaggerating racial injustices.[37]

Just as the Lusk committee began its investigations, Charles Recht was asked to become associate counsel for the Soviet Bureau. His appointment made sense because during the war, Recht had acquired a collective client, the foreign-language federations of the Socialist Party. After the Bolshevik Revolution in Russia, the Russian Socialist Federation (closely aligned with the Soviet Bureau by 1919) had assumed a leading role as spokesperson for the other groups, which included the Lithuanian, Finnish, Hungarian, and Czechoslovakian federations.

Recht, a gifted linguist and inveterate fighter for the underdog, found himself in an anomalous situation. As counsel for the Soviet Bureau, his job was to help "Comrade Martens" protect "nationals." However, as Recht himself noted, "strictly speaking, there was at the time only one citizen of the Soviet Republic in the United States—and that was Martens himself." Nonetheless, despite the refusal of the United States to recognize the Soviet Union, many immigrants from Russia looked to Martens's bureau for protection. The legal cases came to Recht: "This required no change in the character of my work, since I was already defending American workingmen of many nationalities for the Bureau of Legal Advice—including Russian immigrants."[38]

By the time Recht agreed to become counsel for the Soviet Bureau, the affairs of the Bureau of Legal Advice were winding down. Fannie May Witherspoon was extremely busy with the amnesty movement, but the kind of networking tasks she undertook in conjunction with other organizations such as the Workers Liberty Defense Union and the Amnesty League did not translate into a forward-looking strategy for the Bureau of Legal Advice. In the white heat of the Red Scare May Day and June attacks on aliens and radicals, financial support for the Bureau faltered.

Nonetheless, Fannie May Witherspoon struggled to keep the Bureau solvent. On June 6, 1919, she penned a "begging letter" that she posted to a select group of Bureau supporters. Witherspoon allowed herself to gloat a bit with regard to the Ellis Island deportation cases: "When you consider all of the boastful statements in the press about the deportation of thousands of radicals, I think you will agree that we have really put a little halt to this march of autocracy." However, she appreciated the bigger picture and foresaw difficulties ahead: "More constructive than the help to the individuals is the fact that we have thus forced the Bureau of Immigration to reverse itself on many points and to guarantee the legal protection of aliens in the future. For of what avail is it to attempt to get our conscientious objector and political prisoners of foreign birth out of the miserable jails which hold them, if the business interests are going to be able to exile them through the Department of Labor?"[39]

A few days later, Witherspoon lambasted the *New York Times* for its inaccurate report on the Red Special cases. She let the *Times* editor know how outraged she was that the Bureau of Legal Advice had been referred to as a "queer little group in the East." Witherspoon proclaimed indignantly that her association "has had the energy to insist that the heads of the Department of Labor do more than rubber stamp the findings of the Immigration Inspectors, and afford to aliens such scant justice as their own rules provide." Uncharacteristically sarcastic, Witherspoon's angry letter focused on the antidemocratic and repressive features of the Immigration Act of 1918:

> Apparently [it is a deportable offense] to possess and circulate a piece of writing which discusses sabotage or destruction of property in industrial pursuits, and states the case for it; merely to possess such a book or pamphlet and pass it on to another person constitutes advocacy of destruction of property, and therefore brings you within the terms of the present immigration law, although you yourself may disbelieve in sabotage, or any form of violence, and though there is no record that the organization to which you belong has ever officially adopted the piece of writing in question or that it has itself officially advocated similar views. If this is to be a criterion, all persons of wide reading had better purge their library shelves, first of the Bible, and after, of practically every other work of historical subject matter, for the case for violence in pursuit of a social end has been stated many thousands of times since the world began. And if to own is to advocate, no one is safe.[40]

Witherspoon concluded testily with "another small point":

> You stress the word "immediate" in connection with the deportation of those whose cases have been lost in court. You cannot

desire immediate deportation more heartily, apparently, than do these people who have been suffering so many weary months in prison, and who are now waiving their right to appeal . . . to a higher court because of their despair of justice in a country maddened by bomb hysteria. It is a deplorable fact that they leave these shores with a conviction that the courts, our presumed centre of justice, but confirm conclusions already drawn of our institutions throughout a harsh industrial experience.[41]

Within the month, Witherspoon and Tracy Mygatt had taken themselves off to their beloved Maine coast to recoup their energies after a difficult yet stimulating fall and winter of full-time activism and writing for the cause. By the time they left, the Lusk raids and allegations, coming so quickly after the May Day riots in New York City and elsewhere, had accomplished much damage, and "bomb hysteria" infested many communities. Witherspoon and Mygatt no doubt experienced anguish when race riots broke out in major industrial urban areas during July. They also must have followed the actions of Attorney General Palmer with mounting alarm, as he began to spend the $50,000 appropriation that the Department of Justice had been granted by Congress to facilitate his antiradical crusade. In short order, Palmer's department infiltrated leftist groups, sent reports on radicals and their activities to the press, and set up files on thousands of left-wing or left-leaning political activists.[42]

A young man, Edmond Brown, who also assisted Charles Recht in his office, was left in charge of Bureau of Legal Advice affairs while Witherspoon was on vacation. Correspondence between Brown and Witherspoon demonstrates that she was feeling very discouraged about the Bureau's future. In one letter, Witherspoon referred to the Bureau as an "outlawed organization" and predicted that it would soon cease to exist.[43] In this same period, Witherspoon and Bruno Grunzig exchanged views on the Bureau's probable demise. Witherspoon was evidently still toying with the idea of the Bureau assuming legal aid work for small unions, but she also began to speak of amalgamating prodemocracy, prolabor, and civil liberties groups into a "People's Freedom Union." Grunzig enthusiastically supported Witherspoon's scheme for an integrated association and praised Witherspoon for her integrity of purpose. However, his comments hint at an ongoing tension be-

tween the Bureau of Legal Advice and the National Civil Liberties
Bureau. Grunzig's cryptic allusions to unnamed individuals might
have been meant to include Roger Baldwin, who had completed
his prison term. Grunzig seems to have imbibed Witherspoon's
justifiable resentment towards Baldwin, whose need to be at the
center of things had frequently had the effect of placing Witherspoon on the sidelines.[44]

When Witherspoon and Mygatt returned to New York City in
the fall, the nation was in turmoil. Hundreds of political prisoners,
including many COs, were still awaiting their freedom. President
Wilson had suffered an incapacitating stroke at the end of his
cross-country speaking tour to garner support for the Versailles
peace treaty. (He had, at any rate, shown little concern for civil
liberties since the commencement of the war.) From October 2,
1919, until he stepped down from office on March 4, 1921,
Wilson was chief executive in name only; high-ranking politicians
such as Attorney General Palmer held inordinate power, especially
in domestic affairs.[45]

In the fall, Boston police, Pennsylvania steel workers, and Ap-
palachian coal miners went out on strike, and red-scare panic increased. Popular paranoia that a Bolshevik revolution was at hand
heightened in September, when the Socialist Party splintered at its
annual convention in Chicago. Henceforth, two rival parties—the
Communist Party and the Communist Labor Party—competed
with a much reduced Socialist Party for the allegiance of individuals associated with a now fractious and demoralized left. Worse
was to come, however.

By fall 1919, a strident press and an alarmed citizenry were
clamoring for the Department of Justice to undertake more aggressive action against radicals and dissenters. Picking up on the public mood, U.S. senators began to criticize Palmer's department. A
number demanded "new Red Specials" and the deportation of radical agitators. Initially, the failure of the government to deport
most of the Red Special aliens made Palmer and his coworkers
cautious, and they hesitated to proceed with mass deportations. In
the rush of events and circumstances, however, Palmer finally decided to act.

On November 7, 1919—two years to the day after the Bolshevik assumption of power in Russia—a nationwide raid on the
offices of the pro-Soviet Union of Russian Workers took place.

Literally overnight, state and local officials assumed the offensive and on November 8, more raids were conducted against all manner of foreign and left-wing associations. As was the case on November 7, the New York City raids were the most dramatic, as seven hundred zealous police officers invaded seventy-three offices and arrested over five hundred individuals. Most citizens were released, but aliens were detained, pending deportation proceedings.[46]

After the raids, Palmer's star rose meteorically and the U.S. Senate, backed by President Wilson's verbal support in December 1919, seriously considered a peacetime sedition act. However, the General Intelligence Division of the Justice Department had determined that ninety percent of radicals were aliens, and the plan to conduct mass arrests and deportations remained Palmer's preferred approach to the "red menace." He persisted in this strategy even when the House Committee on Immigration—meeting in November 1919—announced that of the six hundred supposed revolutionary aliens who had been arrested between February 1917 and November 1919, only sixty had actually been deported as dangerous anarchists.[47]

The number of deportees was soon to increase, however, in large part as a consequence of the November 1919 "Palmer Raids." Immigration officials held deportation hearings; two hundred and forty-nine individuals were judged either to be anarchists or members of groups that advocated anarchism, and deportation orders were drawn up. Emma Goldman and Alexander Berkman, who expected to be deported given that they had completed their prison terms, became part of this group. Almost all the others, however, were, according to historian Julian Jaffe, "aliens without friends or influence, who possessed only a hazy knowledge of the doctrines of which they were accused." "On the whole," Jaffe states, "they appeared confused and bewildered by the hearings and left the country without a clear understanding of just why they were considered a threat to the security of the United States."[48]

When it became clear that the deportation orders would soon be carried out, the wives of several deportees submitted a petition to Commissioner General of Immigration Caminetti. In an aggrieved tone, the women declared their victimhood. Without their male breadwinners, they insisted, they were "helpless, prostrate and a heavy burden upon the community."[49] They demanded to be deported with their husbands. Secretary of Labor Wilson probably knew of this request, but he chose not to inform the deportees or their lawyers and families of the arranged date for the sailing of the *Buford*, an ancient leaky ship first used in the Spanish-American War for troop transfers. Wilson did, however, telegraph all deportation centers that aliens with families should not be included on the *Buford* passenger list. He hoped, in this way, to give such aliens time to arrange their personal affairs. However, the telegram either arrived too late or was ignored at Ellis Island. Instead, those interned at the Port of New York were told on the evening of December 20 that the *Buford* would leave within a few hours. No communication with the mainland was permitted. The first passengers began boarding at 2 A.M. on Sunday, December 21, 1919. At 6 A.M., the *Buford* set sail.[50]

The next day, several wives of the deportees arrived at the barge office at the Battery to request passes to see their husbands. The *New York Tribune* sensationalized what transpired when the women were informed that their husbands had already departed on the *Buford;* according to the reporter, "a near riot occurred at the Ellis Island Ferry when women became enraged" over the deportation of their menfolk. This disturbance was led by Clara Brook, a twenty-four-year-old Russian whose husband, Abraham Brook, had been arrested during a riot at a demonstration in Washington Square in October 1918. He was found to have been circulating anarchist literature that protested against the presence of American troops in Russia and was ordered deported. The *Tribune* story continued:

> Pushing her way through the crowd, Mrs. Brook, according to the police, shook her fist and shouted: "Down with this dirty, rotten government! They have taken my husband and are taking the husbands, brothers and fathers of all of us away."
>
> While Asa Mitchell, superintendent of the Barge Office, was awaiting the arrival of the police reserves some of the women jammed their fists through a window. After the reserves had quieted the crowd one of the women was called upon to explain what the demonstration was about.
>
> "They arrested my husband," she said. "When I went to find out about him they said, 'Don't worry, he's all right.' I pleaded with them to let me talk to him, but they refused to let me see him. Now when I come back here I learn he is gone on the sea. I'll never see him again."[51]

Clara Brook was arraigned before Magistrate Max Levine at the Tombs Court and found guilty of disorderly conduct; the sentence was suspended for forty-eight hours pending an investigation by a probation officer.

Harry Weinberger was attorney for some of the wives of the deported aliens and was under the impression that arrangement would be made for families to accompany the deportees. After the events of December 22, he sent a telegram to Commissioner Caminetti firmly requesting more definite plans as to when wives and children could join their husbands and fathers in their native land. Accompanying Weinberger's telegram was one written on behalf of the wives who (according to the *Tribune*) had "stormed" the entrance to the Ellis Island ferry. It read in part:

> We have been patient and long-suffering, but the cruelty is driving us to desperation. Already one of your victims has been driven to acts of violence. The result of starvation and heart-pangs rests upon your heads. Has the government of the United States no decency and self-respect? Shall atrocities be visited on Russian women and children? We ask for justice and receive only promises that develop into lies. Are there no Americans left who know the history of their country? In the name of humanity and justice we demand at this time when all the world is about to celebrate the birth of Christ, the name you hold sacred, the right of peace in our hearts. We demand that you unite us with our husbands and fathers.[52]

The *Call,* which also reported on the events at the barge office on December 21, challenged the facts of the *Tribune's* coverage. The protest was not launched by two hundred frenzied men and women "as the capitalist press tried to indicate"; rather, there were "10 mournful women, several with infants in their arms, protesting ineffectually against the deportation of their husbands, which had already occurred." The *Call* version is worth quoting at some length:

> The half score of women appeared at the immigration barge office at the Battery at 9 o'clock this morning and asked for the customary passes issued to visitors to Ellis Island. Mrs. Clara Brook, of 219 Forsyth Street, whose husband, Abe, was among those deported Sunday, acted as spokesman.
>
> Mrs. Brook, when she appeared at the barge office, did not

know that her husband had been exiled and was on his way to an unknown place, presumably Russia.

According to Miss Sophie Kessler, a sister of Mrs. Brook and one of the women in the party, the employee in the barge office, believed to be one named Barr, addressed Mrs. Brook sarcastically: "You will never see your husband again. They'll drown him."

Mrs. Brook, upon whom the events of the last few days have weighed heavily, became hysterical and broke through a glass pane in the little office where passes are issued. Thereupon women in the party began to cry and grow excited. A riot call was sent to Old Slip Station. When coast guards rushed the barge office, a policeman and Superintendent Asa Mitchell managed to subdue the women.[53]

The article recounted Clara Brook's arraignment and conviction for disorderly conduct; her anguished statement, "I'll never see him again," was also quoted.

In the January 10, 1920, issue of *The Survey* magazine, civil liberties reporter Winthrop Lane noted that Brook spent five days in jail. She was jeered at and called a "Bolshevik" by the other women prisoners (who were described in this article as "prostitutes, pickpockets, and so forth"). Lane recorded some of Brook's testimony when she spoke with him: "She cried while she was telling this part of her story. . . . 'I can't express my feelings so good in English,' said Mrs. B_____, 'but maybe it ain't necessary. You understand. Anybody would feel terrible to have a friend taken away without saying good-by, but I am his wife.'"[54]

It is not known if Clara Brook or any of the other thirteen wives and their children were ever reunited with their husbands in the Soviet Union. In 1921, however, Constantine Panunzio's conscientious study of the Red Scare deportation cases confirmed that these women were still in the United States. Panunzio stated sympathetically that these individuals were struggling to secure jobs but that most had young children to care for and found it impossible as a rule to arrange child care. He found that three of the women whom he had interviewed consistently refused public charity. Instead, they "uniformly asked for one thing—the privilege of joining their husbands, wherever they are."[55]

Native-born M. Eleanor Fitzgerald—the "Fitzi" of New York City's anarchist circles—identified with the Russian women who wished to accompany their husbands into exile: her lover Alexander Berkman's request that she be permitted to leave with him as his common law wife was turned down flat. In her autobiography, Emma Goldman (Berkman's lifelong comrade and former lover) recalled that he had emerged from the Atlanta Penitentiary not long before the *Buford* sailed "with the horrors of his experience burned into his soul" and in poor health.[56] Berkman ("Sasha" to close friends) was quite cast down by the forced separation from Fitzgerald. After Berkman and Goldman were deported, Fitzgerald kept in touch with them and visited them in Europe on several occasions in the 1920s. In 1926, Berkman fell in love with Emmy Eckstein, a young German woman from a conventional bourgeois family, with whom he lived the last years of his life. However, Fitzgerald and Berkman remained intimate friends and kept up a correspondence until his death in 1936.[57] Towards the end of the war, Fitzgerald had become the executive manager of the experimental theatre group, the Provincetown Playhouse, a post in which she excelled during the 1920s. With a well-established reputation in the field, Fitzgerald assumed a number of administrative positions in theatrical enterprises; she retired in 1953, two years before her death.[58]

During these stirring and disturbing times, Fannie May Witherspoon was forcing herself to let go of the Bureau of Legal Advice. The war was over and, by 1919, other organizations existed to carry forward the amnesty struggle. The National Civil Liberties Bureau had become a powerful and well-funded group for legal defense. In contrast, the financial resources of the Bureau of Legal Advice, dependent on small donations from poor immigrant and working-class clients and well-wishing movement activists, had dried up by the end of 1919. Undaunted, Witherspoon and others sought (somewhat impulsively) to establish an umbrella People's Freedom Union to consolidate the identity and carry forward the work of the wartime antimilitarist and civil libertarian movements. This initiative, however, failed rapidly.

In this time of sorrowful endings for Witherspoon and for her coworkers, Tracy Mygatt proposed a dramatic action for the amnesty campaign, one that would call forth the exuberant joyfulness in "doing" that had been such a significant aspect of the prewar movement of cultural and political radicals, feminists, and pacifists in New York City. Mygatt's suggestion was to organize an amnesty

23. *People's Freedom Union postcard, December 1919.*
Courtesy of the Swarthmore College Peace Collection.

walk up Fifth Avenue, stopping along the way to picket various churches. The walk could begin on Eleventh Street at the parish house of the Church of the Ascension, an Episcopal church whose minister, Dr. Percy Stickney Grant, had participated in the delegation to Secretary Baker in December 1918 and to which Mygatt and Witherspoon belonged. Grant gave his enthusiastic support to the venture. In a circular letter, Mygatt enjoined people who believed in the "publicity value of this demonstration" to come out on Christmas Day at 10 A.M. "It is precisely because it will be a little hard to come out on Christmas Day," Mygatt declared, "that we know you will want to do so."[59]

Witherspoon recalled in an interview conducted on March 9,

1966, that "when Christmas [1919] came, it was a very beautiful day, with snow . . . and the sun was shining."[60] However, city authorities had refused to grant a permit for the walk. Witherspoon and Mygatt were aware that they were orchestrating an act of civil disobedience and expected trouble. Nonetheless, about three hundred people turned out, including members of Eleanor Fitzgerald's Amnesty League and the "under forty" activists of the Young Democracy. War veterans added variety to the peaceable crowd that assembled at Eleventh Street just west of Sixth Avenue. As people began to enter the Church of the Ascension, the march started. In Witherspoon's words, "At the head of it we had a motor car with several men and women wearing surplices like a choir . . . and singing Christmas carols and Christmas hymns with two trumpeters furnishing the music. And they set forth up the Avenue and the rest of us marched on foot. . . . A young minister led the march, carrying a large American flag."[61] Much of the rest of the story can be gleaned from the prejudiced but detailed coverage of the march in the *New York Times*.[62]

The young Methodist member of the clergy who headed the walk up Fifth Avenue was the Reverend Dr. C. V. Howell. He was followed by two leaders, Florence Lee and Alice Riggs Hunt, and ten others, all garbed in chorister's vestments and bedecked festively in evergreen and holly. They and the others marching behind them (six feet apart in single file) carried placards that read "On Christmas Day We Ask For Amnesty," "Ten Prisoners Have Died For Conscience Sake," and "Peace on Earth—Good Will to Men." Crowds quickly assembled along the avenue to observe the marchers; a large contingent of New York police officers was also on hand. When the demonstrators reached Fourteenth Street, Captain Ashley of the West Twentieth Street Station bellowed: "Turn back; you cannot do this. You have no permit and you have no right to carry those signs." The marchers kept on in silence, and the police attempted to disperse them. The demonstrators persisted, although they were forced to change route: they headed along Fourteenth Street to Sixth Avenue, whence they proceeded unmolested to Twenty-ninth Street and then back over to Fifth Avenue. "One block up the avenue," reported the *Times*, "the police were upon them again. The column wavered and broke, and the flagbearer was the only one to get by." Requests to desist from their protest reached the ears of the marchers from time to time from sidewalk observers such as Major Lorillard Spencer, "a man of soldierly bearing" and the Chair of the American Legion's Committee on the Suppression of Anti-American Activities.

The participants in the walk persevered. As they zigzagged their way uptown, trying to stay together as a group, five individuals (including two pro-amnesty war veterans) were arrested at points along the route for disorderly conduct. Spectators interfered with the marchers and tore the placards from them. One indignant placard-destroying serviceman was furious when he discovered that one of the demonstrators was a war veteran like himself. In an allusion to the departure of the *Buford* several days beforehand, he expostulated: "[I]f it is true [that you are a veteran], I am ashamed of you. If you don't like the way things are run here, then why the hell don't you get out of here? You should have gone last Sunday morning."

Only about fifty marchers continued on at this point. Hostile onlookers assailed them with "hoots and jeers" at Broadway and Herald Square. Witherspoon remembered that she and Mygatt had brought up the rear of the march and "didn't know just what was happening up ahead. . . . [A]s we finally learned, a great many people were roughly handled by the police and 'Peace on Earth— Good Will to Men' was snatched from them and thrown down and the signs broken up."[63] After reaching as far as Fifty-fifth Street, the marchers headed back to the Church of the Ascension, where they heard Witherspoon declare the demonstration a success. The next day, she filed a formal complaint against the police. The inquiry that followed determined that the Christmas Day paraders had been within their legal rights to protest as they had, and the police officers who had been on duty at the demonstration received a reprimand for their rough behavior towards the "hikers."[64] More important from Witherspoon's point of view, however, was the "enormous publicity" that the amnesty movement gained as a result of the demonstration: "In that way it really was a success, though apparently a failure."[65]

This is the last glimpse we have of Fannie May Witherspoon as a movement leader in the context of the World War I–era pacifist civil liberties movement. The Red Scare had not abated, however. On the contrary, it moved into high gear at this time, and a monumental legal struggle lay ahead for individuals such as Charles Recht. As counsel for hundreds of alien deportees arrested in the highly irregular Palmer Raids of early January 1920, Recht found himself at the center of another chapter in civil liberties history that did not really conclude until alien deportations ceased in 1921.

Fortunately for the future of U.S. democracy, well-placed liberals such as Assistant Secretary of Labor Louis Post finally made common cause with the few remaining radicals who like Recht had not been deported, silenced, browbeaten into apathy, or just plain worn out, and brought the deportation fiasco to a halt. Post used his authority to cancel thousands of deportation orders in 1920: of the close to four thousand "red" cases that he reviewed, only seven hundred deportations were sustained. In his book on the subject, Post exposed a "pernicious delirium" that he defined as a spirit "hostile to American ideals of government." After reviewing the "appalling facts" of the red crusade, Post concluded with an cautionary note that speaks across the decades to contemporary times:

> Had the public sentiment that made this crusade possible been a product of considerable American thought, instead of a temporary delirium, the democracy of our Republic would have barely escaped destruction by the very forces that were operating professedly for its preservation. The episode might be safely forgotten were it not that it may serve as a warning to the American people to be alert, even in delirious periods, for the protection of American liberties. Lawless persecutions of resident aliens, though only symptoms of a popular frenzy, might easily lead on, if the delirium persisted, to comprehensive policies that would turn our Republic backward upon its democratic course. Americans cannot afford to ignore their traditional admonition that "eternal vigilance is the price of liberty."[66]

Fannie May Witherspoon had held high hopes for an inclusive, politically radical civil libertarian organization when she, along with Tracy Mygatt and a few others, attempted to get the People's Freedom Union off the ground. The times were inauspicious for a new departure, however, and Witherspoon in 1920 did not possess the material resources and the physical and mental fortitude to carry on in the old way. Depending on the good will of movement people and of grateful clients, as she had in the crisis of the war, no longer sufficed in the aggressively reactionary postwar period. Furthermore, the left-wing, feminist, pacifist-oriented (or at least antimilitarist) war-era movement culture was now increasingly divided against itself. Wobblies, evolutionary socialists (the rump Socialist Party members or "right wing"), and factionalized communist and anarchist groups engaged in bitter, self-defeating debates and power struggles. Feminists were caught in these fissures as well, facing new challenges over theoretical and strategic issues of equality and difference in the environment of gender backlash that followed in the wake of warmaking. As Joan Jensen has demonstrated, pacifist feminists were especially preoccupied with the need to establish realistic agendas for the struggles ahead.[67] The wartime coalition—pacifists, feminists, political and cultural radicals, and civil libertarians of various political views—that Witherspoon and her coworkers had helped to bring into purposeful action had receded temporarily. It would take different circumstances, fresh challenges, and the infusion of a new generation of activists to revitalize movement culture.

After the Bureau of Legal Advice closed its doors, Witherspoon and Mygatt retreated for a time into private life. Both women devoted most of their energy to their writing careers. They had little money but managed to support themselves with part-time jobs and with income derived from very modest family bequests. In the 1920s, they collaborated on two books with religious themes.[68] Creative writing remained a primary activity for Mygatt throughout her life; Witherspoon wrote less as she grew older but maintained engagement in literary production.

In the midst of World War I, Witherspoon had written to a friend in Atlanta, Georgia, Alice Holdship Ware, that she and Mygatt thought of her as one of the "real intellectuals." Witherspoon elaborated: "I don't mean it as the Socialists mean it; I mean one of the people who go through life refusing to be irretrievably bound to one philosophy and one set of ideas. We are always interested in your kind because we happen to belong to the other kind ourselves, 'join-up-for-life,' so to speak."[69]

Witherspoon and Mygatt did indeed prove themselves to be unswerving activists for peace and for human rights over their long and productive lives. After the Great War, they helped to establish in 1921 a separatist absolute pacifist group, the Women's Peace Union of the Western Hemisphere; Mygatt played a crucial role in the association's attempt to get the U.S. Congress to pass a consti-

24. Charles Recht with his dog Budo upon return from the Soviet Union, December 1922. Courtesy of UPI/Corbis-Bettmann.

tutional amendment against war in the 1930s.[70] Witherspoon and Mygatt also assisted Jessie Wallace Hughan when she spearheaded the founding of the mixed-gender absolute pacifist War Resisters League, still in existence today.[71] During World War II, Witherspoon worked within the War Resisters League to help a new generation of conscientious objectors make their stand; in this same period she and Mygatt were also active in the national Women's Committee to Oppose Conscription. In the 1950s, Mygatt faced down McCarthyite allegations against her and went on to become a leader in the Campaign for World Government. Witherspoon and Mygatt became members of the NAACP and championed the civil rights movement of the 1950s and 1960s. In 1968, Witherspoon, at age 82, organized a Bryn Mawr alumnae petition protesting the war in Vietnam; it was signed by one thousand women and was printed in the *New York Times*. Letters from Witherspoon to newspaper editors and to public officials flowed from her pen on many peace-related topics until only days before her death on December 16, 1973, just three weeks after Mygatt passed away. Each, after her own fashion, had proved herself to be (as Witherspoon had predicted) a join-up-for-life thinker and doer.

Charles Recht also kept on the remarkable course he had set himself during World War I. He remained the chief legal advisor to the Soviet Union until the United States finally recognized that state in 1933. He developed his literary interests further and published translations of plays as well as a collection of his own verse.[72] Recht was "tailed" for years by Department of Justice officials but managed, always with dignity and a disarming warmth of spirit, to maintain his professionalism and his personal integrity. When he died in 1964, he left behind a unique legacy in the field of civil liberties law.

❧ 7 ❧

Creating a Peace Culture

*Our files . . . contain material of which someone will
make effective use, I hope, in working against militarism as an institution for the future.*
—Frances M. Witherspoon, 1918

On several occasions in 1917 and 1918, Fannie May Witherspoon considered the need to keep track of events from the point of view of the rebels against war, the radical dissenting pacifists and civil libertarians who were committed to holding the line against the culture of violence (the war culture) that threatened to engulf U.S. society. She particularly wished to see the deeds of the wartime "feminine COs" written into the historical record. The needs of the moment, however, decreed otherwise.

Fannie May Witherspoon was herself a key actor in the "high significant moments" of the wartime peace and civil liberties movement. She was both an ordinary person and an extraordinary one. Witherspoon belonged to a generation of bright, privileged, well-educated white women who had taken inspiration from feminist foremothers to push themselves beyond conventional reform work towards radical engagement with the world. Ironically, the debilitating conditions and ugliness of the home front war supplied Witherspoon with a stimulating challenge and scope for her considerable talents.

When assessing Witherspoon's role as the real head of the Bureau of Legal Advice, it is apparent that her personal determination and commitment insured its survival in very difficult circumstances. This self-described "daughter and sister of lawyers" felt comfortable with legal matters. Witherspoon relished being in charge of the Bureau and its work. She was competent and confident about getting things done and could be canny and adroit in her interactions with powerful authority figures and bureaucrats. Witherspoon's experience in the suffrage and socialist movements before the war had trained her how to build coalitions, and she put what she had learned to effective use during the war. She also enjoyed immersing herself in the particular and the concrete: as Recht had observed, the Bureau of Legal Advice (at least at its inception) had "no ultimate purpose"; rather, the point was to assess a situation, organize a response, and then get on with the task at hand.

A quality of moral seriousness was a key aspect of Witherspoon's character and influenced in crucial ways how she handled the leadership of the Bureau of Legal Advice as well as her other commitments. As we have seen, Witherspoon considered herself to be a Christian socialist, and although she expressed her pacifist stand in secular terms, New Testament teachings on nonviolence informed her credo. When the Socialist Party splintered in 1919, she firmly rejected the communist path and remained in the Socialist Party. Moreover, Witherspoon steadfastly insisted on women's right to full citizenship status within the nation; she was appointed to the advisory committee of the National Woman's Party (NWP) in 1917 and remained an unswerving advocate of the NWP-sponsored Equal Rights Amendment all her life.

Witherspoon's commitments to feminism, socialism, pacifism, and the inviolability of individual conscience enabled her to develop a fundamental critique of the patriarchal warmaking state. Although she never theorized the relation between gender and war in any sustained way, Witherspoon connected the two. As early as 1916, in the pages of the *New York Call,* Witherspoon declared: "The state of gigantic armies and navies is the anti-social state, as it is the anti-feminist state. Its essence is discrimination, arbitrary distinctions. It presupposes inequalities, a superior and an inferior, an owning class and a propertyless and exploited class, which will at once furnish the means of the military incubus, monetary and human, and be its chief victim. It must also be an aristocracy of sex, bullets to back ballots."[1]

Witherspoon carried this radical assessment of the patriarchal warmaking state with her into her civil liberties work. She believed, as did her feminist-socialist comrades, that root and branch change both in productive and in affective relations among people was imperative. Such transformative change would require time, however; it was a process, or as Witherspoon once remarked, "an on and on road." The point was to be there, on the well-trodden path.

Idealism, a comradely spirit, and an empathetic identification with the marginalized, the maligned, and the outcast should not blind us to the anger, resentment, and even envy that women such as Witherspoon experienced as the female other in a patriarchal world. World War I, as Charles Recht at one point glibly asserted, was "strictly a male affair," and Witherspoon comprehended that this reality infused movement subculture as well. Witherspoon often became exasperated with the latitude that Recht sometimes took with regard to his responsibilities as chief counsel, upon occasion publicly taking too much credit for himself at the expense of the Bureau. Further, she was often annoyed at and outmaneuvered by Roger Baldwin's controlling and intimidating tactics towards "her" group, the "little Bureau of care." At times, this anger spurred Witherspoon to confront and to take charge, but in other instances, she succumbed to churlishness and defeatism.

Nonetheless, this consciousness of gender inequality also prompted movement women such as Witherspoon to unite to fight injustice on many fronts and increased their ability to find common ground with other oppressed groups. This understanding evolved and expanded for movement women as victims of wartime repression multiplied. Witherspoon spoke often (as did other civil libertarians) of reinstating "traditional freedoms," but she had a keen sense of history and as a feminist (and a socialist) recognized that reinstatement was not the issue, for civil liberties customarily had been accorded only to propertied native-born white men.[2] During the war, Witherspoon and other women civil libertarians fought especially hard to establish the legitimacy of legal protections for outsiders, such as enemy aliens, radicals, and conscientious objectors. In fighting for these outsiders, feminist civil libertarians were also fighting for themselves, as women.

When we turn to consider additional dimensions of women's involvement in the peace and civil liberties movement of World War I America, we are drawn to the story of the female COs and their male CO counterparts. Here we refer not only to the young women (such as Elsie Knepper and Frieda Ledermann Jasmagy) who visited "their boys" in military prisons but also to the women civil libertarians (Witherspoon, Ella Reeve Bloor, Anna Davis, and others) who established close ties of their own devising with objectors.

It is one of the paradoxes of World War I that conscription brought to the fore a host of contesting voices on the meaning of manliness. Despite the state's insistence that the warrior-citizen ideal represented the highest standard of manliness during war, many men, be they native-born or foreign-born, rejected a soldier identity for themselves and found a number of rationales for so doing. Indeed, a plethora of manliness ideals among different regions, classes, and races of men during the World War I era can now be identified.[3]

In the press of circumstances, the "feminine COs" and some of the objectors whom they aided learned that war (as feminist theorists today argue) is a gendered process. Such individuals sometimes employed this insight to develop novel antimilitarist protest strategies. That is, they came to see that the militarized state of their times could not prosecute war if men refused to be men (combat-ready soldiers) and women refused to be women (patriotic moral mothers). Objectors (such as Bruno Grunzig) who found themselves grappling with the dilemma of how to be manly and pacifist at the same time had great difficulty rejecting all aspects of the soldier ideal, despite their refusal to fight. Others, however, such as Howard Moore and Evan Thomas, found it easier. The women, for their part, struggled to retain nurturant aspects of a moral mother ideal at the same time as they distanced themselves from the wartime patriotic moral mother construct. A "motherist" and pacifist ethos seemed to attach itself to a vision of the autonomous woman citizen in the minds of the feminine COs, or more accurately, feminist COs.[4] From our contemporary vantage point, what seems striking is not that these men and women failed fully to transform themselves but that they made the attempt.

At the public, political level, the Bureau of Legal Advice accomplished quite a bit. Here we are reminded that this group was organized by a coalition of left-wing groups composed of women and men with the same overriding objective: to protect the civil liberties of individuals—especially those on the left—who came into conflict with the law during the war. It is certain that the mixed-gender character of the Bureau of Legal Advice strengthened its influence. For example, Witherspoon secured John L. Elliot as chair of the Bureau; Elliot, prominent in social reform and founding member of the Ethical Culture Society, was also on the directing committee of the National Civil Liberties Bureau. Other male members of the Bureau of Legal Advice's executive committee at one time or another included Roger Baldwin, Jacob Hillquit (lawyer and brother of Morris Hillquit), and Arthur Leeds (treasurer, also an attorney); of course, Charles Recht served as chief counsel. Witherspoon understood that to be effective politically, women civil libertarians had to work cooperatively with men and to manipulate patriarchal privilege to the advantage of the cause whenever possible.[5]

Witherspoon found it difficult to let go of the Bureau when it became clear that circumstances militated against its continuance. Her last effort to shore up the fortunes of the pacifist civil liberties movement of the war era, the establishment of the People's Freedom Union, ended almost before it had begun. Roger Baldwin testified before the New York state senate's committee on radical activities (the infamous Lusk committee) that the People's Freedom Union "practically abandoned its work in January 1920" and that "such of their activities as have been continued are in the hands of the American Civil Liberties Union."[6]

Despite its brief existence, however, it is instructive to look at what Witherspoon and other movement comrades hoped to accomplish with the People's Freedom Union. Most simply stated, the Union aimed for solidarity of purpose among all movement groups and causes. Here is Witherspoon's explanation, written on November 28, 1919, to her sister feminist and pacifist in Chicago, Lola Maverick Lloyd:

What I am doing here is attempting to put together in one big covering federation all of the groups in New York standing for peace and freedom. We had become so utterly disorganized in these months since the armistice that one felt one would like to flee the scene and go off and grow roses, which seems theoretically to be the conventional occupation for wornout pacifists. Just at the time, however, that I touched bottom in despair over this question, I succeeded in making a few people see the thing

as I did. . . . Our slogan is: One-Big-Union of specialized committees for the particular job, whatever that is—Lift the Block-
ade on Russia, Fight Mexican Intervention, Release Political
Prisoners, etc. One of the best things about what is happening is
that we are reviving a great many people who had dropped away
from the movement and are getting in fresh new blood.[7]

On January 14, 1920, a People's Freedom Union appeal was
published (probably authored by Witherspoon) and was entitled
"An Open Letter to Rational Americans." "People of cultural sta-
bility and sound mind" were importuned to support the People's
Freedom Union. It was suggested that the "heresy-hunting" planted
during the war seemed to have struck permanent root: "Lynching
parties chanting the hymn of liberty as cloak for their own sadistic
fury formed themselves during the war into a hideous procession
that still passes the windows of the less secure, and the bodies of
negroes and white working class leaders swing in lonely places—
milestones of our public degradation." To remedy such wrongs,
the People's Freedom Union had been formed.[8]

The ambitious One Big Union enterprise faded quickly into
the bleak, reactionary landscape of the postwar years. Nonetheless,
its predecessor—the peace and freedom movement of the war
era—had accomplished much. This was due in large part to the
fact that the Bureau of Legal Advice and the other New York City
groups with which it worked possessed the One Big Union vision.
We cannot explain the victories that the movement accomplished
on behalf of thousands of ordinary people in varied circumstances
without this understanding. Seen in this light, it becomes difficult
to single out the Bureau of Legal Advice for its unique achievements. At the same time, it becomes almost impossible to imagine
the inclusive feminist-pacifist, civil libertarian movement of the
World War I era without the Bureau's contributions.

Hence, explicit acknowledgment of the Bureau of Legal Advice's accomplishments in the field of civil liberties needs to be
made. As Fannie May Witherspoon and Joy Young were so fond of
declaring, their Bureau was the only legal aid group in New York
City to counsel draftees and their families free of charge. It was
also the only association to represent individuals in magistrates'
courts who could not afford to pay for an attorney. This meant that
the Bureau of Legal Advice handled thousands of cases for mostly

immigrant, working-class people and thereby made a real difference in the lives of individuals who had nowhere else to turn for help.

The Bureau was not alone in advising COs of their legal rights before they were inducted into military service, but it was the only group in New York City whose members kept track of all COs in the vicinity and maintained personal contact with them through visits and correspondence once objectors were in military camps.[9] Because of this, the Bureau was able to make timely and well-documented reports on the treatment of COs in the army to appropriate military and government officials and to provide the National Civil Liberties Bureau with crucial information for its own lobbying work on behalf of COs. Fannie May Witherspoon took the initiative in the campaign to end manacling of military prisoners as a punishment, and she was justifiably proud of the Bureau of Legal Advice's work when Secretary of War Baker abolished the practice on December 6, 1918. Her success in organizing the high-profile Baker delegation (Christmas 1918) also resulted in some amelioration of conditions for military prisoners in the period immediately following the war.

The founding of the Friends of COs in Witherspoon's own home was a brilliant sleight of hand. This group took on propaganda and lobbying tasks, efforts that the Bureau of Legal Advice could not be seen to be doing. Some months after its establishment, Witherspoon admitted that the Friends of COs was really a subcommittee of her Bureau. The Friends helped to establish the legitimacy of the amnesty movement in the eyes of the public. Individuals within this group such as Theodore Lunde were instrumental in bringing military prison atrocities to the attention of Congress in 1919.

The networking and coalition-building skills of Witherspoon (and of other Bureau of Legal Advice executive committee members such as Ella Reeve Bloor) were truly astounding. The efforts that women on the left made to connect groups across the country in the drive to secure amnesty is a story that still needs to be told in more detail. Nonetheless, we can appreciate the way that Witherspoon teamed up so effectively with Eleanor Fitzgerald of the League for the Amnesty of Political Prisoners and with the leaders of other similar groups. This chapter in the affairs of the Bureau of Legal Advice draws out the supple activist style of left-wing women and helps to underline their enduring political power, despite the repressive climate of the war years and the overlapping Red Scare hysteria.

The Ellis Island deportee saga accentuates the partnership of Charles Recht and feminist-socialist Caroline Lowe, who in the name of workers' trade union rights and first amendment freedoms fought a successful battle to overturn the deportation orders for over two score Wobblies. The legal precedents that Recht and Lowe set in these cases facilitated the efforts of Assistant Secretary of Labor Louis Post and other liberals to curb some of the worst excesses of the "deportations delirium" and other similar Red Scare outrages. Once more, we might ask ourselves: What would this period of history have looked like without the Bureau of Legal Advice?

It is important to capture the elusive idealism that underlay these concrete achievements and that concentrated the energies of the individuals associated with the World War I pacifist civil liberties movement. Such people, whether they were activists or "friends" of the movement, were aware of the historic significance of their peace work, and they believed that they could influence the shape of things to come. Fear and hope intermingled in their thoughts, but a forward-looking confidence predominated. For instance, in August 1918, objector Harry Maximon sent a message to Joy Young from military prison: "Please tell Grunzig and the other boys that I hope to meet them all after the war and to cooperate with them in the building of the great palace of peace, of beauty, and of dreams, which will surely come true when the dreamers awake after this terrible nightmare."[10] Other objectors and activists expressed themselves similarly. One month before the war ended, Frieda Ledermann Jasmagy wrote to her in-laws: "I am beginning to grow impatient now, and cry very often all by myself, but I will still make an effort to keep up and prepare for better things."[11] Shortly after the war ended, Ella Reeve Bloor wrote to her good friend Anna Davis: "Oh, my dear sister, pray that the courage to *go* on will come to us all, so that we may make this country of ours safe for the free souls of the coming generation."[12]

In the early 1920s, after the worst of Red Scare mania had receded, representatives from several absolute pacifist organiza-

25. Jessie Wallace Hughan, 1922. Courtesy of Margaret Rockwell Finch.

tions—notably the Fellowship of Reconciliation, the Women's Peace Society, and the Women's Peace Union of the Western Hemisphere—worked together over a period of several years to establish a secular mixed-gender absolute pacifist association, the War Resisters League (WRL). Formally constituted in 1925, the League's founder was Jessie Wallace Hughan. From the outset, Fannie May Witherspoon and Tracy Mygatt were dedicated League members. Those associated with the fledgling organization held the conviction that individuals could end war by refusing to support war; enrolled members pledged in writing never to support war. Hughan, who served as the executive secretary of the League for two decades, never wavered in her belief that the time to work

26. *Frances Witherspoon, 1933. Courtesy of the Swarthmore College Peace Collection.*

for peace was in periods between wars. She and other WRL members did not doubt that future wars were inevitable.

The WRL remained small in the interwar period; its membership never exceeded 1,100. The League was not established to launch a mass movement, however; rather, in Hughan's words, it existed to create a "determined minority" who would refuse their services in wartime: "Wars cannot be fought . . . unless men enlist in armies, unless women contribute their savings, unless workers manufacture and transport munitions."[13] Witherspoon had described the World War I conscientious objector as "a stranger in a strange land" who spoke a language no one understood. The men and women who became members of the WRL—some of whom,

27. Tracy Mygatt, 1933. Courtesy of the Swarthmore College Peace Collection.

like Evan Thomas, had been objectors during the Great War—were not strangers to each other and they did speak a common language. In banding together, they committed themselves to the idea of a world without war and worked concretely on specfic projects with other liberal and radical organizations when WRL principles were not endangered. Under Hughan's tutelage, the League's purpose was clarified; in the interwar period, she developed a clearly reasoned theory of nonviolent resistance to war which was influenced by Quaker thought and by the teachings of Mohandas Gandhi.[14]

Witherspoon and Mygatt, like Hughan, Evan Thomas, and other League members, appreciated that the institutionalization of war in a democratic and patriarchal state was woven into the gender identities, beliefs, attitudes, language, and behaviors of its citizenry. Their World War I experiences as critics and outsiders—as antimilitarists, feminist pacifists, conscientious objectors, and civil libertarians— had convinced them that it was important to strengthen efforts to build peace-oriented communities. Thus, the WRL benefited from the peace and civil liberties movements of the Great War, and the sense of its members that they were part of an evolving peace culture became more focused in the period between the wars—especially in the 1930s, when the spread of fascism in Europe sparked fears that another world war was probable.[15]

When war became a reality for the American people in 1941, the WRL became a strong advocate on behalf of the conscientious objector and worked with other groups to influence the state to accept a more lenient policy towards objectors than had existed during World War I. After the war, young war resisters who had absorbed many insights from their pacifist forebears began to argue that the nonviolent theory and practice of the WRL had to be revised to accommodate the needs of a broader movement for social justice.

The history of the League's role in the civil rights movement of the 1950s and 1960s and in the draft resistance and peace movement of the 1960s awaits its chronicler.[16] However, a gendered analysis will doubtless reveal that League members rejected not only the premise that war is ethically acceptable but also its corollary, that the just warrior and the beautiful soul are desirable citizen ideals.

When we reflect upon the history of the women and men of the peace and freedom movement in World War I America, we can identify the coming-into-being of a peace culture, a new way of thinking about and behaving in the world. The people whose lives we have glimpsed experienced the imperative to combat war and to build peace, a process that they perceived was at once political and personal. Despite the tensions, conflicts, and uncertainties that assailed them at every turn, they labored indefatigably for concrete outcomes at the same time as they sought lives of happiness for themselves and those they loved. Doubtless such individuals, were they alive today, would agree with feminist peace activist and theoretician Ursula Franklin that "pacifism is not anti-war, pacifism is the advocacy of a way of life in which the roots of war are attacked and war is unnecessary."[17]

Notes
Bibliography
Index

Notes

Abbreviations

ACLU	American Civil Liberties Union [Papers]
AUAM	American Union Against Militarism [Papers]
CLB	Caroline Lexow Babcock [Papers]
CR	Charles Recht [Papers]
EGB	Emily Greene Balch [Papers]
EPF	Emergency Peace Federation [Papers]
JWH	Jessie Wallace Hughan [Papers]
LAPP	League for the Amnesty of Political Prisoners [Papers]
LDC	League for Democratic Control [Papers]
LDU	Liberty Defense Union [Papers]
LML	Lola Maverick Lloyd [Papers]
MHC	Michigan Historical Collection
MMR	Mercedes M. Randall [Papers]
NWP	National Woman's Party
NYBLA	New York Bureau of Legal Advice [Papers]
NYPL	New York Public Library
RS	Rebecca Shelley [Papers]
SCPC	Swarthmore College Peace Collection
SL	Arthur and Elizabeth Schlesinger Library, Radcliffe College
TDM/FW	Tracy D. Mygatt and Frances M. Witherspoon [Papers]
TIL	Tamiment Institute Library, New York University
WIL	Women's International League
WPP/NYC	Woman's Peace Party, New York City Branch [Papers]

Introduction

1. For example, Paul L. Murphy's important study *World War I and the Origin of Civil Liberties in the United States* (New York: Norton, 1979) does not refer to the Bureau of Legal Advice or to its founder, Frances Witherspoon. Donald Johnson, in *The Challenge to American Freedoms: World War I and the Rise*

of the American Civil Liberties Union (Lexington: Univ. of Kentucky Press, 1963), makes only a passing reference to the Bureau of Legal Advice. Samuel Walker's recent full-scale history of the ACLU, *In Defense of American Liberties: A History of the ACLU* (New York: Oxford Univ. Press, 1990), mentions the Bureau of Legal Advice once, mistakenly assuming that in 1918, the Bureau was absorbed by the forerunner of the ACLU, the National Civil Liberties Bureau. In fact, the Bureau remained an independent entity until its demise in late 1919; see Frances H. Early, "Feminism, Peace, and Civil Liberties: Women's Role in the Origins of the World War I Civil Liberties Movement," *Women's Studies: An Interdisciplinary Journal* 18, nos. 1–2 (1990): 95–115.

2. G. R. Elton, *The Practice of History* (Melbourne, Australia: Fontana, 1967), 20.

Prologue

1. *New York Evening Post,* Apr. 2, 1917; newspaper clipping in EPF, SCPC.

2. All quotations in this paragraph were culled from a small collection of files and pamphlets, EPF, SCPC.

3. Frances M. Witherspoon and Tracy D. Mygatt, reminiscences, Oral History Research Office, Columbia Univ., 1966, 12. All citations are to a transcription of an original interview.

4. Witherspoon and Mygatt, reminiscences, 18. The lawyer was Harry Weinberger. The case of "People vs. Loewe DeBoer," written up by Weinberger, parallels the story that Witherspoon recounts; see "People vs. Loewe DeBoer," box 3, folder 9, American Legal Defense League, Harry Weinberger Papers, Yale University Library. In an autobiographical essay, Weinberger referred to a "distinguished Dutch historian, engaged in research into the early colonial history of New York City," for whom he obtained a writ of habeas corpus after this individual had been arrested and sent to Bellevue Hospital for observation; see Harry Weinberger, "A Rebel's Interrupted Autobiography," *American Journal of Economics and Sociology* 2, no. 1 (Oct. 1942): 117.

5. Mercedes M. Randall, the biographer of Emily Greene Balch and a comrade of Balch as well as of Witherspoon and other pacifist women of the World War I era, described Witherspoon as "implacably gentle" in *Improper Bostonian: Emily Greene Balch* (New York: Twayne, 1964), 217.

1. Fannie May Witherspoon and the Founding of the Bureau of Legal Advice

1. Frances M. Witherspoon's contribution to *Record of 1908,* Bryn Mawr Archives.

2. Ibid.

3. Frances M. Witherspoon, "Breakfast in a Bag," *Patent Trader,* Feb. 5, 1961; newspaper clipping in box 6, TDM/FMW, SCPC.

4. Frances M. Witherspoon to Mercedes M. Randall, Oct. 25, 1958, box 1, MMR, SCPC.

5. Frances M. Witherspoon, notes on influences that have contributed to Frances Witherspoon's pacifism, box 6, TDM/FMW, SCPC.

6. Witherspoon to Randall, Oct. 25, 1958.

7. Minnie Clapp, diary TDM/FMW, SCPC.

8. "Tracy Dickinson Mygatt," in *The Biographical Cyclopaedia of American Women,* Vol. 2, ed. Erma Conkling Lee (New York: Franklin W. Lee, 1925), 132–34; newspaper clipping, box 11, scrapbook, TDM/FMW, SCPC.

9. The relationship between the two girls is described in *Julia Newberry's Diary* (New York: Norton, 1933) and in Tracy D. Mygatt, *Julia Newberry's Sketch Book or the Life of Two Future Old Maids* (New York: Norton, 1934). A quote from Newberry (12) captures the romance and allure of a relationship that achieved the quality of "legend" in Mygatt's childhood: "My cousin Minnie Clapp & I, Julia R. Newberry . . . have long since decided that we will never marry but be two jolly old maids & live in a house of our own. . . . We do not expect to be at all melancholy but to give balls, dinners & every sort of entertainment except teafights. . . . We shall be happy to receive visits from all our friends, young & old bachelors, married & unmarried ladies, everybody except children which we respectfully request may be left behind."

10. The child was Jesse Kaufman, son of Ida and Abe Kaufman, good friends both of Fannie May Witherspoon and of Tracy Mygatt. Abraham Kaufman, interview by author, Port Charlotte, Fla., May 10, 1989.

11. Carroll Smith-Rosenberg, "The Female World of Love and Ritual: Relations Between Women in Nineteenth-Century America," *Signs: A Journal of Women in Culture and Society* 1 (Autumn 1975): 1–29.

12. See Barbara Miller Solomon, *In the Company of Educated Women: A History of Women and Higher Education in America* (New Haven, Conn.: Yale Univ. Press, 1985); Louise A. Tilly, "Women, Politics, and Change," in *Women, Politics, and Change,* ed. Louise A. Tilly and Patricia Gurin (New York: Russell Sage Foundation, 1990), 1–32; and, for Britain, Martha Vicinus, *Independent Women: Work and Community for Single Women, 1850–1920* (London: Virago, 1985).

13. Nancy Manahan, "Future Old Maids and Pacifist Agitators: The Story of Tracy Mygatt and Frances Witherspoon," *Women's Studies Quarterly* 10, no. 1 (Spring 1982): 10–13.

14. Lillian Faderman, *Surpassing the Love of Men: Romantic Friendship and Love Between Women from the Renaissance to the Present* (New York: William Morrow, 1981), 17–18. For a thoughtful discussion of the conceptual and methodological complexities involved in the biographical rendering of lesbian women's lives, see Liz Stanley, "Romantic Friendships? Some Issues in Researching Lesbian History and Biography," *Women's History Review* 1, no. 2 (1992): 193–216.

15. Kaufman, interview; Margaret Rockwell Finch, interview by author, New Rochelle, N.Y., June 15, 1989.

16. I am indebted to Margaret Rockwell Finch, who permitted me to read the diaries and family correspondence of her two aunts, Evelyn Hughan and Jessie Wallace Hughan, who were among Witherspoon's and Mygatt's closest friends. Margaret Finch's mother, Marjorie Hughan Rockwell (the sister of Evelyn and Jessie), told her daughter that Witherspoon was "in love hopelessly with a married man and then his wife died and before they could marry he died too." The quote is from a notation among the Hughan family papers, in the possession of Margaret Rockwell Finch.

17. The term "Boston marriage" was coined in the late nineteenth century to describe relationships between two unrelated, often professional women, who chose to make homes together for economic or affectional reasons. See Angela Howard Zophy's entry, "Boston Marriages," in *Handbook of American Women's History,* ed. Angela Howard Zophy and Frances M. Kavenik (New York: Garland, 1990), 86. Zophy notes that some of these relationships included sexual intimacy; she also points out that Boston marriages provided women who chose careers with "a reasonable alternative to remaining at home as well as a long-term relationship with a peer."

18. See Blanche Wiesen Cook, "Female Support Networks and Political Activism: Lillian Wald, Crystal Eastman, Emma Goldman," in *A Heritage of Her Own,* ed. Nancy F. Cott and Elizabeth H. Pleck (New York: Simon and Schuster, 1979), 412–44; Judith Schwarz, *Radical Feminists of Heterodoxy: Greenwich Village 1912–1940* (Lebanon, N.H.: New Victoria, 1982); and Suzanne Lebsock, "Women and American Politics, 1880–1920," in *Women, Politics, and Change,* ed. Tilly and Gurin, 35–62. Lebsock argues that the case can be made for "a woman's political culture" in the period that she investigates.

19. Newspaper clipping, box 11, scrapbook, TDM/FMW, SCPC.

20. Ibid.

21. Bryn Mawr alumnae bulletin clipping, box 11, scrapbook, TDM/FMW, SCPC.

22. "Tracy Dickinson Mygatt," 135.

23. Nancy F. Cott, *The Grounding of Modern Feminism* (New Haven, Conn.: Yale Univ. Press, 1987), 37.

24. Ibid., 35.

25. Mari Jo Buhle, *Women and American Socialism, 1870–1920* (Urbana: Univ. of Illinois Press, 1981), 234.

26. Newspaper clipping, box 11, scrapbook, TDM/FMW, SCPC.

27. Buhle, 235.

28. The letter was published in the local paper, the *Meridian Evening Star,* Oct. 1915; newspaper clipping in box 11, scrapbook, TDM/FMW, SCPC.

29. Newspaper clipping [late 1914], box 11, scrapbook, TDM/FMW, SCPC.

30. See David Patterson, *Toward a Warless World: The Travail of the American Peace Movement, 1887–1914* (Bloomington: Indiana Univ. Press, 1976) and Charles Chatfield, *For Peace and Justice: Pacifism in America, 1914–1941* (Knoxville: Univ. of Tennessee Press, 1971).

31. The New York City branch of the national Woman's Peace Party remained uncompromisingly antiwar even after the United States became a belligerent in 1917. See Barbara Steinson, *American Women's Activism in World War I* (N.Y.: Garland, 1982) and Harriet Hyman Alonso, *Peace as a Women's Issue: A History of the U.S. Movement for World Peace and Women's Rights* (Syracuse, N.Y.: Syracuse Univ. Press, 1993).

32. "Anti-Enlistment League Statement," JWH, MRF.

33. Frances M. Witherspoon to Dr. Maria Montessori, Jan. 13, 1917, reel 12.15, correspondence, 1916–19, WPP/NYC, SCPC.

34. Harriet Hyman Alonso, "A Shared Responsibility: The Women and

Men of the People's Council of America for Democracy and Terms of Peace, 1911–1919" (master's thesis, Sarah Lawrence College, 1982).

35. See James R. Mock and Cedric Larson, *Words that Won the War: The Story of the Committee on Public Information 1917–1919* (1939; reprint, New York: Russell and Russell, 1968) and Stephen L. Vaughn, *Holding Fast the Inner Lines: Democracy, Nationalism, and the Committee on Public Information* (Chapel Hill: Univ. of North Carolina Press, 1980).

36. Woodrow Wilson made this statement in a private conversation. Quoted in Randall, 232.

37. Minutes, Apr. 5 conference meeting, EPF, SCPC.

38. On Young's involvement in the National Woman's Party, see Inez Haynes Irwin, *The Story of the Woman's Party* (1921; reprint, New York: Kraus, 1971).

39. Others in attendance were Mr. Schaffer of the Naturalization Aid Bureau (affiliated with *The Forward*), Mrs. Neumann Zilberman, Elizabeth Freeman, Irwin St. John Tucker, Mrs. Russell, and Winter Russell. Minutes, Apr. 5 conference meeting.

40. Harry Weinberger to Margaret Lane, May 3, 1917, reel 12.15, correspondence, 1916–19, WPP/NYC, SCPC; and EPF, SCPC.

41. Frances M. Witherspoon to Theresa Mayer, May 3, 1917, reel 12.15, correspondence, 1916–19, WPP/NYC, SCPC. As early as April 25, the *New York Call* reported that Witherspoon was "in charge of free speech cases" for the Emergency Peace Federation.

42. Hereafter referred to as the Bureau of Legal Advice. Minutes of the executive committee of the Bureau of Legal First Aid, [May 22, 1917], reel 1, box 1, file 13, NYBLA, TIL. The eight women were Frances Witherspoon, Marion B. Cothren, Adelma Burd, Elinor Byrns, Jessie Ashley, Margaret Lane, Martha Gruening, and Mrs. Russell. An earlier meeting was held on May 11, which may actually represent the first organizational effort of the Bureau. See "History of the Bureau of Legal First Aid," reel 1, box 1, file 8, NYBLA, TIL.

43. Minutes of the AUAM executive committee, Apr. 30, 1917, reel 10.1, AUAM, SCPC. The pamphlet by Thomas appeared in May.

44. Minutes, May 7 and May 28, 1917, reel 10.1, AUAM, SCPC; Roger Baldwin, "Recollections of a Life in Civil Liberties—I," *The Civil Liberties Review* 2, no. 2 (1975): 51–54.

45. Minutes of June 2, June 4, and June 15, 1917, reel 10.1, AUAM, SCPC; Crystal Eastman to Emily Greene Balch, June 14, 1917, cited in *Crystal Eastman on Women and Revolution,* ed. Blanche Wiesen Cook (New York: Oxford Univ. Press, 1978), 260.

46. Minutes, June 4, 1917, reel 10.1, AUAM, SCPC.

47. Norman Thomas to Jane Addams, June 6, 1917, reel 12.4, correspondence, 1916–19, WPP/NYC, SCPC.

48. Minutes, summer and fall 1917, reel 10.1, AUAM, SCPC.

49. "History of the Bureau of Legal First Aid," reel 1, box 1, file 8, NYBLA, TIL; Conference on Legal First Aid, reel 1, box 1, file 4, NYBLA, TIL. (File 4 is mistakenly labeled as July 18, 1918; the meeting took place July 18, 1917.) Frances M. Witherspoon to Emily Greene Balch, July 25, 1917, series 2, box 13, EGB, SCPC.

50. "Proposed Aims," reel 1, box 1, file 4, NYBLA, TIL.

51. Woodrow Wilson quoted in Blanche Wiesen Cook, "Woodrow Wilson and the Antimilitarists, 1914–1917" (Ph.D. diss., Johns Hopkins Univ., 1970), 215.

52. No-Conscription League Aims [1917], box 10, RS, MHC; No-Conscription League flyers, World War I Espionage Cases, RG 28, 47480, Records of the U.S. Postal Service, National Archives, Washington, D.C.

2. Free Speech and Personal Behavior in Wartime

1. *New York Times*, June 3, 1917, 1.

2. Press release, 1917, reel 9, box 12, file 1, NYBLA, TIL.

3. See Martha Gruening, "National Association for the Advancement of Colored People (Houston: An NAACP Investigation)," *The Crisis* (Nov. 1917): 14–19.

4. Charles Recht, "Objection Overruled," unpublished memoir, 178–79, CR, TIL. In his reminiscences, Recht mistakenly referred to Gruening's adopted child (born 1912) as Joe Butts. Gruening and her son lived abroad from 1923 to 1931, during which time she worked as a freelance journalist and David attended the Odenwald Schule in Germany; he became a student at City College of New York upon their return to the United States. She remained active in the NAACP until her death in 1937. See Martha Gruening file, Smith College Alumnae Archives, Northhampton, Mass.

5. *Froken Julie* had been translated from Swedish into German; Recht's English translation was based on the German edition. See August Strindberg, *Countess Julia*, trans. Charles Recht (Philadelphia: Brown Brothers, 1912).

6. Recht, "Objection Overruled," esp. 1–14, 137, 154–61.

7. Ibid., 171.

8. Ibid., 29.

9. Various correspondence, minutes, press releases, and newspaper clippings, NYBLA, TIL. See as well Harriot Stanton Blatch, *Challenging Years: The Memoirs of Harriot Stanton Blatch* (1940; reprint, Westport, Conn.: Hyperion, 1976), 109–110; Buhle, 276–78; and Caroline Lexow Babcock, "Elinor Byrns: 1876–1957. Recollections of Her Life," 1, CLB, SL.

10. Secretary's reports, reel 1, box 2, file 20, NYBLA, TIL.

11. Miscellaneous files, EPF, SCPC.

12. *New York Times*, Sept. 21, 1917, *New York Tribune*, Sept. 23, 1917, and *New York Call*, Sept. 29, 1917; newspaper clippings in box 3, scrapbook, NYBLA, SCPC.

13. *New York Call*, Nov. 21, 1917, and *New York Evening World*, Nov. 16, 1917; newspaper clippings in box 3, scrapbook, NYBLA, SCPC; and *The New York Bureau of Legal Advice Yearbook, 1918*, 1, box 10, TDM/FMW, SCPC.

14. *Yearbook, 1918*, 4.

15. Ibid.

16. Rose Samet to Charles Recht, quoted in Recht, "Objection Overruled," 211. See also *Yearkbook, 1918*, 4–5.

17. *Yearbook, 1918*, 5.

18. Magistrate Mancusco, quoted in ibid.

19. Quoted in *New York Call,* Mar. 20, 1919, newspaper clipping in box 3, scrapbook, NYBLA, SCPC.

20. Frances M. Witherspoon to Elinor Byrns, Apr. 2, 1919, reel 12.15, correspondence, 1916–19, WPP/NYC, SCPC.

21. Howard K. Beale, *Are American Teachers Free? An Analysis of Restraints upon the Freedom of Teaching in American Schools* (1936; reprint, New York: Octagon, 1972), 36.

22. Rough draft of pamphlet written by Charles Recht on Gertrude Pignol's case, untitled, reel 4, box 5, file 14, NYBLA, TIL. Pignol's statement "No, I do not . . ." is quoted in this draft.

23. *Yearbook, 1918,* 6.

24. Ibid.

25. Charles F. Howlett, "Quaker Conscience in the Classroom: The Mary S. McDowell Case," *Quaker History* 83 (Fall 1994): 99–115.

26. Various newspaper clippings, 1917 and 1918, box 3, scrapbook, NYBLA, SCPC. Samuel D. Schmalhausen, Thomas Mufson, and A. Henry Schneer, teachers at De Witt Clinton High School, were placed on trial before the board of education in December 1917, after having been suspended in the preceding month on charges of "'holding views subversive of discipline and tending to undermine good citizenship.'" Newspaper clipping, *New York Tribune,* Dec. 3, 1917.

27. Various newspaper clippings for 1917 and 1918, box 3, scrapbook, NYBLA, SCPC. See as well Beale, 22–40 and 50–51, and various files, JWH, SCPC.

28. *Yearbook, 1918,* 7. This statement was quoted by corporation counsel Charles McIntyre during Pignol's May 7 trial and appears on page 86 of the trial transcript; McIntyre attributed the statement to Commissioner of Education Finley. See reel 5, box 5, file 24, NYBLA, TIL.

29. Kathleen Kennedy, "'We Mourn for Liberty in America': Socialist Women, Anti-militarism, and State Repression, 1914–1922" (Ph.D. diss., Univ. of California at Irvine, 1992), esp. 214–21. When not vicious, accusations could be quite petty. For instance, some coworkers sought to discredit Gertrude Pignol by testifying about the content of conversations with her that dated back many years; others spoke of her fondness for a brooch she often wore that bore a cornflower on one side and a picture of the recent Kaiser's grandfather on the other (a childhood souvenir from Pignol's father). See *Yearbook, 1918,* 6–7.

30. Various newspaper clippings, 1917, box 3, scrapbook, NYBLA, SCPC.

31. "The Case of Fedotoff and Taichin: History of Defendants," pamphlet, 2, reel 4, box 5, file 3, NYBLA, TIL. Witherspoon wrote this pamphlet, although no authorship is given in it.

32. Ibid.; press release, Mar. 26, 1918, reel 9, box 12, file 2, NYBLA, TIL; press release, n.d., reel 4, box 5, file 3, NYBLA, TIL; *Yearbook, 1918,* 10.

33. "Case of Fedotoff and Taichin," 6.

34. Ibid., 6–8.

35. Newspaper clipping [1914 or 1915], box 11, scrapbook, TDM/FMW, SCPC.

36. Newspaper clippings, n.d., and various correspondence, LDU, SCPC.

37. Liberty Defense Union flyer, LDU, SCPC. In August, under Flynn's leadership, the Liberty Defense Union became the Workers Liberty Defense Union so that it could focus on the plight of labor people imprisoned under war legislation for union activities. After the armistice, the Union worked for the release of all political prisoners, a topic that will be taken up in chapter 5.

38. Various files, LDU, SCPC.

39. Joy Young to Henry Carliss, July 5, 1918, reel 4, box 5, file 3, NYBLA, TIL.

40. Frances M. Witherspoon to Charles Recht, Dec. 12, 1917, reel 3, box 4, file 5, NYBLA, TIL.

41. Frances M. Witherspoon to Charles Recht, Jan. 30, 1918, reel 3, box 4, file 5, NYBLA, TIL.

42. Frances M. Witherspoon to Charles Recht, June 3, 1918, reel 3, box 4, file 5, NYBLA, TIL.

43. Ibid.

44. Frances M. Witherspoon to Charles Recht, Apr. 24, 1919, reel 3, box 4, file 5, NYBLA, TIL.

45. Ibid.

46. Frances M. Witherspoon to the editor, *New York Evening Call,* Dec. 7, 1917, reel 2, box 2, file 16, NYBLA, TIL. Two weeks later, on Dec. 21, Witherspoon wrote again with the same complaint about the *Call*'s "habit always to de-capitalize us . . . we feel a little shocked as we continue to find ourselves thus treated."

47. Charles Recht to Charles Ervin, July 8, 1919, reel 2, box 2, file 22, NYBLA, TIL.

48. Kathleen Kennedy argues that antimilitarist socialist men, in common with nonsocialist men, preferred women to be essentially domestic and motherly. See Kathleen Kennedy, "Declaring War on War: Gender and the American Socialist Attack on Militarism, 1914–1917," *Journal of Women's History* 7, no. 2 (Summer 1995): 27–51.

49. Witherspoon and Mygatt, reminiscences, 20.

50. Frances M. Witherspoon to Roger Baldwin, Dec. 1, 1917, reel 3, box 3, file 20, NYBLA, TIL.

51. Frances M. Witherspoon to Roger Baldwin, Dec. 6, 1917, reel 3, box 3, file 20, NYBLA, TIL.

52. Frances M. Witherspoon to Roger Baldwin, Jan. 15, 1918, reel 3, box 3, file 20, NYBLA, TIL.

53. Walker, 46. For a biographical study of Baldwin's life, see Peggy Lamson, *Roger Baldwin: Founder of the American Civil Liberties Union* (Boston: Houghton Mifflin, 1976).

54. Baldwin, 54.

55. Ibid. A refreshing alternative male perspective on Rebecca Shelley and her work was articulated by Frederick Lynch, who later became secretary of the Church Peace Union. In a letter to Shelley, Lynch declared: "I did want to say to you . . . how much I admire the superb way in which you have carried through the great things you have set your hands to, and the indomitable will and

unflinching courage you have shown." Frederick Lynch to Rebecca Shelley, Mar. 11, 1917, RS, MHC.

56. Witherspoon and Mygatt, reminiscences, 10.

57. Frances M. Witherspoon to Rebecca Shelley, Nov. 16, 1932, RS, MHC.

58. F. P. Keppel to Roger Baldwin, Aug. 1, 1918, reel 2, vol. 15, ACLU, NYPL.

59. Roger Baldwin to F. P. Keppel, Aug. 2, 1918, reel 2, vol. 15, ACLU, NYPL.

60. Joy Young to F. P. Keppel, Aug. 9, 1918, reel 2, vol. 15, ACLU, NYPL.

61. Surveillance officers of the Military Intelligence Division identified the NYBLA for the first time in March 1918 and reported regularly thereafter to the Department of Justice Bureau of Investigation on the Bureau's activities. The reports reveal the mounting alarm among military and Justice Department officials with regard to dissenters, radicals, and their defenders, but historians need to consult these records with care. The intelligence officers who reported to higher officials often conveyed inaccurate information, which was tinged with hysteria against all outsiders. The Bureau's yearbook of 1918, for instance, was reported to be "on the borderline of espionage cases" and could "be construed as German propaganda," according to one Military Intelligence Division report originating out of New York City. See memo of John M. Dunn, Dec. 19, 1918, Records of the War Department General and Special Staffs Military Intelligence Division, 1917–1941, RG 165, National Archives, Washington, D.C. Similar pronouncements can be found in the Investigative Case Files of the Bureau of Investigation, 1908–1922, Records of the Federal Bureau of Investigation, RG 65, National Archives, Washington, D.C.

62. Joy Young to Frances M. Witherspoon, n.d., box 1, NYBLA, SCPC.

3. Conscription's Home Front Victims and Enemy Aliens

1. David M. Kennedy, *Over Here: The First World War and American Society* (New York: Oxford Univ. Press, 1980), 148. Kennedy notes that the lack of conscription in the first months of war in Great Britain and Canada resulted in the deaths of many college-educated volunteers and men previously employed in essential wartime work. The Wilson administration sought to avoid such a turn of events in the United States with its comprehensive conscription bill.

2. See Vaughn.

3. Woodrow Wilson, quoted in ibid., 150.

4. Frances M. Witherspoon, "Proposed Activities and Program," n.d., reel 1, box 1, file 8, NYBLA, TIL.

5. "Hilda [Kovner] Adel," interview in *Anarchist Voices: An Oral History of Anarchism in America,* ed. Paul Avrich (Princeton, N.J.: Princeton Univ. Press, 1995), 60–61.

6. In fall 1918, the Bureau was forced to move to a new office at 128 East Twenty-eighth Street; the Fellowship of Reconciliation was also housed at this address.

7. Report of "Illegal Conduct of Registrars, Registration Day, June 5,

1917," reel 1, box 1, file 9, NYBLA, TIL. In one of the 42 cases, the clerk's alleged misconduct was not described. Because so much of the Bureau's work came to focus on COs and their families as the war progressed, they will be dealt with in detail in chapter 4.

8. In spring and summer 1917, the New York Municipal Marriage Chapel recorded a great increase in marriages. Mark Sullivan, *Our Times: The United States, 1900–1925* (New York: Scribner's, 1933), 5:308–9.

9. Warren S. Tyron, "The Draft in World War I," *Current History* (June 1968): 367.

10. Ibid., 368. The total number of men serving in the armed services by war's end—including drafted men, voluntary enlistments, and those already in service when war was declared—was just short of five million.

11. *New York Call,* Sept. 22, 1917, newspaper clipping in box 3, scrapbook, NYBLA, SCPC.

12. Samuel McCune Lindsay, "Purpose and Scope of War Risk Insurance," *Annals of the American Academy of Political and Social Science* 79 (1918): 52–68, and Lieutenant-Colonel S. H. Wolfe, "Eight Months of War Risk Insurance Work," *Annals of the American Academy of Political and Social Science* 79 (1918): 68–79.

13. Various newspaper clippings for Sept. 1917, box 3, scrapbook, NYBLA, SCPC.

14. Martin Conboy to the Bureau of Legal Advice, July 24, 1918, reel 8, box 9, file 41, NYBLA, TIL.

15. Frances M. Witherspoon to Leavitt J. Hunt, May 6, 1918, reel 8, box 9, file 64, NYBLA, TIL.

16. Leavitt J. Hunt to Frances M. Witherspoon, May 17, 1918, reel 8, box 9, file 64, NYBLA, TIL.

17. The various correspondence for the Nardone case is found in reel 8, box 10, file 3, NYBLA, TIL.

18. Ibid.

19. Yenta Lumin to the Bureau of Legal Advice [English translation], Oct. 4, 1918, reel 8, box 9, file 29, NYBLA, TIL. The Urechie that Lumin mentions is probably the small town of Ureki near the eastern edge of the Black Sea in present-day Georgia.

20. Various correspondence, reel 8, box 9, file 29, NYBLA, TIL.

21. Pershing, quoted in Wolfe, 76.

22. Lindsay, 57.

23. Mary Willcox Glenn, "Purpose and Methods of a Home Service Section," *Annals of the American Academy of Political and Social Science* 79 (1918): 98.

24. A flyer of the Bureau that was printed in early 1918 noted that four thousand exemption and dependency cases had been handled; by November 1918, the figure cited in the *Yearbook* was five thousand. See flyer, box 1, NYBLA, SCPC, and *Yearbook,* 19.

25. William Gibbs McAdoo quoted in David Kennedy, *Over Here,* 105.

26. David Kennedy, *Over Here,* 143.

27. See Vaughn; H. C. Peterson and Gilbert C. Fite, *Opponents of War, 1917–1919* (Madison: Univ. of Wisconsin Press, 1957); Joan M. Jensen, *The*

Price of Vigilance (Chicago: Rand McNally, 1968); and John Carver Edwards, *Patriotism in Pinstripe: Men of the National Security League* (Washington, D.C.: Univ. Press of America, 1982).

28. See Mock and Larson.

29. Woodrow Wilson, quoted in Frederick C. Luebke, *Bonds of Loyalty: German Americans and World War I* (DeKalb: Northern Illinois Univ. Press, 1974), 234.

30. See Mock and Larson.

31. David Kennedy, *Over Here*, 61.

32. Bessie Louise Pierce, *Public Opinion and the Teaching of History* (1926; reprint, New York: Da Capo, 1970), 110.

33. During and especially immediately following the war, African Americans were victimized by urban mobs outside the South. At immediate issue was job competition as blacks migrated to the northern states to labor in mass production industries, but the underlying force was racism, fed by the wartime notion of 100 percent Americanism, which identified all African Americans as permanent aliens in their own country. This theme will be developed further in chapter 5.

34. Peterson and Fite, 57–58.

35. Ibid., 78–79.

36. See Peterson and Fite, 202–7, for a vivid description of the lynching and of the national response to it.

37. Murphy, 131.

38. Jensen, *Price of Vigilance*, 61.

39. Newspaper clipping, box 3, scrapbook, NYBLA, SCPC.

40. Luebke, 294.

41. Woodrow Wilson quoted in ibid., 247.

42. Luebke, 255–56. Luebke calls these sites of detainment "concentration camps."

43. During the weeks leading up to the war declaration by Congress, there was some discussion among President Wilson's chief advisors of the existence within the nation of peaceful enemy aliens and of the need to protect them from violence. Over the course of the war, government officials and the press occasionally spoke of "friendly" or "neutral" aliens, but the idea that a peaceful enemy alien could exist within the country during wartime disappeared. A nativist repugnance of all things foreign informed public discourse on what was generally perceived to be "the alien problem." See especially Jensen, *Price of Vigilance;* Mock and Larson; and Luebke.

44. *New York Herald,* Nov. 26, 1917, newspaper clipping in box 3, scrapbook, NYBLA, SCPC.

45. All quotes in this paragraph in ibid.

46. Newspaper clipping, *Tacoma (Wash.) Ledger* Nov. 27, 1917, reel 7, vol. 65, ACLU, NYPL.

47. Jensen employs the term "home front war" in her meticulous and thought-provoking study of the American Protective League, *Price of Vigilance.* See also the now classic and still invaluable study by William Preston Jr., *Aliens and Dissenters: Federal Suppression of Radicals, 1903–1933* (1963; reprint, New York: Harper Torchbook, 1966).

48. In the country at large, there were two and one-half million immigrant men of draftable age.

49. Quoted in David Kennedy, *Over Here,* 157. Kennedy points out that in May 1918, quotas were changed and assessed on the basis of men in class I, the most eligible category.

50. Whitman (correspondence with Frances M. Witherspoon) quoted in the *New York Call* (newspaper clipping), Sept. 20, 1917, box 3, scrapbook, NYBLA, SCPC.

51. Ibid.

52. Correspondence between the Bureau and various government officials in the War Department and camp commanders is extensive. See various correspondence files, esp. reel 1, box 2, file 6, and reel 4, box 4, files 16 and 17, NYBLA, TIL, and Bureau correspondence with the War Department, box 1, NYBLA, SCPC.

53. *New York Call,* Sept. 27, 1917, newspaper clipping in box 3, scrapbook, NYBLA, SCPC.

54. Various files on reel 4, NYBLA, TIL.

55. *New York Journal,* Nov. 12, 1917, newspaper clipping in box 3, scrapbook, NYBLA, SCPC. In telegram correspondence to Witherspoon in January 1918, Crowder reiterated that enemy aliens were excluded from military liability even if declarants. Those already in service illegally were instructed to contact the Adjutant General of the Army, because Crowder's authority as provost marshal ceased with an individual's induction into the army; see reel 4, box 4, file 17, NYBLA, TIL. One month later, the National Civil Liberties Bureau representative in Washington, D.C., Lawrence Todd, informed Witherspoon that conscripted alien enemies had to request release from the camp commandant, who would then relay the proposal to the adjutant general's office. Todd also noted that it was not to be publicly announced that enemy aliens could obtain official discharges; each case had to be taken up individually. Witherspoon was most annoyed and recognized the harsh implications of such a policy: "If no blanket order is to be issued, and if upon each man, no matter how often he may have sought his discharge, the burden of proof still rests, I presume we can only hope for success once in a while in an individual case." Various correspondence, reel 4, box 4, file 14, NYBLA, TIL.

56. Austrian Max Pfloun, a Bureau client, is representative. In an August 1917 deposition to local board #10 in the Bronx, Pfloun requested a reversal of his induction order. He pointed out that he had two brothers fighting in the Austrian army on the western front and quoted an 1871 Austrian law, still in effect, stating that the death penalty for "high treason" could be imposed on Austrians returning to their homelands who had served in the army of an enemy country. The local board's decision does not appear in the records. See reel 8, box 10, file 12, NYBLA, TIL.

57. Newspaper clippings, Oct. and Nov. 1917, box 3, scrapbook, NYBLA, SCPC.

58. In Latin *certiorari* means "to be informed of." A writ of certiorari requires an inferior court to supply to a superior court a certified record of a particular case. The purpose of the writ is to determine whether there have been

irregularities in the case in question. An injunction is an order requiring a person or persons to do a particular act or to refrain from doing a particular act. On certiorari, see Henry Campbell Black, *Black's Law Dictionary,* 6th ed. (St. Paul, Minn.: West, 1990), 228.

59. Quoted in *Yearbook, 1918,* 14, box 10, TDM/FMW, SCPC.

60. Ibid.

61. Quotation of Ex-parte Pfefer vs. Bell, in Charles Recht, "Mobilizing the Judicia," 11, reel 1, box 2, file 17, NYBLA, TIL.

62. Ibid., 12.

4. Feminist Pacifists and Conscientious Objectors

1. See Jean Bethke Elshtain, *Women and War* (New York: Basic Books, 1987); Cynthia Enloe, *Does Khaki Become You? The Militarisation of Women's Lives,* 2nd ed. (London: Pandora Press; New York: Unwin Hyman, 1988); and Betty A. Reardon, *Sexism and the War System* (New York: Teachers College Press, 1985). Elshtain is particularly insightful in her explication of the "just warrior" and "beautiful soul" constructs. She has noted that a counter ideal of the "woman warrior" has existed from time immemorial and has never completely disappeared in western culture. In like manner, Elshtain identifies the ideal of the pacific male, although historically this latter religiously-based construct has lacked the popular appeal of the woman warrior ideal. She employs the just warrior and beautiful soul constructs in the context of western cultural development over the past two centuries. The literature on gender and war is now extensive; useful anthologies of interdisciplinary approaches to this topic include Margaret Randolph Higonnet, Jane Jensen, Sonya Michel, and Margaret Collins Weitz, eds., *Behind the Lines: Gender and the Two World Wars* (New Haven, Conn.: Yale Univ. Press, 1987); Eva Isaksson, ed., *Women and the Military System* (Hertfordshire, Eng.: Harvester-Wheatsheaf, 1988); Jean Bethke Elshtain and Sheila Tobias, eds., *Women, Militarism, and War: Essays in History, Politics, and Social Theory* (Savage, Md.: Rowman and Littlefield, 1990); and Miriam Cooke and Angela Woollacott, eds., *Gendering War Talk* (Princeton, N.J.: Princeton Univ. Press, 1993). Also important is Joan W. Scott, "Women and War: A Focus for Rewriting History," *Women's Studies Quarterly* 12, no. 2 (Summer 1984): 2–6, and a number of essays published in a special issue of *Women's Studies Quarterly,* edited by Linda Rennie Forcey and Amy Swerdlow, entitled "Rethinking Women's Peace Studies" (23, nos. 3–4 [Fall/Winter 1995]). See especially the articles in the section "Gender and the Culture of Militarism."

2. See Enloe; Michele J. Shover, "Roles and Images of Women in World War I Propaganda," *Politics and Society* 5 (1975): 469–86, and, on a related topic, Linda Schott, "Jane Addams and William James on Alternatives to War," *Journal of the History of Ideas* 54, no. 2 (Apr. 1993): 241–54.

3. Gerald Edwin Shenk, " 'Work or Fight': Selective Service and Manhood in the Progressive Era" (Ph.D. diss., Univ. of California at San Diego, 1992), 18. A useful general history of U.S. manhood is E. Anthony Rotundo, *American Manhood: Transformations in Masculinity from the Revolution to the Modern Era* (New York: Basic Books, 1993). On the formation of a self-conscious white male elite

concept of manliness in the Progressive era, see John D'Emilio and Estelle B. Freedman, *Intimate Matters: A History of Sexuality in America* (New York: Harper and Row, 1988), 203–15. Of interest as well is J. A. Mangan and James Walvin, eds., *Manliness and Morality: Middle-Class Masculinity in Britain and America, 1800–1940* (Manchester, Eng.: Manchester Univ. Press, 1987). A fascinating new study, which draws insightfully upon feminist and postmodern theories of gender, is Gail Bederman, *Manliness & Civilization: A Cultural History of Gender and Race in the United States, 1880–1917* (Chicago: Univ. of Chicago Press, 1995). The historical literature on masculinity is most extensive for the Victorian era; see, for instance, Mark Carnes and Clyde Griffen, eds., *Meanings for Manhood: Constructions of Masculinity in Victorian America* (Chicago: Univ. of Chicago Press, 1990).

4. Kathleen Kennedy, "'We Mourn for Liberty,'" 10.

5. Ibid., 86. See also Kathleen Kennedy, "Declaring War on War." Of related interest in the Australian context is Joy Damousi, "Socialist Women and Gendered Space: The Anti-Conscription and Anti-War Campaigns of 1914–1918," *Labour History* [Australia] 4 (1991): 1–15.

6. Bureau of Legal Advice flyer [May 1917], reel 1, box 1, file 15, NYBLA, TIL.

7. The exact number of objectors, according to the War Department, was 3,989. See Norman Thomas, *Is Conscience a Crime?* (1923; reprint, New York: Garland, 1972), 14.

8. For a useful overview of the history of conscientious objectors in the United States, see John Whiteclay Chambers II, "Conscientious Objectors and the American State from Colonial Times to the Present," in *The New Conscientious Objection: From Sacred to Secular Resistance*, ed. Charles C. Moskos and John Whiteclay Chambers II (New York: Oxford Univ. Press, 1993), 23–46.

9. The pamphlet provided facts regarding exemptions from military service under the Selective Service Act. It was distributed widely by the American Union. See Norman Thomas, *Conscription and the "Conscientious Objector" to War* (Washington, D.C.: American Union Against Militarism, May 1917), box 10, RS, MHC.

10. In his pamphlet on the CO, Thomas mentioned that the Bureau of Legal Advice (initially called the Bureau of Legal First Aid) was already established and advised that "communications regarding cases in and about New York should be addressed to this bureau." Thomas, *Conscription*, 7.

11. It was left to the discretion of local board officials to decide which sects or churches possessed creeds that warranted CO exemption.

12. "Selective Service Regulations, 1917," in *Conscience in America: A Documentary History of Conscientious Objection in America, 1757–1967*, ed. Lillian Schlissel (New York: E. P. Dutton, 1968), 133.

13. In the first draft call, the registration form contained just one line in which to write one's reason for requesting exempt status; many individuals did not realize that they could request CO status on this form. In the second and subsequent draft calls, registrants were provided with a questionnaire, which included a section entitled "religious conviction against war." If a local draft board ruled a registrant to be a religious CO on the basis of the completed

questionnaire, he was provided with a certificate that exempted him from combatant service. The drafted man was still in the army but was eligible for "such military service as may be declared noncombatant by the President of the United States." See "Selective Service Questionnaire (Form 1001), 1917," in Schlissel, 134–35.

14. A useful chronological overview of the evolution of the war administration's policies towards COs is found in Johnson.

15. Bureau flyer [May 1917], reel 1, box 1, file 15, NYBLA, TIL.

16. Recht, "Objection Overruled," 186.

17. John W. Chambers, "Introduction" to *The Conscientious Objector,* by Walter Guest Kellogg (1919; reprint, New York: Garland, 1972), 8.

18. There were exceptions, however. Some military personnel could not tolerate sustained abuse against objectors. For example, objector William Breidert related an incident at Fort Riley where some rough treatment occurred as a result of "some petty officers [who] forgot themselves. . . . One of the sergeants [*sic*] that was put in charge of us is in the hospital suffering from a nervous breakdown. He sure has my sympathy as he was quite a likable old chap." William Breidert to Marie [surname absent], Aug. 7, 1918, box 2, NYBLA, SCPC.

19. Chambers, "Introduction," 9.

20. At war's end, the War Department identified an estimated 171,000 men as draft evaders. Schlissel, 130.

21. Thomas, *Is Conscience a Crime?* 18.

22. Chambers, "Introduction," 12.

23. The War Department reported that 1,300 men "originally accepted or were assigned to noncombatant service." Ninety-nine men joined the Friends Reconstruction Unit in France. Thomas, *Is Conscience a Crime?* 15.

24. Copy of memorandum for the adjutant-general, Apr. 23, 1918, box 1, NYBLA, SCPC. The order went out to military authorities on April 27. Earlier, in December 1917, Baker had expanded the concept of conscientious objector when he sent a secret directive to military authorities instructing them to treat men with "personal scruples against war . . . in the same manner as other conscientious objectors." Order as quoted by Johnson, 33.

25. Bureau of Legal Advice notes, box 1, NYBLA, SCPC.

26. Walter Nelles to President Woodrow Wilson, Apr. 16, 1918, reel 12.3, COs, 1917–18, WPP/NYC, SCPC. The letter made extensive use of Gellert's own diary and included excerpts from his court-martial, which took place December 14, 1917. It makes chilling reading. At one point, the gentle young man, whom Nelles described as "tolerant, sweet-tempered, and utterly an idealist," was put in solitary confinement for three months and was given two slices of bread per meal. The cell was so cold that he was eventually removed to a hospital, where he was found to be suffering from chilblains and fallen arches from lack of exercise. Just before his court-martial, Gellert was kept standing at attention for many hours in a blizzard. He was interviewed frequently by officers. Gellert was at Camp Upton from October 1917 until early January 1918. He was never allowed to see his family or friends again after removal to Fort Hancock.

27. Recht, "Objection Overruled," 187.

28. Norman Thomas noted that this term was used to measure "not the quality of a man's sincerity but the absoluteness of his refusal to make any terms with the government under conscription." Thomas, *Is Conscience a Crime?* 2, n. 1.

29. Schlissel, 131. Forty COs were court-martialed and given long prison sentences before the board of inquiry was established. A number of objectors were still in military camps pending final disposition of their cases when the armistice was signed.

30. The best known are Ernest L. Meyer, *Hey! Yellowbacks: The War Diary of a Conscientious Objector* (New York: John Day, 1930); Harold Studley Gray, *Character "Bad": The Story of a Conscientious Objector* (1934; reprint, New York: Garland, 1971); Julius Eichel, *The Judge Said "20 Years": The Story of a Conscientious Objector in World War I* (New York: War Resisters League, 1981); Howard W. Moore, *Plowing My Own Furrow* (1985; reprint, Syracuse, N.Y.: Syracuse Univ. Press, 1993); and Charles Chatfield, ed., *The Radical "No": The Correspondence and Writings of Evan Thomas on War* (New York: Garland, 1974). See also R. Alfred Hassler, *Conscripts of Conscience: The Story of Sixteen Objectors to Conscription* (1942) and Arle Brooks and Robert J. Leach, *Help Wanted! The Experiences of Some Quaker Conscientious Objectors* (1940) (reprinted in one volume, New York: Garland, 1971), and Roderick Seidenburg, "I Refuse to Serve," *American Mercury* (Jan. 1932): 91–99. Unfortunately, memoirs of African American objectors have not been published. According to Norman Thomas, few African Americans became objectors and those who did were generally objectors on religious grounds; see *Is Conscience a Crime?* 21–22. Standard histories of the African American experience during World War I stress men's struggle, against the odds, to become combat soldiers and officers (and, thereby, bona fide soldier citizens). See, for instance, John Hope Franklin and Alfred A. Moss Jr., *From Slavery to Freedom: A History of African Americans,* 7th ed. (New York: McGraw Hill, 1994), 325–30.

31. See, for instance, Peterson and Fite; David Kennedy, *Over Here;* and Johnson. Norman Thomas's *Is Conscience a Crime?* (first published in 1923) is the only book-length treatment of World War I objector history; A new and comprehensive history is required.

32. Various files on CO clients, reels 6 and 7, NYBLA, TIL. Also useful is a handwritten list of mostly absolutist objectors compiled over a number of months by at least four different people, presumably objectors in their respective camps. Completed sometime in February 1919, when some objectors had already been discharged, the profile of 236 men reveals that there were twice as many political objectors as religious objectors (155 to 72) and 157 citizens. Names of men who were Bureau clients appear on the list; eighteen of these 22 men were either socialist or humanitarian COs. There were several "colored" objectors on the list but none of them were Bureau clients. See box 2, NYBLA, SCPC.

33. Howard Moore, another political objector and a friend of Grunzig's during and after the war, told me in an interview conducted at his home in Cherry Valley, N.Y., on Aug. 23, 1991, that during the war years "Bruno Grunzig was in love with Frances Witherspoon."

34. Anna N. Davis to Frances M. Witherspoon, Dec. 7, 1918, reel 5, box 6, file 2, NYBLA, TIL.

35. [Frances M. Witherspoon], *Who Are the Conscientious Objectors?* (Brooklyn, N.Y.: Committee of 100 Friends of Conscientious Objectors, 1919), 15, reel 5, box 6, file 2, NYBLA, TIL. Witherspoon's name does not appear on the pamphlet as the author, but a letter to Charles Recht confirms that she wrote it.

36. Ibid., 19.

37. Shenk, 572.

38. Bruno Grunzig to Frances M. Witherspoon, June 23, 1918, box 2, NYBLA, SCPC. Grunzig mentioned that forty "colored men" were part of this debased group, but added that by their own admission, they "had tried to duck and then if arrested agree to fight." He also related a stereotypically racist incident in a casual, unreflecting manner: "We were then searched and everything taken away even unto a few cigarette papers, newspapers, pencil and an empty whiskey flask which one colored boy claimed he had carried with him since his marriage, 4 years ago, it having been presented to him, quite full, as a wedding present."

39. Bruno Grunzig to Frances M. Witherspoon, July 11, 1918, box 2, NYBLA, SCPC.

40. Bruno Grunzig to Frances M. Witherspoon, Aug. 6, 1918, box 2, NYBLA, SCPC.

41. Bruno Grunzig to Tracy D. Mygatt, May 7, 1919, box 2, NYBLA, SCPC. Six months later, Grunzig had modified his view of the Molokan objectors, as the following comment in a letter to Witherspoon indicates: "I am glad that Tracy is doing so well with her plays. I liked *Good Friday,* first rate with the reservations made some time ago. We received one copy here a few weeks ago, and everybody thought it was really very powerful. The little sketch will always call to mind those fine, big Molokan boys before whom one almost stood is awe. Just as simple as children but with an appeal to one's heart that was just an undeniable. They were great stuff and Tracy did them up in excellent style." Bruno Grunzig to Frances M. Witherspoon, Nov. 1, 1919, box 6, TDM/FMW, SCPC. Thomas declared that the Molokans were the "religious sectarians best loved by their fellow-objectors in Fort Leavenworth Military Prison"; see the discussion of Molokans in Thomas, *Is Conscience a Crime?* 50–54, 150–54.

42. Quoted in Joyce L. Kornbluh, *Rebel Voices: An Anthology* (Ann Arbor: Univ. of Michigan Press, 1984): 316.

43. Bruno Grunzig to Frances M. Witherspoon, July 11, 1918, box 2, NYBLA, SCPC.

44. Bruno Grunzig to Frances M. Witherspoon, Aug. 9 and Nov. 12, 1918, box 2, NYBLA, SCPC. The word "negro" appeared on the right margin of the letter beside Morgan's name; "colored" appeared in parentheses beside Clayton's name. The occasional references to an African American objector in the Bureau of Legal Advice files, whether in letters, camp treatment reports, or objector lists, show the name followed with the word "colored" or "negro" in parentheses. No substantive discussion of African American objectors appears in any of the sources I have examined. Norman Thomas's jocular and dismissive attitude towards African American objectors makes obnoxious but instructive

reading today, particularly his derisive account of a Camp Upton "devoutly religious colored brother"—reminiscent of the character of Uncle Tom in Harriet Beecher Stowe's mid-nineteenth-century best-selling novel, *Uncle Tom's Cabin*—complete with quotes written in the Joel Chandler Harris "Uncle Remus" dialect. Both Thomas's story and the one recounted by Grunzig (see note 38) reinforce the "soft" racist view of the "good" African American man as an earnest, naive individual with a childlike trust in simple Christian verities. See Thomas, *Is Conscience a Crime?* 133.

45. Bruno Grunzig to Frances M. Witherspoon, July 19, 1918, box 2, NYBLA, SCPC.

46. Bruno Grunzig to Frances M. Witherspoon, Aug. 9, 1918, box 2, NYBLA, SCPC.

47. Bruno Grunzig to Frances M. Witherspoon, Nov. 1, 1918, box 2, NYBLA, SCPC.

48. Bruno Grunzig to Frances M. Witherspoon, Nov. 12, 1918, box 2, NYBLA, SCPC.

49. Grunzig was, at the same time, anxious to distance himself from some religious objectors whom he perceived as effeminate and to bind himself tightly in comradeship with "Reds" whom he saw as unambiguously masculine in their behavior. George Chauncy Jr. argues that a multiplicity of sexual discourses coexisted in civilian and in military communities during the war years. However, effeminate behavior rather than specific kinds of sexual activities or choice of sexual partner seemed to be the most widely accepted standard among men for determining male sexual identity as either—in the popular parlance of the day—"queer" or "straight." Grunzig's hostility towards the "religious nuts and their effeminate ways" takes on new meaning in light of Chauncey's findings. See George Chauncy Jr., "Christian Brotherhood or Sexual Perversion? Homosexual Identities and the Construction of Sexual Boundaries in the World War I Era," in *Hidden from History: Reclaiming the Gay and Lesbian Past,* ed. Martin Bauml Duberman, Martha Vicinus, and George Chauncey Jr. (New York: New American Library, 1989), 294–317. Of related interest is Kevin White, *The First Sexual Revolution: The Emergence of Male Heterosexuality in Modern America* (New York: New York Univ. Press, 1993).

50. Grunzig to Witherspoon, Nov. 12, 1918.

51. Statement of Miss Navard, box 2, NYBLA, SCPC.

52. Statement of Mrs. William Jasmagy, box 2, NYBLA, SCPC.

53. Statement of Miss Navard.

54. Ibid.

55. Statement of Mrs. William Jasmagy.

56. Statement of Miss Navard.

57. Ibid.

58. Spiller's attitude reflected a common assumption that pacifist men were cowards and unfit for marriage. For instance, on February 25, 1917, the *New York Times* reported approvingly that girl students of the Tewksbury School in Scarsdale, New York, had been advised to refuse to marry pacifists or men with pacifist tendencies. Part of the speech was quoted: "Always throughout life remember that the man who will not defend his country will not defend his

wife, his child, his home. Do not marry such a man. Do not have such among your friends. Make the first test of the young men you admit to your acquaintance, their patriotism. Carry this formula throughout life: No man who is not a patriot is to be trusted with a woman's welfare."

59. Statement of Mrs. Brandon, box 2, NYBLA, SCPC.

60. During the war, military and government officials aligned with a number of progressive reformers in an attempt to lessen the perceived threat of venereally-infected prostitutes to the health of soldiers. In some literature, prostitutes were likened to alien enemies, and in some areas of the country, draconian measures to arrest, quarantine and imprison, and reform prostitutes were instituted. By the end of the war, "a girl problem" was deemed to exist, whereby even "respectable" girls and women were viewed as potential or actual "bad girls" who threatened the health and morals of enlisted men. For a detailed discussion on this topic, see Alan M. Brandt, *No Magic Bullet: A Social History of Venereal Disease in the United States since 1880* (New York: Oxford Univ. Press, 1985), esp. chapter 2. See also Lieutenant George J. Anderson, "Making the Camps Safe for the Army," *Annals of the American Academy of Political and Social Sciences* 79 (1918): 143–51, and Henrietta S. Additon, "Work Among Delinquent Women and Girls," *Annals of the American Academy of Political and Social Sciences* 79 (1918): 152–66.

61. Frances M. Witherspoon to Mrs. William Jasmagy, Jan. 18, 1919, reel 6, box 7, file 19, NYBLA, TIL.

62. Frances M. Witherspoon to Mabel Higgins, Oct. 25, 1918, reel 6, box 7, file 19, NYBLA, TIL.

63. Frances M. Witherspoon to Mrs. W. J. Jasmagy, [Oct. 1918], reel 6, box 7, file 34, NYBLA, TIL.

64. This was in reference to Louis Kramer, a political prisoner at the Essex County Penitentiary in Caldwell, New Jersey; Frances M. Witherspoon to Jessie Lee Sheppard, July 23, 1919, reel 4, box 4, file 11, NYBLA, TIL. Sheppard had offered to visit Kramer under the auspices of the Bureau of Legal Advice.

65. See Ella Reeve Bloor, *We Are Many: An Autobiography* (New York: International Publishers, 1940). Bloor's papers are located in the Sophia Smith Collection, Women's History Archive, Smith College, Northampton, Mass.

66. Mrs. William Jasmagy to "Mother Bloor," Jan. 7, 1919, reel 6, box 7, file 19, NYBLA, TIL.

67. Ella Reeve Bloor to Anna N. Davis, Dec. 30, 1918, reel 6, box 7, file 19, NYBLA, TIL.

68. Thomas, *Is Conscience a Crime?* 155.

69. A typescript manuscript of ten pages, entitled "Report of Treatment of Conscientious Objectors at the Camp Funston Guard House," exists in the Bureau files; the report consists mostly of Ben Breger's diary. See box 2, NYBLA, SCPC. This report was published in pamphlet form under the same title (see same archive) in December 1918 by the Friends and Relatives of Conscientious Objectors. The National Civil Liberties Bureau published a pamphlet on these and other instances of brutal treatment against COs, and one of its branches in Chicago, headed by Lenetta M. Cooper (a frequent correspondent of Witherspoon's), published another version of the Camp Funston outrages, as they came

to be known, entitled *What Happens in Military Prisons: The Public is Entitled to the Facts* [1919], general correspondence, 1919, LML, NYPL. In January 1919, a congressional investigation was held on the treatment of objectors in military camps and prisons; parts of the Camp Funston diary were read into the Congressional Record. See speech of Hon. Charles H. Dillon, *Introducing Examples of Brutalities, Tortures, and Deaths to Political Prisoners Under Military Régime* (Washington, D.C.: Government Printing Office, 1919).

70. See, for example, Walter Nelles to Woodrow Wilson, Apr. 16, 1918, reel 12.3, COs, 1917–18, WPP/NYC, SCPC.

71. Stephen M. Kohn, *Jailed For Peace: The History of American Draft Law Violations, 1658–1985* (Westport, Conn.: Greenwood, 1986), 29.

72. Moore, *Plowing My Own Furrow*, 136.

73. Howard Moore to Frances M. Witherspoon, Dec. 19, 1919, box 2, NYBLA, SCPC.

74. Excerpt from William Jasmagy's court-martial records, reel 6, box 7, file 19, NYBLA, TIL.

75. A small number of Molokans had emigrated from Russia to the United States after 1903, at about the same time as the Dukhobors, on the understanding that they would be exempt from military service. The Molokans were vegetarians and were guided by the Holy Spirit to be nonresistants. By 1917, they had become prosperous farmers in Arizona. See Thomas, *Is Conscience a Crime?* 50–54, 149–55.

76. Evan W. Thomas to Colonel Sedgwick Rice, Nov. 5, 1918, box 1, NYBLA, SCPC.

77. Bulletin [of the National Civil Liberties Bureau], box 1, NYBLA, SCPC; excerpts from *Political Prisoners in Federal Military Prisons, 1918,* published by the National Civil Liberties Bureau, in Schlissel, 150–59. Some of the documents cited in this pamphlet were supplied to the Civil Liberties Bureau by the Bureau of Legal Advice.

78. Moore, *Plowing My Own Furrow*, 137.

79. Excerpts from Judge Mayer's remarks in imposing sentence, in Schlissel, 148–49.

80. Erling Lunde, quoted in [Witherspoon], *Who Are the Conscientious Objectors?* 18.

81. [Witherspoon], *Who Are the Conscientious Objectors?* 13.

82. Evan W. Thomas, Howard W. Moore, Erling H. Lunde, and Harold S. Gray to Newton Baker, Aug. 21, 1918, box 2, NYBLA, SCPC.

83. Moore, *Plowing My Own Furrow*, 122.

84. Ibid., 125–26.

85. Frances M. Witherspoon, "If This Happened in Russia," [Nov. 1918], reel 3, box 4, file 19, NYBLA, TIL.

86. Ibid.

87. Ibid.

88. [Witherspoon], *Who Are the Conscientious Objectors?* 3.

89. Thomas's pamphlet, *War's Heretics: A Plea for the Conscientious Objector,* is reproduced in the Garland edition of Thomas's book *Is Conscience a Crime?* It was originally issued by the Civil Liberties Bureau in August 1917.

90. [Witherspoon], *Who Are the Conscientious Objectors?* 18–19.

91. Press release of the War Department News Bureau, no. 9, Dec. 6, 1918, box 2, NYBLA, SCPC. This was the first time the administration used the term "political prisoner"; the term "conscientious objector" does not appear in this document.

5. The Push for Amnesty

1. Joy Young to Frances M. Witherspoon [July or Aug. 1918], box 1, NYBLA, SCPC.

2. *New York Times,* Sept. 1, 1918, newspaper clipping in box 3, scrapbook, NYBLA, SCPC.

3. Fannie May Witherspoon and Jessie Ashley, letters, Oct. 1918 and Jan. 1919, reel 1, box 2, file 4, NYBLA, TIL.

4. Emma Goldman, *Living My Life,* abridged ed., eds. Richard and Anna Maria Drinnon (New York: New American Library, 1977), 676.

5. Recht, "Objection Overruled," draft of chapter 11, part 2 ("The *Masses* Trial"), 10–12.

6. Frances M. Witherspoon to Anna R. Brenner, Oct. 17, 1918, reel 1, box 2, file 9, NYBLA, TIL.

7. Frances M. Witherspoon to Laura Hughes Lunde, Nov. 18 and 25, 1918, box 1, NYBLA, SCPC.

8. Frances M. Witherspoon to Laura Hughes Lunde, Nov. 26, 1995, box 1, NYBLA, SCPC.

9. Barbara Roberts, "Women Against War, 1914–1918: Francis Benyon and Laura Hughes," in *Up and Doing: Canadian Women and Peace,* ed. Janice Williamson and Deborah Gorham (Toronto: Women's Press, 1989): 48–65, and "Women's Peace Activism in Canada," in *Beyond the Vote: Canadian Women and Politics,* ed. Joan Sangster and Linda Kealey (Toronto: Univ. of Toronto Press, 1989), 279–85.

10. On Gertrude Richardson, see the compelling study by Barbara Roberts, *A Reconstructed World: A Feminist Biography of Gertrude Richardson* (Montreal: McGill-Queen's Univ. Press, 1996).

11. Frances M. Witherspoon to William Simpson, Nov. 25, 1918, reel 3, box 3, file 20, NYBLA, TIL. In her secretary's report to the Bureau for November, Witherspoon wrote in reference to the Friends of COs: "A committe was appointed to work up a 'spontaneous uprising of indignant families and friends.'" See reel 1, box 2, file 20, NYBLA, TIL. By mid-summer 1919, Witherspoon admitted to a Bureau correspondent that the Friends of COs "are in a way a sub-committee of this organization on whose stationery I write you, and of which I am secretary." Frances M. Witherspoon to Miss V. Thomas, June 18, 1919, reel 5, box 6, file 4, NYBLA, TIL.

12. Roger Baldwin traveled to Chicago in April 1917 to facilitate the establishment of the American Liberty Defense League. However, the Civil Liberties Bureau, in Albert De Silver's words, "adopted the policy when it was formed not to authorize any branch organizations, but to cooperate as fully as possible with all organizations who had in mind purposes similar to ours." See

Albert De Silver to Lenetta Cooper, Feb. 23, 1919, reel 12, vol. 98, ACLU, NYPL. The League for Democratic Control was established in April 1917 as the Boston branch of the American Union Against Militarism. See LDC, SCPC.

13. For an insightful study of a second echelon feminist pacifist leader, see Melanie Gustafson, "Lola Maverick Lloyd: 'Truly a Live Wire and a Brick' . . . a Militant Pacifist" (Master's thesis, Sarah Lawrence College, 1983).

14. Press release, box 1, NYBLA, SCPC. The notion of "character" was central to the Victorian bourgeois ideal of manliness. Arnaldo Testi examines this theme in his insightful article "The Gender of Reform Politics: Theodore Roosevelt and the Culture of Masculinity," *Journal of American History* 81, no. 4 (Mar. 1995): 1509–33; see also Bederman.

15. Frances M. Witherspoon to Mrs. Frank Moore, Dec. 28, 1918, reel 5, box 6, file 2, NYBLA, TIL.

16. Frances M. Witherspoon to Lenetta Cooper, Dec. 28, 1918, reel 5, box 6, file 2, NYBLA, TIL.

17. Witherspoon and Mygatt, reminiscences, 28.

18. Thomas, *Is Conscience a Crime?* 197.

19. Howard Moore was badly beaten about the face in one incident, resulting in broken bones in one hand for the officer who had administered the beating. On another occasion, a fire hose was aimed for many minutes into the CO barracks at Douglas, resulting in physical injuries and mental anguish for several objectors. One man became hysterical and suffered temporary insanity in the aftermath of the hosing. See Moore, *Plowing My Own Furrow*, chapter 18.

20. Witherspoon was apprised of this situation through the women's civil liberties networking channels, which reached to the west coast by 1919. See, for instance, forwarded letter of Marion S. Alderton to Eleanor Fitzgerald, Sept. 10, 1919, reel 2, box 3, file 11, NYBLA, TIL, and excerpt of letter from Margaret Stanislawsky, Sept. 21 [1919], box 1, NYBLA, SCPC. Witherspoon's and Theodore Lunde's exchange of letters with War Department officials and the commandant of the Alcatraz military prison is found in Bureau files; Lunde also wrote to members of Congress with regard to this issue. See reel 5, box 6, file 5, NYBLA, TIL.

21. Thomas, *Is Conscience a Crime?* 236–43, 249. Thomas does not provide the first names of Grosser and Simmons; a newspaper clipping in the Bureau of Legal Advice records supplies Grosser's forename but not that of Simmons. The near-invisibility of African American COs in the secondary sources and the scattered nature of references in primary materials underscore the need for a comprehensive study of this topic. John H. Stanfield II addresses this need in his article "The Dilemma of Conscientious Objection for Afro-Americans," in ed. Moskos and Chambers, 47–56. On the treatment of COs in this postwar period see Moore, *Plowing My Own Furrow*, esp. chapters 16 through 19.

22. Thomas, *Is Conscience a Crime?* 275.

23. Chicago activists Theodore Lunde and Lenetta Cooper were mainly responsible for this. In January 1919, the *New York World* published a five-part series on conditions in military prisons, which helped to bring attention to the plight of political prisoners, including COs, in such institutions.

24. The article appeared in the Feb. 1, 1919, issue.

25. Frances M. Witherspoon to Theodore Lunde, Jan. 30, 1919, reel 3, file 16, NYBLA, TIL. See also correspondence of released objectors to the Bureau, box 2, NYBLA, SCPC.

26. Circular letter of the Friends of COs, June 1919, reel 5, box 6, file 2, NYBLA, TIL.

27. Roger Baldwin, quoted in the *Milwaukee Leader,* Mar. 11, 1919, newspaper clipping in box 3, scrapbook, NYBLA, SCPC.

28. Joseph Kantor to Jules Wortsmann, July 1, 1919; Frances M. Witherspoon to Joseph Kantor, July 11, 1919; Joseph Kantor to Frances M. Witherspoon, July 15, 1919; and Frances M. Witherspoon to Joseph Kantor, Aug. 8, 1919, reel 5, box 6, file 5, NYBLA, TIL.

29. Stephen M. Kohn provides a useful overview in *American Political Prisoners: Prosecution Under the Espionage and Sedition Acts* (Westport, Conn.: Praeger, 1994).

30. See discussion, chapter 2.

31. Ella Reeve Bloor to Frances M. Witherspoon, July 10, 1919, reel 2, box 2, file 8, NYBLA, TIL.

32. Goldman, 652; Lucy Robins Lang, *Tomorrow Is Beautiful* (New York: MacMillan, 1948), 122; and Paul Avrich, *The Modern School Movement: Anarchism and Education in the United States* (Princeton, N.J.: Princeton Univ. Press, 1980), 246–48.

33. *New York Tribune,* Apr. 8, 1918, newspaper clipping in reel 7, vol. 65, ACLU, NYPL.

34. Circular Letter of the League for the Amnesty of Political Prisoners, May 15, 1918, LAPP, SCPC.

35. *New York Tribune,* Nov. 27, 1918, newspaper clipping in box 3, scrapbook, NYBLA, SCPC.

36. Goldman, 647–48.

37. De Silver's wife, Margaret Burnham, was a Quaker from Philadelphia and a suffragist. For a sympathetic portrayal of De Silver by one of his colleagues in the legal profession who was also active in the Civil Liberties Bureau, see Walter Nelles, *A Liberal in Wartime: The Education of Albert De Silver* (New York: Norton, 1940).

38. Mrs. Stanley J. Clark to the National Civil Liberties Bureau, Dec. 13, 1918, reel 12, vol. 98, ACLU, NYPL. Stanley Clark was a socialist and, in 1918, a political prisoner; Dorothy Clark, his wife, worked tirelessly in the amnesty campaign. See Mary D. Brite, "Civil Liberties in the United States during and after World War I," unpublished manuscript, SCPC.

39. Goldman, 667; Alice Wexler, *Emma Goldman in America* (Boston: Beacon, 1984), 183–84. After the war, Inglis became the first curator of the University of Michigan Labadie Collection in Ann Arbor. Her papers are now on deposit in the Labadie Collection.

40. Agnes Inglis to Albert De Silver, Dec. 13, 1918, reel 12, vol. 98, ACLU, NYPL.

41. Agnes Inglis to Albert De Silver, Feb. 20, 1919, reel 12, vol. 98, ACLU, NYPL.

42. Agnes Inglis to Albert De Silver, Apr. 19, 1919, reel 12, vol. 98, ACLU, NYPL.

43. Albert De Silver to Agnes Inglis, Apr. 23, 1919, reel 12, vol. 98, ACLU, NYPL.

44. Victor Berger helped to organize the Socialist Party in 1901. He was editor of the *Milwaukee Leader* and was the first socialist to be elected to the U.S. Congress in 1910. Berger was elected five additional times, serving three terms in the House of Representatives in the 1920s. During World War I, he was convicted of conspiracy under the Espionage Act, although the Supreme Court later overturned the verdict.

45. Albert De Silver to Elizabeth Thomas, Mar. 24, 1919, reel 12, vol. 98, ACLU, NYPL.

46. Elizabeth Thomas to Albert De Silver, May 23, 1919, reel 12, vol. 98, ACLU, NYPL.

47. Elizabeth Thomas to Albert De Silver, July 2 and 17, 1919, and Albert De Silver to Elizabeth Thomas, July 21, 1919, reel 12, vol. 98, ACLU, NYPL.

48. Julian F. Jaffe, *Crusade Against Radicalism: New York During the Red Scare, 1914–1924* (Port Washington, N.Y.: Kennekat, 1972), 100. For more detail on the fortunes of the Socialist Party in this era see Buhle; James Weinstein, *The Decline of Socialism in America, 1912–1925* (New York: Monthly Review Press, 1967); David A. Shannon, *The Socialist Party of America: A History* (New York: MacMillan, 1955); and Ray Ginger, *The Bending Cross: A Biography of Eugene Victor Debs* (New Brunswick, N.J.: Rutgers Univ. Press, 1949).

49. Frances M. Witherspoon to Lenetta Cooper, June 10, 1919, reel 5, box 6, file 4, NYBLA, TIL.

50. Lenetta Cooper to Frances M. Witherspoon, June 13, 1919, reel 5, box 6, file 4, NYBLA, TIL. Members of the Chicago Amnesty Committee included Lenetta Cooper, Lola Maverick Lloyd, Eleanor Daggett Karsten, Ellen Gates Starr, Sophonisba Breckenridge, Seymour Stedman, and Sherwood Anderson.

51. Undated letter, reel 12, vol. 98, ACLU, NYPL.

52. Secretary-Treasurer of the National Women's Trade Union League to Albert De Silver, June 27, 1919, reel 12, vol. 98, ACLU, NYPL.

53. Louise Hunt to Albert De Silver, July 12, 1919, reel 12, vol. 98, ACLU, NYPL; Albert De Silver to Louise Hunt, July 17, 1919, reel 23, vol. 98, ACLU, NYPL.

54. *Labor Free Your Prisoners,* pamphlet, 4, reel 2, box 3, file 11, NYBLA, TIL.

55. Goldman, 648.

56. Lucy Robins, *War Shadows: A Documentary Story of the Struggle for Amnesty* (New York: Central Labor Bodies Conference for the Release of Political Prisoners, 1922). As correctives to Robins's self-aggrandizing interpretation of events, see Brite; Elizabeth Gurley Flynn, *The Rebel Girl* (New York: International Publishers, 1955); Rosalyn Fraad Baxandall, *Words on Fire: Elizabeth Gurley Flynn* (New Brunswick, N.J.: Rutgers Univ. Press, 1987); and Helen C. Camp, *Iron in Her Soul: Elizabeth Gurley Flynn and the American Left* (Pullman: Washington State Univ. Press, 1995). Also informative is Frank L. Grubbs, *The*

Struggle for Labor Loyalty: Gompers, the A. F. of L., and the Pacifists, 1917–1920 (Durham, N.C.: Duke Univ. Press, 1968).

57. Kathleen Kennedy, "'We Mourn For Liberty,'" 289. Socialist women such as Meta Berger set up a Socialist Party amnesty office in 1921 and did effective lobbying work among members of Congress in the two years it took until all political prisoners had been released. Kennedy's study provides a gendered analysis of the Children's Crusade for Amnesty, which was organized and led by Kate Richards O'Hare in 1922. O'Hare, who had served time in the Missouri State Penitentiary after being found guilty of uttering seditious speech during the war, was one of the Socialist Party's most inspiring public speakers. As Kennedy points out, however, her views were considered extreme by key male leaders of the Socialist Party such as Victor Berger.

58. Frances M. Witherspoon to M. Eleanor Fitzgerald, May 26, 1919, reel 2, box 3, file 11, NYBLA, TIL.

59. Frances M. Witherspoon to M. Eleanor Fitzgerald, July 21, 1919, reel 2, box 3, file 11, NYBLA, TIL.

60. M. Eleanor Fitzgerald to Frances M. Witherspoon, July 17, 1919, and Frances M. Witherspoon to M. Eleanor Fitzgerald, July 21, 1919, reel 2, box 3, file 11, NYBLA, TIL.

61. Ella Reeve Bloor to Frances M. Witherspoon, Mar. 9, 1919, reel 2, box 2, file 8, NYBLA, TIL.

62. Frances M. Witherspoon to Lenetta Cooper, Jan. 15, 1919, reel 5, box 6, file 2, NYBLA, TIL.

63. Frances M. Witherspoon to Theodore Lunde, Feb. 14, 1919, reel 3, box 4, file 16, NYBLA, TIL.

64. Franklin and Moss, 357.

65. Ida B. Wells-Barnett published several pamphlets on the topic, including *A Red Record, Tabulated Statistics and Alleged Causes of Lynching in the U.S.,* which has been reprinted in Mildred I. Thompson, *Ida B. Wells: An Exploratory Study of an American Black Woman, 1893–1930* (New York: Carlsen, 1990). In her writings, Wells-Barnett challenged the South's rape myth and attacked the credulity of white public opinion on this issue. See also Ida B. Wells-Barnett, *Crusade for Justice: The Autobiography of Ida B. Wells* (Chicago: Univ. of Chicago Press, 1970). In 1919, the NAACP published *Thirty Years of Lynching in the United States, 1889–1918,* and the association began to campaign in earnest for a federal law against lynching. An antilynching bill was introduced by Representative L. C. Dyer of Missouri in 1921; the bill passed the House but was defeated in the Senate. In 1922, Mary Burnett Talbert, an NAACP board member, followed on the heels of Ida B. Wells-Barnett to assemble a coalition of African American women into the Anti-Lynching Crusaders. In 1930, a white southern woman, Jessie Daniel Ames, established the Association of Southern Women for the Prevention of Lynching. Despite all of this work, no antilynching bill ever succeeded in passing both houses of Congress to become law. For further references on women's antilynching organizations see the entries for Ida B. Wells-Barnett, Mary Burnett Talbert, Jessie Daniel Ames, the NAACP, and the Association of Southern Women for the Prevention of Lynching, in ed. Zophy and Kavenik. Also useful is Patricia A. Gozemba and Marilyn L. Hum-

phrie, "Women in the Anti–Ku Klux Klan Movement, 1865–1984," *Women's Studies International Forum* 12, no. 1 (1989): 35–40.

66. In a now-famous July 1918 editorial in *The Crisis,* the organ of the NAACP, one of the foremost spokespersons for African American civil rights, W. E. B. Du Bois, urged blacks to "forget our special grievances and close ranks shoulder to shoulder with our own white citizens and the allied nations that are fighting for democracy." After the war, Du Bois thought differently; he mused bitterly that perhaps "passive resistance by 12 million to war activity might have saved the world for black and white," and he confessed: "I did not realize the full horror of war and its wide impotence as a method of social reform." A. Philip Randolph and Chandler Owen, the young militant Black socialist editors of *The Messenger,* took issue with Du Bois's wartime advice. Owen wrote with conviction: "Since when has the subject race come out of a war with its rights and privileges accorded for such participation?" Quotations by Du Bois from Neil A. Wynn, *From Progressivism to Prosperity: World War I and American Society* (New York: Holmes and Meier, 1986), 175, 191; quotation by Owen from Jervis Anderson, *A. Philip Randolph: A Biographical Portrait* (New York: Harcourt, Brace, Jovanovich, 1973), 112. See also Mark Ellis, "W. E. B. Du Bois and the Formation of Black Opinion in World War I: A Commentary on 'The Damnable Dilemma,'" *Journal of American History* 81, no. 4 (Mar. 1995): 1584–90, and William Jordan, "'The Damnable Dilemma': African American Accommodation and Protest During World War I," *Journal of American History* 81, no. 4 (Mar. 1995): 1162–83.

67. By the end of April 1917, black volunteers had filled up four regular Army and eight National Guard black units. The administration, wedded to a segregated fighting force, delayed the first draft call for African Americans until September 1917. David Kennedy, *Over Here,* 160, and Jane Lang Scheiber and Harry N. Scheiber, "The Wilson Administration and the Wartime Mobilization of Black Americans, 1917–1918," *Labor History* 10 (1969): 433–58.

68. Peterson and Fite, 88, and Elliot M. Rudwick, *Race Riot at East St. Louis, July 2, 1917* (1964; reprint, New York: Atheneum, 1972).

69. See discussion, chapter 2.

70. In 1910, the African American population of New York City was 91,709; by 1920, as a result of the war era migration of blacks out of the rural South and into urban-industrial areas of the North and Midwest, the figure was 152,467. Gilbert Osofsky, *Harlem: The Making of a Ghetto,* 2nd ed. (New York: Harper and Row, Harper Torchbooks, 1971), 128.

71. Frances M. Witherspoon, "Breakfast in a Bag," *The Patent Trader,* Feb. 5, 1961, box 6, TDM/FMW, SCPC.

72. See discussion, chapter 4.

73. Moore, *Plowing My Own Furrow,* 133.

74. For a contemporary report of the strike, which includes some discussion of the race riot that sparked the prisoners' revolt, see Winthrop Lane, "The Strike at Fort Leavenworth," *The Survey* 41 (Feb. 15, 1919): 687–93. Secondary sources skirt over the race issue embedded in the early history of the strike, before CO involvement resulted in the deletion of the demand of some whites for the establishment of racial segregation in prison.

75. Mygatt does not seem to question the southern rape myth: in one lynching episode, she shows the murdered man to have been innocent, but in another, there is no suggestion that the African American man who was lynched might not have raped a young factory worker. In fact, by implying that the second lynch victim might have been guilty, Mygatt enhances the moral character of the white female protagonist, Margaret Clay, who condemns the mob murder regardless of the victim's actual guilt or innocence. At one point in the play, Margaret (obviously with Mygatt's point of view) denounces the history of the rape of black women under slavery but then reveals her assumption that African Americans are less civilized than whites; Margaret tells her husband that the rape of black women by white men is "a thousand times worse . . . with a thousand years of civilization behind them, than black, with scarcely a hundred." Mygatt's play was published in *The Drama* (Nov. 1929): 42–48. A copy is found in box 2, TDM/FMW, SCPC.

76. Review of *The Noose* in the *New York Call,* [Apr. 1919], newspaper clipping in box 2, TDM/FMW, SCPC.

77. Franklin and Moss, 348.

78. Ibid., 350.

79. See William M. Tuttle Jr., *Race Riot: Chicago in the Red Summer of 1919* (New York: Atheneum, 1977).

80. Lewis Mumford, "Patriotism and its Consequences," *The Dial* 46 (Apr. 1919): 406.

81. Baxandall, 27.

6. The Ellis Island Deportees

1. Jensen, *Price of Vigilance,* 78.

2. Biographical information on Caroline Lowe is found in Buhle, 151–56, 173, 216, 319, and 327. Lowe was born in Cottom, Essex County, Ontario, on November 28, 1874. Her mother was the descendant of a Loyalist family that had migrated to Canada during the American Revolution. Lowe's father was employed as an itinerant timber worker in the American Midwest during her childhood. Her papers are in the possession of Pittsburg State University, Special Collections, Axe Library, Pittsburg, Kans.

3. In Latin, *habeas corpus* means "you have the body." A habeas corpus ad subjiciendum, the most common form of habeas corpus writs, is an established legal device in England and the United States for challenging illegal confinement. Such a writ is a directive to the authority detaining someone to produce that person ("the body"). The aim of the writ is to test the legality of the detention not to determine whether the imprisoned individual is guilty or innocent. Habeas corpus is guaranteed by the U.S. Constitution (article I) and by state constitutions. See Black, 709–10.

4. John Higham, *Strangers in the Land: Patterns of American Nativism 1860–1925* (1963; reprint, New York: Atheneum, 1971), esp. 222–24. See also Tuttle; 3–31; and Stanley Coben, "A Study in Nativism: The American Red Scare of 1919–20," *Political Science Quarterly* 79, no. 1 (Mar. 1964): 52–75.

5. Preston, 191.

6. Testimonies of some of these men attest to the horrid prison conditions that detained Wobblies were forced to endure. See, for instance, [Statement of John Morgan, Deportee], box 1, NYBLA, SCPC, and Anonymous, "My Experience in the Deportation Wave," box 1, NYBLA, SCPC.

7. See Recht, "Objection Overruled," 239–64, and Preston, 181–207.

8. George Vanderveer's key role in the antideportation efforts of the IWW is discussed in Preston, esp. 196–97.

9. Preston, 197. Preston does not, however, refer directly to Lowe or Recht, except in a footnote. The Bureau of Legal Advice is not mentioned.

10. Recht, "Objection Overruled," 252.

11. All quotations in this paragraph from Recht, "Objection Overruled," 252–54.

12. One of the thirty-nine men apprehended was labeled Swiss, but he eventually proved that he had been born in the United States. Thus, the number of Wobblies to be deported became 38 instead of 39.

13. Deportation case record as quoted in Kate Holladay Claghorn, *The Immigrant's Day in Court* (New York: Harper, 1923), 355. In 1919, Charles Recht supplied Claghorn (who was a faculty member of the New York School of Social Work) with material for her projected book. See Frances M. Witherspoon to John L. Elliot, July 21, 1919, reel 2, box 2, file 21, NYBLA, TIL.

14. Recht quotations from the brief in "Objection Overruled," 259–60.

15. Claghorn, 337.

16. Recht, "Objection Overruled," 262.

17. Press release, Feb. 13, 1919, reel 9, box 12, file 3, NYBLA, TIL.

18. Press release, Feb. 14, 1919, reel 9, box 12, file 3, NYBLA, TIL.

19. "Under the Shadow of Liberty" [n.d.], flyer, box 1, NYBLA, SCPC.

20. Caroline A. Lowe, circular letter, Mar. 20, 1919, box 1, NYBLA, SCPC.

21. Newspaper clippings, reel 6, vol. 52, ACLU, NYPL.

22. Ibid.

23. The newspaper that the group published was called *Frayhayt* (Freedom). In an oral interview, Hilda Kovner Adel recalled that she had helped to print up the leaflets and had accompanied Steimer and others to a factory to distribute them. One of their number, Hyman Rosansky, informed on Steimer and four others, who were then arrested by the police. It appears that Kovner narrowly escaped an unenviable fate. She met her future husband, Sam Adel, in the Frayhayt group. See Adel, 60–61.

24. *New York Call,* Feb. 14, 1919, newspaper clipping in reel 6, vol. 52, ACLU, NYPL.

25. Frances M. Witherspoon to Elinor Byrns, Apr. 7, 1919, reel 2, box 2, file 11, NYBLA, TIL.

26. For a thorough discussion of this controversy within the feminist movement of the period, see Susan D. Becker, *The Origins of the Equal Rights Amendment: American Feminism Between the Wars* (Westport, Conn.: Greenwood, 1981); see also Cott.

27. Witherspoon to Byrns, Apr. 7, 1919. Witherspoon also pointed out that Charles Recht had discovered two other deportations of "immoral" women

in his study of immigration law. See Charles Recht, *American Exclusion and Deportation Laws* (New York: Workers Defense Union, 1919), 5.

28. Witherspoon to Byrns, Apr. 7, 1919.

29. *Workers' Defense Bulletin* no. 3 (Sept. 1919), 5, reel 4, box 4, file 24, NYBLA, TIL.

30. This case—Abrams et al. vs. U.S.—secured a central place in legal history when it was reviewed by the Supreme Court in 1919. The majority opinion sustained the lower court's conviction, which was based on the "clear and present danger" standard formulated some months previously by Supreme Court Justice Oliver Wendell Holmes Jr. In effect, the words expressed in the leaflets distributed by the defendants were deemed, in the circumstances of war, to encourage "evils" (in this instance, lack of support for the war), which Congress had the responsibility to prevent. Interestingly, however, in the Abrams case, Holmes dissented from the majority opinion, which was based on his own earlier interpretation of the relationship between words and intended deeds. In his minority dissent, Holmes argued that the content of the distributed leaflets revealed no "literal" intent to interfere with the war effort, and his revised thinking (a broadening of the parameters of his own "clear and present danger" standard) represented a benchmark in the history of free speech protections under the Constitution. The legal scholarship on this case is extensive. For a well-crafted history of the Abrams case, see Richard Polenberg, *Fighting Faiths: The Abrams Case, the Supreme Court, and Free Speech* (New York: Viking Penguin, 1987); for an article-length treatment, see Fred Ragan, "Justice Oliver Wendell Holmes, Jr., Zechariah Chafee, Jr., and the Clear and Present Danger Test for Free Speech: The First Year, 1919," *Journal of American History* 58 (June 1971): 24–45.

31. Goldman, 706.

32. Recht, "Objection Overruled," 221–22.

33. Circular letter to editor by Elizabeth Gurley Flynn for the Workers Defense Union, July 2, 1919, reel 4, box 4, file 24, NYBLA, TIL. This suspicion of governmental use of agents provocateurs was explored several years after the fact by Louis Post, the assistant secretary of labor during the deportation crisis. Post questioned the Department of Justice thesis that the bomb incidents were the work of radical agitators. Why, he asked, did officials fail to uncover the perpetrators? Post also discussed the "fixed mental attitude" of Justice Department detectives, which might have led them to ignore leads not to their liking or thinking. See Louis F. Post, *The Deportations Delirium of Nineteen-Twenty: A Personal Narrative of an Historic Official Experience* (Chicago: Charles H. Kerr, 1923), 44.

34. See Robert Murray, *Red Scare: A Study in National Hysteria, 1919–1920* (1955; reprint, New York: McGraw-Hill, 1964). Murray's interpretation of the chronology of events is accepted by other historians, including Jaffe, Higham, and Preston.

35. Murray, 75.

36. Text of act as quoted in ibid., 98.

37. Murray, 98–102. Stevenson had achieved notoriety when he appeared in January 1919 before a Senate Judiciary Committee headed by Lee Overman

that was charged with investigating left-wing activities in the United States. Stevenson produced a list of sixty-two eminent citizens whom he labeled dangerous radicals; among the names were Jane Addams, Lillian D. Wald, and Oswald Garrison Villard. Tracy Mygatt and Jessie Wallace Hughan were also included on the list, but Witherspoon joked about being left off of this "Who's Who" of radicalism. The allegations against such prominent individuals were outrageous, and Secretary of War Baker was forced to distance himself from Stevenson and the list. In a public statement, Baker avowed that the list contained "names of people of great distinction, exalted purity of purpose, and lifelong devotion to the highest interests of America and mankind." Quoted in Jaffe, 120.

38. Recht, "Objection Overruled," 310.

39. Frances M. Witherspoon to J. G. Phelps Stokes, June 6, 1919, reel 4, box 4, file 11, NYBLA, TIL.

40. Frances M. Witherspoon to the editor of the *New York Times*, June 11, 1919, reel 4, box 5, file 19, NYBLA, TIL. It is interesting that in this letter, Witherspoon signs off as "Frances M." rather than as "Fannie May." Bruno Grunzig noticed that Witherspoon had begun to publish articles as "Frances M. Witherspoon" about this time. See Frances M. Witherspoon, "The Lumberjack and the Constitution," *The World Tomorrow* 2, no. 5 (May 1919): 133–34, for a comprehensive summary of the Red Special deportation cases.

41. Witherspoon to editor of the *Times*, June 11, 1919.

42. On the enhanced role of military intelligence in this period with regard to domestic security concerns, see Joan M. Jensen, *Army Surveillance in America, 1775–1980* (New Haven, Conn.: Yale Univ. Press, 1991), and Roy Talbert Jr., *Negative Intelligence: The Army and the American Left, 1917–1941* (Jackson: Univ. Press of Mississippi, 1991).

43. Brown cites Witherspoon's comment in his letter to her of Sept. 2, 1919, reel 1, box 1, folder 19, NYBLA, TIL.

44. Bruno Grunzig to Frances M. Witherspoon, Nov. 1, 1919, box 6, TDM/FMW, SCPC.

45. Harry N. Scheiber, *The Wilson Administration and Civil Liberties, 1917–1921* (Ithaca, N.Y.: Cornell Univ. Press, 1960). Historian Robert Ferrell has observed that after his stroke, Wilson was turned "into a shell of a man, incompetent to occupy the office of President." See Robert H. Ferrell, *Woodrow Wilson and World War I, 1917–1921* (New York: Harper and Row, 1985), 156.

46. Ferrell, 197.

47. Ibid., 205.

48. Jaffe, 183–84. In this group were 199 members of the Union of Russian Workers, apprehended during the Palmer Raids; 43 anarchists whose deportation had been determined before the roundup of Russian Workers; and seven who were public charges, criminals, or misfits. See Murray, 207.

49. "Deport Us, Too," *New York Call*, Dec. 20, 1919, newspaper clipping in reel 6, vol. 52, ACLU, NYPL.

50. Claghorn, 436–37.

51. *New York Tribune*, Dec. 23, 1919, newspaper clipping in reel 6, vol. 52, ACLU, NYPL.

52. Ibid.

53. *New York Call,* Dec. 23, 1919, newspaper clipping in reel 6, vol. 52, ACLU, NYPL.

54. Quoted in Winthrop Lane, "The Buford Widows," *The Survey* 43, no. 11 (Jan. 10, 1920), 391.

55. Constantine M. Panunzio, *The Deportation Cases of 1919–1920* (1921; reprint, New York: Da Capo, 1970), 89.

56. Goldman, 698. At one point, Berkman was put in solitary for protesting the death of an African American convict who was shot in the back by a guard. Candace Falk, *Love, Anarchy, and Emma Goldman* (New York: Holt, Rinehart and Winston, 1984), 285.

57. The relationships between and among Fitzgerald, Goldman, Berkman, and Eckstein are sensitively explored in Falk.

58. Eleanor Fitzgerald's papers are held by the University of Wisconsin at Milwaukee, Manuscript Collections, Golda Meir Library. For her crucial leadership role in the Provincetown Playhouse theatre group, see Helen Deutsch and Stella Hanau, *The Provincetown: A Story of the Theatre* (1931; reprint, New York: Russell and Russell, 1972). Charles Recht was involved in the Playhouse in its early years, as was Harry Weinberger, who served as the Playhouse lawyer. Among the cultural and political radicals and playwrights who became members of the Provincetown Playhouse were John Reed, Max Eastman, George Cram Cook, Susan Glaspell, Floyd Dell, Ida Rauh, Eugene O'Neill, Hutchins Hapgood, and Mary Heaton Vorse.

59. Quoted in Robins, 97. Robins expressed disdain for the group in whose name Mygatt wrote the letter, the Free Political Prisoners Committee of the People's Freedom Union. She cited Mygatt's letter in full but prefaced this with the comment that the group was "mainly organized by women, upon the emotional spur of the moment [and] disbanded just as suddenly."

60. Witherspoon and Mygatt, reminiscences, 30.

61. Ibid.

62. *New York Times,* Dec. 26, 1919, 1, 3. Except for the observations attributed to Fannie May Witherspoon, the facts of the Christmas Day walk have been culled from the *Times* reportage of the event.

63. Witherspoon and Mygatt, reminiscences, 31.

64. Witherspoon and Mygatt, reminiscences, 31; David Hirshfield, Commissioner of Accounts, City of New York, to Frances M. Witherspoon, Jan. 5, 1920, box 1, NYBLA, SCPC.

65. Witherspoon and Mygatt, reminiscences, 31.

66. Post, 327.

67. Joan M. Jensen, "All Pink Sisters: The War Department and the Feminist Movement in the 1920s," in *Decades of Discontent: The Women's Movement, 1920–1940,* ed. Lois Schark and Joan M. Jensen (Westport, Conn.: Greenwood, 1983): 199–222.

68. Tracy D. Mygatt and Frances M. Witherspoon, *The Glorious Company of the Apostles* (New York: Harcourt Brace, 1928), and Tracy D. Mygatt and Frances M. Witherspoon, *Armour of Light* (New York: Holt, 1930). Both books were reviewed positively; *The Glorious Company* was the more acclaimed of the two and received a full-page review in the *New York Times.*

69. Frances M. Witherspoon to Alice Holdship Ware, Feb. 25, 1919, reel 4, box 4, file 25, NYBLA, TIL.

70. See Harriet Hyman Alonso's fine study, *The Women's Peace Union and the Outlawry of War, 1921–1942* (Knoxville: Univ. of Tennessee Press, 1990).

71. Frances H. Early, "Revolutionary Pacifism and War Resistance: Jessie Wallace Hughan's 'War against War,'" *Peace and Change* 20, no. 3 (July 1995): 307–28. Witherspoon and Mygatt remained active members of the War Resisters League and, in 1961, received the organization's Peace Award in recognition of their "dedicated service to the struggle against war and for a peaceful world." Copy of Peace Awards, box 10, TDM/FMW, SCPC.

72. Charles Recht, *Manhattan Made, Poems* (New York: H. Liveright, 1930).

7. Creating a Peace Culture

1. Frances M. Witherspoon, "Women and the Military," *New York Call,* [1916], newspaper clipping in box 11, TDM/FMW, SCPC.

2. See Preston for a scholarly treatment of this thesis.

3. See, for instance, Shenk and Chauncy.

4. The work of feminist philosopher Sara Ruddick comes to mind here. See particulary Sara Ruddick, "Preservative Love and Military Destruction," in *Mothering: Essays in Feminist Theory,* ed. J. Trebilcot (Totowa, N.J.: Rowman and Allanheld, 1984), 231–62; "Maternal Thinking and Peace Politics," *Journal of Education* 167 (1985): 97–112; and "The Rationality of Care," in ed. Elshtain Tobias, 229–54.

5. For an in-depth analysis of this reality for women political activists in an earlier period, see Kathryn Kish Sklar, 'Hull House in the 1890s: A Community of Women Reformers," *Signs: A Journal of Women in Culture and Society* 10 (1985): 658–77.

6. Baldwin, quoted in New York State Joint Legislative Committee Investigating Seditious Activities, *Revolutionary Radicalism: Its History, Purpose and Tactics* (Albany: Lyons, 1920), 2, 1991. After the war, Witherspoon served for a time on committees of the American Civil Liberties Union, which was established in 1920 as the successor to the National Civil Liberties Bureau.

7. Frances M. Witherspoon to Lola Maverick Lloyd, Nov. 28, 1919, general correspondence, LML, NYPL. The founders of the IWW referred to its industrially organized association of workers as "One Big Union"; the founders of the People's Freedom Union appreciated that the public would make the connection between their One Big Union and that of the Wobblies.

8. "An Open Letter to Rational Americans," box 1, NYBLA, SCPC.

9. The League for Democratic Control in Boston did much the same for "their boys."

10. Harry Maximon to Joy Young, Aug. 5, 1918, box 2, NYBLA, SCPC.

11. Frieda Lederman Jasmagy to Mr. and Mrs. W. J. Jasmagy, Oct. 14, 1918, box 2, NYBLA, SCPC.

12. Ella Reeve Bloor to Anna N. Davis, Dec. 30, 1918, reel 6, box 7, file 19, NYBLA, TIL.

13. Jessie Wallace Hughan, "Direct Attack Upon War," *The Social Preparation* [1923], 13, JWH, SCPC.

14. Early, "Revolutionary Pacifism," 322–24.

15. I have found Elise Boulding's definition of a peace culture conceptually useful in this study: "A peace culture is a mosaic of historical identities, attitudes, values, behaviors, and institutional patterns that leads people to live nurturantly with one another." See Elise Boulding, "Feminist Inventions in the Art of Peacemaking: A Century Overview," *Peace and Change* 20, no. 4 (Oct. 1995): 436. Barton Hacker, in a thoughtful essay, argues for the significance of the anarcha-feminist component in women's historic and contemporary peace work. Hacker posits that if one assumes that military institutions and states are inseparable from patriarchy (a theoretical position he terms "anarcha-feminist"), then "the proper question becomes how women and other outsiders might focus their opposition to military institutions and strengthen efforts to build peace-oriented communities." Hacker continues: "I have no answers, but that at least, I think, is the right question." This "right question" has been a recurrent one among women peace-makers (and, at times, "other outsiders") for much of this century. See Barton Hacker, "From Military Revolution to Industrial Revolution: Armies, Women and Political Economy in Early Modern Europe," in *Women and the Military System,* ed. Eva Isaksson (Hertfordshire, Eng.: Harvester-Wheatsheaf, 1988), 25. Also of interest is Frances H. Early, "New Historical Perspectives on Gendered Peace Studies," *Women's Studies Quarterly* 23, nos. 3–4 (Fall/Winter 1995): 22–31.

16. For a careful reconstruction of early WRL history, see Michael David Young, "'Wars Will Cease When Men Refuse to Fight': The War Resisters League 1925–1950" (Honors essay, Brown Univ., 1975). See also Early, "Revolutionary Pacifism."

17. Ursula Franklin, "Comment," in *Women and Peace: Theoretical, Historical and Practical Perspectives,* ed. Ruth Pierson (London: Croom Helm, 1987), 24. Franklin is a member of the Voice of Women of Canada.

Bibliography

Manuscript Collections

Bryn Mawr College Archives, Bryn Mawr, Pa.
   Alumnae Records.
Hughan Family Papers and Jessie Wallace Hughan Papers.
   Courtesy of Margaret Rockwell Finch.
University of Michigan Historical Collections, Bentley Historical Library,
   Ann Arbor, Mich.
   Rebecca Shelley Papers.
National Archives, Washington, D.C.
   Records of the Federal Bureau of Investigation, RG65.
   Records of the War Department General and Special Staffs Military In-
      telligence Division, 1917–1941, RG 165.
   U.S. Postal Service Records, RG 28.
New York Public Library, New York, N.Y.
   American Civil Liberties Union Papers (microfilm copy).
   Lola Maverick Lloyd Papers.
Pittsburg State University Special Collections, Axe Library, Pittsburg, Kans.
   Caroline Lowe Papers.
Princeton University Seeley G. Mudd Manuscript Library, Princeton, N.J.
   American Civil Liberties Union Archives (photo collection).
Arthur and Elizabeth Schlesinger Library on the History of Women in Amer-
   ica, Radcliffe College, Cambridge, Mass.
   Caroline Lexow Babcock Papers.
Smith College Archives, Northampton, Mass.
   Martha Gruening File, Alumnae Records.
Sophia Smith Collection, Women's History Archive, Smith College, North-
   ampton, Mass.
   Ella Reeve Bloor Papers.

Swarthmore College Peace Collection, Swarthmore, Pa.
    American Union Against Militarism Papers.
    Emily Greene Balch Papers.
    Henry Wadsworth Longfellow Dana Papers.
    Emergency Peace Federation Papers.
    Jessie Wallace Hughan Papers.
    League for the Amnesty of Political Prisoners Papers.
    League for Democratic Control Papers.
    Liberty Defense Union Papers.
    Tracy D. Mygatt and Frances M. Witherspoon Papers.
    New York Bureau of Legal Advice Papers.
    Mercedes M. Randall Papers.
    Woman's Peace Party Papers (New York City Branch).
Tamiment Institute Library, New York University, New York, N.Y.
    Elizabeth Gurley Flynn Papers.
    New York Bureau of Legal Advice Papers.
    Charles Recht Papers.
University of Wisconsin at Milwaukee Manuscript Collections, Golda Meir
    Library, Milwaukee, Wisc.
    M. Eleanor Fitzgerald Papers.
Yale University Library, New Haven, Conn.
    Harry Weinberger Papers.

Books, Articles, Pamphlets, and Unpublished Works

Additon, Henrietta. "Work Among Delinquent Girls and Women." *Annals
    of the American Academy of Political and Social Sciences* 79 (1918): 152–66.
Adel, Hilda [Kovner]. "Hilda Adel." In *Anarchist Voices: An Oral History of
    Anarchism in America,* edited by Paul Avrich, 60–61. Princeton, N.J.:
    Princeton Univ. Press, 1995.
Alonso, Harriet Hyman. *Peace as a Woman's Issue: A History of the U.S. Movement for
    World Peace and Women's Rights.* Syracuse, N.Y.: Syracuse Univ. Press, 1993.
————. "A Shared Responsibility: The Women and Men of the People's
    Council of America for Democracy and Terms of Peace, 1911–1919."
    Master's thesis, Sarah Lawrence College, 1982.
————. *The Women's Peace Union and the Outlawry of War, 1921–1942.*
    Knoxville: Univ. of Tennessee Press, 1990.
Anderson, George J. "Making the Camps Safe for the Army." *Annals of the
    American Academy of Political and Social Sciences* 79 (1918): 143–51.
Anderson, Jervis. *A. Philip Randolph: A Biographical Portrait.* New York:
    Harcourt, Brace, Jovanovich, 1973.
Avrich, Paul. *The Modern School Movement: Anarchism and Education in the
    United States.* Princeton, N.J.: Princeton Univ. Press, 1980.

Baldwin, Roger. "Recollections of a Life of Civil Liberties—I." *The Civil Liberties Review* 2, no. 2 (1975): 39–72.

Baxandall, Rosalyn Fraad. *Words on Fire: Elizabeth Gurley Flynn.* New Brunswick, N.J.: Rutgers Univ. Press, 1987.

Beale, Howard K. *Are American Teachers Free? An Analysis of Restraints upon the Freedom of Teaching in American Schools.* 1936. Reprint. New York: Octagon, 1972.

Becker, Susan D. *The Origins of the Equal Rights Amendment: American Feminism Between the Wars.* Westport, Conn.: Greenwood, 1981.

Bederman, Gail. *Manliness & Civilization: A Cultural History of Gender and Race in the United States, 1880–1917.* Chicago: Univ. of Chicago Press, 1995.

Black, Henry Campbell. *Black's Law Dictionary.* 6th ed. St. Paul, Minn.: West, 1990.

Blatch, Harriot Stanton. *Challenging Years: The Memoirs of Harriot Stanton Blatch.* 1940. Reprint. Westport, Conn.: Hyperion, 1976.

Bloor, Ella Reeve. *We Are Many: An Autobiography.* New York: International Publishers, 1940.

Boulding, Elise. "Feminist Inventions in the Art of Peacemaking: A Century Overview." *Peace and Change: A Journal of Peace Research* 20, no. 4 (Oct. 1995): 408–38.

Brandt, Alan M. *No Magic Bullet: A Social History of Venereal Disease in the United States since 1880.* New York: Oxford Univ. Press, 1985.

Brite, Mary D. "Civil Liberties in the United States during and after World War I." Swarthmore College Peace Collection. Unpublished paper.

Brooks, Arle, and Robert J. Leach. *Help Wanted! The Experiences of Some Quaker Conscientious Objectors.* 1940. Reprint. New York: Garland, 1971.

Buhle, Mari Jo. *Women and American Socialism, 1870–1920.* Urbana: Univ. of Illinois Press, 1981.

Camp, Helen C. *Iron in Her Soul: Elizabeth Gurley Flynn and the American Left.* Pullman: Washington State Univ. Press, 1995.

Carnes, Mark, and Clyde Griffin, eds. *Meanings for Manhood: Constructions of Masculinity in Victorian America.* Chicago: Univ. of Chicago Press, 1990.

Chambers, John Whiteclay II. "Conscientious Objectors and the American State from Colonial Times to the Present." In *The New Conscientious Objection: From Sacred to Secular Resistance,* edited by Charles C. Moskos and John Whiteclay Chambers II, 23–46. New York: Oxford Univ. Press, 1993.

———. Introduction to *The Conscientious Objector,* by Walter Guest Kellogg, 5–18. 1919. Reprint. New York: Garland, 1972.

Chatfield, Charles. *For Peace and Justice: Pacifism in America, 1914–1941.* Knoxville: Univ. of Tennessee Press, 1971.

————, ed. *The Radical "No": The Correspondence and Writings of Evan Thomas on War.* New York: Garland, 1974.

Chauncy, George, Jr. "Christian Brotherhood or Sexual Perversion? Homosexual Identities and the Construction of Sexual Boundaries in the World War I Era." In *Hidden from History: Reclaiming the Gay and Lesbian Past,* edited by Martin Bauml Duberman, Martha Vicinus, and George Chauncy Jr., 294–317. New York: New American Library, 1989.

Claghorn, Kate Holladay. *The Immigrant's Day in Court.* New York: Harper, 1923.

Coben, Stanley. "A Study in Nativism: The American Red Scare of 1919–20." *Political Science Quarterly* 79, no. 1 (Mar. 1964): 52–75.

Cook, Blanche Wiesen. "Female Support Networks and Political Activism: Lillian Wald, Crystal Eastman, Emma Goldman." In *A Heritage of Her Own,* edited by Nancy F. Cott and Elizabeth H. Pleck, 412–44. New York: Simon and Schuster, 1979.

————. "Woodrow Wilson and the Antimilitarists, 1914–1917." Ph.D. diss., John Hopkins Univ., 1970.

————, ed. *Crystal Eastman on Women and Revolution.* New York: Oxford Univ. Press, 1978.

Cooke, Miriam, and Angela Woollacott, eds. *Gendering War Talk.* Princeton, N.J.: Princeton Univ. Press, 1993.

Cott, Nancy F. *The Grounding of Modern Feminism.* New Haven, Conn.: Yale Univ. Press, 1987.

Damousi, Joy. "Socialist Women and Gendered Space: The Anti-Conscription and Anti-War Campaigns of 1914–1918." *Labour History* [Australia] 4 (1991): 1–15.

D'Emilio, John, and Estelle B. Freedman. *Intimate Matters: A History of Sexuality in America.* New York: Harper and Row, 1988.

Deutsch, Helen, and Stella Hanau. *The Provincetown: A Story of the Theatre.* 1931. Reprint. New York: Russell and Russell, 1972.

Dillon, Charles H. *Introducing Examples of Brutalities, Tortures, and Deaths to Political Prisoners Under Military Régime.* Washington, D.C.: Government Printing Office, 1919.

Early, Frances H. "Feminism, Peace, and Civil Liberties: Women's Role in the Origins of the World War I Civil Liberties Movement." *Women's Studies: An Interdisciplinary Journal* 18, nos. 1–2 (1990): 95–115.

————. "New Historical Perspectives on Gendered Peace Studies." *Women's Studies Quarterly* 23, nos. 3–4 (Fall-Winter 1995): 22–31.

————. "Revolutionary Pacifism and War Resistance: Jessie Wallace Hughan's 'War Against War.'" *Peace and Change: A Journal of Peace Research* 20, no. 3 (July 1995): 307–28.

Edwards, John Carver. *Patriots in Pinstripe: Men of the National Security League.* Washington, D.C.: Univ. Press of America, 1982.

Eichel, Julius. *The Judge Said "20 Years": The Story of a Conscientious Objector in World War I.* New York: War Resisters League, 1981.

Ellis, Mark. "W. E. B. Du Bois and the Formation of Black Opinion in World War I: A Commentary on 'The Damnable Dilemma.'" *Journal of American History* 81, no. 4 (Mar. 1995): 1584–90.

Elshtain, Jean Bethke. *Women and War.* New York: Basic Books, 1987.

Elshtain, Jean Bethke, and Sheila Tobias, eds. *Women, Militarism, and War: Essays in History, Politics, and Social Theory.* Savage, Md.: Rowman and Littlefield, 1990.

Elton, G. R. *The Practice of History.* Melbourne, Australia: Fontana, 1967.

Enloe, Cynthia. *Does Khaki Become You? The Militarisation of Women's Lives.* 2nd ed. London: Pandora Press; New York: Unwin Hyman, 1988.

Faderman, Lillian. *Surpassing the Love of Men: Romantic Friendship and Love Between Women from the Renaissance to the Present.* New York: William Morrow, 1981.

Falk, Candace. *Love, Anarchy, and Emma Goldman.* New York: Holt, Rinehart, and Winston, 1984.

Ferrell, Robert H. *Woodrow Wilson and World War I, 1917–1921.* New York: Harper and Row, 1985.

Flynn, Elizabeth Gurley. *The Rebel Girl.* New York: International Publishers, 1955.

Forcey, Linda Rennie, and Amy Swerdlow, eds. "Rethinking Women's Peace Studies." Special issue of *Women's Studies Quarterly* 23, nos. 3–4 (Fall/Winter 1995).

Franklin, John Hope, and Alfred A. Moss Jr. *From Slavery to Freedom: A History of African Americans.* 7th ed. New York: McGraw Hill, 1994.

Franklin, Ursula. "Comment." In *Women and Peace: Theoretical, Historical and Practical Perspectives,* ed. by Ruth Pierson, 24. London: Croom Helm, 1987.

Ginger, Ray. *The Bending Cross: A Biography of Eugene Victor Debs.* New Brunswick, N.J.: Rutgers Univ. Press, 1949.

Glenn, Mary Willcox. "Purpose and Methods of a Home Service Section." *Annals of the American Academy of Political and Social Science* 79 (1918): 97–105.

Goldman, Emma. *Living My Life.* Abridged Ed. Edited by Richard and Anna Maria Drinnon. New York: New American Library, 1977.

Gozemba, Patricia A., and Marilyn L. Humphrie. "Women in the Anti–Ku Klux Klan Movement, 1865–1984." *Women's Studies International Forum* 12, no. 1 (1989): 35–40.

Gray, Harold Studley. *Character "Bad": The Story of a Conscientious Objector.* 1934. Reprint. New York: Garland, 1971.

Grubbs, Frank L. *The Struggle for Labor Loyalty: Gompers, the A. F. of L., and the Pacifists, 1917–1920.* Durham, N.C.: Duke Univ. Press, 1968.

Gruening, Martha. "National Association for the Advancement of Colored People (Houston: An NAACP Investigation)," *The Crisis* (Nov. 1917): 14–19.

Gustafson, Melanie. "Lola Maverick Lloyd: 'Truly a Live Wire and a Brick'. . . a Militant Pacifist." Master's thesis, Sarah Lawrence College, 1983.

Hacker, Barton. "From Military Revolution to Industrial Revolution: Armies, Women and Political Economy in Early Modern Europe." In *Women and the Military System,* edited by Eva Isaksson, 11–29. Hertfordshire, Eng.: Harvester-Wheatsheaf, 1988.

Hassler, R. Alfred. *Conscripts of Conscience: The Story of Sixteen Objectors to Conscription.* 1942. Reprint. New York: Garland, 1971.

Higham, John. *Strangers in the Land: Patterns of American Nativism 1860–1925.* 1963. Reprint. New York: Atheneum, 1971.

Higonnet, Margaret Randolph, Jane Jensen, Sonya Michel, and Margaret Collins Weitz, eds. *Behind the Lines: Gender and the Two World Wars.* New Haven, Conn.: Yale Univ. Press, 1987.

Howlett, Charles F. "Quaker Conscience in the Classroom: The Mary S. McDowell Case." *Quaker History* 83 (Fall 1994): 99–115.

Irwin, Inez Haynes. *The Story of the Woman's Party.* 1921. Reprint. New York: Kraus, 1971.

Isaksson, Eva, ed. *Women and the Military System.* Hertfordshire, Eng.: Harvester-Wheatsheaf, 1988.

Jaffe, Julian F. *Crusade Against Radicalism: New York During the Red Scare, 1914–1924.* Port Washington, N.Y.: Kennekat, 1972.

Jensen, Joan M. "All Pink Sisters: The War Department and the Feminist Movement in the 1920s." In *Decades of Discontent: The Women's Movement, 1920–1940,* edited by Lois Schark and Joan M. Jensen, 199–222. Westport, Conn.: Greenwood, 1983.

———. *Army Surveillance in America, 1775–1980.* New Haven, Conn.: Yale Univ. Press, 1991.

———. *The Price of Vigilance.* Chicago: Rand McNally, 1968.

Johnson, Donald. *The Challenge to American Freedoms: World War I and the Rise of the American Civil Liberties Union.* Lexington: Univ. of Kentucky Press, 1963.

Jordan, William. "'The Damnable Dilemma': African-American Accommodation and Protest During World War I." *Journal of American History* 81, no. 4 (Mar. 1995): 1562–83.

Kennedy, David M. *Over Here: The First World War and American Society.* New York: Oxford Univ. Press, 1980.

Kennedy, Kathleen. "Declaring War on War: Gender and the American Socialist Attack on Militarism, 1914–1918," *Journal of Women's History* 7, no. 2 (Summer 1995): 27–51.

———. " 'We Mourn for Liberty in America': Socialist Women, Antimilitarism, and State Repression, 1914–1922." Ph.D. diss., Univ. of California at Irvine, 1992.

Kohn, Stephen M. *American Political Prisoners: Prosecutions Under the Espionage and Sedition Acts.* Westport, Conn.: Praeger, 1994.

———. *Jailed For Peace: The History of American Draft Law Violations, 1658–1985.* Westport, Conn.: Greenwood, 1986.

Kornbluh, Joyce L. *Rebel Voices: An Anthology.* Ann Arbor: Univ. of Michigan Press, 1984.

Lamson, Peggy. *Roger Baldwin: Founder of the American Civil Liberties Union.* Boston: Houghton Mifflin, 1976.

Lane, Winthrop. "The Buford Widows." *The Survey* 43, no. 11 (Jan. 10, 1920): 391–92.

———. "The Strike at Fort Leavenworth." *The Survey* 41 (Feb. 15, 1919): 687–93.

Lang, Lucy Robins. *Tomorrow is Beautiful.* New York: MacMillan, 1948.

Lebsock, Suzanne. "Women and American Politics, 1880–1920." In *Women, Politics and Change,* edited by Louise A. Tilly and Patricia Gurin, 35–62. New York: Russell Sage Foundation, 1990.

Lindsay, Samuel McCune. "Purpose and Scope of War Risk Insurance." *Annals of the American Academy of Political and Social Science* 79 (1918): 52–68.

Luebke, Frederick C. *Bonds of Loyalty: German Americans and World War I.* DeKalb: Northern Illinois Univ. Press, 1974.

Manahan, Nancy. "Future Old Maids and Pacifist Agitators: The Story of Tracy Mygatt and Frances Witherspoon." *Women's Studies Quarterly* 10, no. 1 (Spring 1982): 10–13.

Mangan, J. A., and James Walvin, eds. *Manliness and Morality: Middle-Class Masculinity in Britain and America, 1800–1940.* Manchester, Eng.: Manchester Univ. Press, 1987.

Meyer, Ernest L. *Hey! Yellowbacks: The War Diary of a Conscientious Objector.* New York: John Day, 1930.

Mock, James R., and Cedric Larson. *Words that Won the War: The Story of the Committee on Public Information 1917–1919.* 1939. Reprint. New York: Russell and Russell, 1968.

Moore, Howard W. *Plowing My Own Furrow.* 1985. Reprint. Syracuse, N.Y.: Syracuse Univ. Press, 1993.

Mumford, Lewis. "Patriotism and its Consequences." *The Dial* 46 (Apr. 1919): 406–7.

Murphy, Paul L. *World War I and the Origin of Civil Liberties in the United States.* New York: Norton, 1979.

Murray, Robert. *Red Scare: A Study in National Hysteria, 1919–1920.* 1955. Reprint. New York: McGraw-Hill, 1964.

Mygatt, Tracy D. *Julia Newberry's Sketch Book or the Life of Two Future Old Maids.* New York: Norton, 1934.

————. "The Noose." *The Drama* (Nov. 1929): 42–48.

Mygatt, Tracy D., and Frances M. Witherspoon. *Armour of Light.* New York: Holt, 1930.

————. *The Glorious Company of the Apostles.* New York: Harcourt Brace, 1928.

Nelles, Walter. *A Liberal in Wartime: The Education of Albert De Silver.* New York: Norton, 1940.

Newberry, Julia. *Julia Newberry's Diary.* New York: Norton, 1933.

New York State Joint Legislative Committee Investigating Seditious Activities. *Revolutionary Radicalism: Its History, Purpose and Tactics.* Vol. 2. Albany: Lyons, 1920.

Osofsky, Gilbert. *Harlem: The Making of a Ghetto.* 2nd ed. New York: Harper and Row, Harper Torchbooks, 1971.

Panunzio, Constantine M. *The Deportation Cases of 1919–1920.* 1919. Reprint. New York: Da Capo, 1970.

Patterson, David. *Toward a Warless World: The Travail of the American Peace Movement, 1887–1914.* Bloomington: Indiana Univ. Press, 1976.

Peterson, H. C., and Gilbert C. Fite. *Opponents of War, 1917–1919.* Madison: Univ. of Wisconsin Press, 1957.

Pierce, Bessie Louise. *Public Opinion and the Teaching of History.* 1926. Reprint. New York: Da Capo, 1970.

Polenberg, Richard. *Fighting Faiths: The Abrams Case, the Supreme Court, and Free Speech.* New York: Viking Penguin, 1987.

Post, Louis F. *The Deportations Delirium of Nineteen-Twenty: A Personal Narrative of an Historic Official Experience.* Chicago: Charles H. Kerr, 1923.

Preston, William, Jr. *Aliens and Dissenters: Federal Suppression of Radicals, 1903–1933.* 1963. Reprint. New York: Harper Torchbook, 1966.

Ragan, Fred. "Justice Oliver Wendell Holmes, Jr., Zechariah Chafee, Jr., and the Clear and Present Danger Test for Free Speech: The First Year, 1919." *Journal of American History* 58 (June 1971): 24–45.

Randall, Mercedes M. *Improper Bostonian: Emily Greene Balch.* New York: Twayne, 1964.

Reardon, Betty A. *Sexism and the War System.* New York: Teachers College Press, 1985.

Recht, Charles. *American Exclusion and Deportation Laws.* New York: Workers Defense Union, 1919.

————. *Manhattan Made, Poems.* New York: Liveright, 1930.

————. "Objection Overruled." Tamiment Institute Library (Charles Recht Papers). Unpublished memoirs.

Roberts, Barbara. *A Reconstructed World: A Feminist Biography of Gertrude Richardson.* Montreal: McGill-Queen's Univ. Press, 1996.

————. "Women Against War, 1914–1918: Francis Benyon and Laura Hughes." In *Up and Doing: Canadian Women and Peace,* ed. by Janice Williamson and Deborah Gorham, 48–65. Toronto: Women's Press, 1989.

————. "Women's Peace Activism in Canada." In *Beyond the Vote: Canadian Women and Politics,* edited by Joan Sangster and Linda Kealey, 279–85. Toronto: Univ. of Toronto Press, 1989.

Robins, Lucy. *War Shadows: A Documentary Story of the Struggle for Amnesty.* New York: Central Labor Bodies Conference for the Release of Political Prisoners, 1922.

Rotundo, E. Anthony. *American Manhood: Transformations in Masculinity from the Revolution to the Modern Era.* New York: Basic Books, 1993.

Ruddick, Sara. "Maternal Thinking and Peace Politics." *Journal of Education* 167 (1985): 97–112.

————. "Preservative Love and Military Destruction." In *Mothering: Essays in Feminist Theory,* edited by J. Trebilcot, 231–62. Totowa, N.J.: New Jersey: Rowman and Allanheld, 1984.

————. "The Rationality of Care." In *Women, Militarism and War: Essays in History, Politics, and Social Theory,* edited by Jean Bethke Elshtain and Sheila Tobias, 229–54. Savage, Md.: Rowman and Littlefield, 1990.

Rudwick, Elliot M. *Race Riot at East St. Louis, July 2, 1917.* 1964. Reprint. New York: Atheneum, 1972.

Scheiber, Harry N. *The Wilson Administration and Civil Liberties, 1917–1921.* Ithaca, N.Y.: Cornell Univ. Press, 1960.

Scheiber, Jane Lang, and Harry N. Scheiber. "The Wilson Administration and the Wartime Mobilization of Black Americans, 1917–1918." *Labor History* 10 (1969): 433–58.

Schlissel, Lillian, ed. *Conscience in America: A Documentary History of Conscientious Objection in America, 1757–1967.* New York: Dutton, 1968.

Schott, Linda. "Jane Addams and William James on Alternatives to War." *Journal of the History of Ideas* 54, no. 2 (Apr. 1993): 241–54.

Schwarz, Judith. *Radical Feminists of Heterodoxy: Greenwich Village 1912–1940.* Lebanon, N.H.: New Victoria, 1982.

Scott, Joan W. "Women and War: A Focus for Rewriting History." *Women's Studies Quarterly* 12, no. 2 (Summer 1984): 2–6.

Seidenburg, Roderick. "I Refuse to Serve." *AmericanMercury* (Jan. 1932): 91–99.

Shannon, David A. *The Socialist Party of America: A History.* New York: Macmillan, 1955.

Shenk, Gerald Edwin. "'Work or Fight': Selective Service and Manhood in the Progressive Era." Ph.D. diss., Univ. of California at San Diego, 1992.

Shover, Michele J. "Roles and Images of Women in World War I Propaganda." *Politics and Society* 5 (1975): 469–86.

Sklar, Kathryn Kish. "Hull House in the 1890s: A Community of Women Reformers." *Signs: A Journal of Women in Culture and Society* 10 (1985): 658–77.

Smith-Rosenberg, Carroll. "The Female World of Love and Ritual: Relations Between Women in Nineteenth-Century America." *Signs: A Journal of Women in Culture and Society* 1 (Autumn 1975): 1–29.

Solomon, Barbara Miller. *In the Company of Educated Women: A History of Women and Higher Education in America.* New Haven, Conn.: Yale Univ. Press, 1985.

Stanfield, John H., II. "The Dilemma of Conscientious Objection for Afro-Americans." In *The New Conscientious Objection: From Sacred to Secular Resistance,* edited by Charles C. Moskos and John Whiteclay Chambers II, 47–56. New York: Oxford Univ. Press, 1993.

Stanley, Liz. "Romantic Friendships? Some Issues in Researching Lesbian History and Biography." *Women's History Review* 1, no. 2 (1992): 193–216.

Steinson, Barbara. *American Women's Activism in World War I.* New York: Garland, 1982.

Strindberg, August. *Countess Julia.* Trans. Charles Recht. Philadelphia: Brown, 1912.

Sullivan, Mark. *Our Times: The United States, 1900–1925.* Vol. 5. New York: Scribner's, 1933.

Talbert, Roy, Jr. *Negative Intelligence: The Army and the American Left, 1917–1941.* Jackson, Miss.: Univ. Press of Mississippi, 1991.

Testi, Arnaldo. "The Gender of Reform Politics: Theodore Roosevelt and the Culture of Masculinity." *Journal of American History* 81, no. 4 (Mar. 1995): 1509–33.

Thomas, Norman. *Conscription and the "Conscientious Objector" to War.* Washington, D.C.: American Union Against Militarism, 1917.

———. *Is Conscience a Crime?* 1923. Reprint. New York: Garland, 1972.

Thompson, Mildred I. *Ida B. Wells-Barnett: An Exploratory Study of an American Black Woman, 1893–1930.* New York: Carlsen, 1990.

Tilly, Louise A. "Women, Politics, and Change." In *Women, Politics, and Change,* edited by Louise A. Tilly and Patricia Gurin, 1–32. New York: Russell Sage Foundation, 1990.

"Tracy Dickinson Mygatt." In *The Biographical Cyclopaedia of American Women,* edited by Erma Conkling Lee, vol. 2, 132–37. New York: Franklin W. Lee, 1925.

Tuttle, William M., Jr. *Race Riot: Chicago in the Red Summer of 1919.* New York: Atheneum, 1977.

Tyron, Warren S. "The Draft in World War I." *Current History* (June 1968): 339–44, 367–68.

Vaughn, Stephen L. *Holding Fast the Inner Lines: Democracy, Nationalism, and the Committee on Public Information.* Chapel Hill: Univ. of North Carolina Press, 1980.

Vicinus, Martha. *Independent Women: Work and Community For Single Women, 1850–1920.* London: Virago, 1985.

Walker, Samuel. *In Defense of American Liberties: A History of the ACLU.* New York: Oxford Univ. Press, 1990.

Weinberger, Harry. "A Rebel's Interrupted Autobiography." *American Journal of Economics and Sociology* 2, no. 1 (Oct. 1942): 111–22.

Weinstein, James. *The Decline of Socialism in America, 1912–1925.* New York: Monthly Review Press, 1967.

Wells-Barnett, Ida B. *Crusade for Justice: The Autobiography of Ida B. Wells.* Chicago: Univ. of Chicago Press, 1970.

Wexler, Alice. *Emma Goldman in America.* Boston: Beacon, 1984.

Witherspoon, Frances M. "The Lumberjack and the Constitution." *The World Tomorrow* 2, no. 5 (May 1919): 133–34.

[Witherspoon, Frances M.] *Who Are the Conscientious Objectors?* Brooklyn, N.Y.: Committee of 100 Friends of Conscientious Objectors. 1919.

Wolfe, Lieutenant-Colonel S. H. "Eight Months of War Risk Insurance Work." *Annals of the American Academy of Political and Social Science* 79 (1918): 68–79.

Wynn, Neil A. *From Progressivism to Prosperity: World War I and American Society.* New York: Holmes and Meier, 1986.

Young, Michael David. "'Wars Will Cease When Men Refuse to Fight': The War Resisters League 1925–1950." Honors essay, Brown Univ., 1975.

Zophy, Angela Howard, and Frances M. Kavenik, eds. *Handbook of American Women's History.* New York: Garland, 1990.

Oral Histories and Interviews

Finch, Margaret Rockwell. Interview by author. New Rochelle, N.Y., June 15, 1989.

Kaufman, Abraham. Interview by author. Port Charlotte, Fla., May 10, 1989.

Moore, Howard. Interview by author. Cherry Valley, N.Y., Aug. 23, 1991.

Witherspoon, Frances M. and Tracy D. Mygatt. Reminiscences. Oral History Research Office, Columbia Univ., 1966.

Newspapers and Journals

New York Call
New York Times
The Survey
The World Tomorrow

Index

Page numbers in *italics* denote illustrations.